BABY, YOU ARE MY RELIGION

GENDER, THEOLOGY AND SPIRITUALITY

Series Editor: Lisa Isherwood, University of Winchester

Gender, Theology and Spirituality examines the gendered nature of theology and spirituality. Volumes in the series explore a range of topics, often employing materialist and radical readings, and frequently questioning the notion of gender itself. The series aims to expand the boundaries of theology and spirituality through an engagement with embodied knowledge and critical praxis.

BABY, YOU ARE MY RELIGION

Women, Gay Bars, and Theology Before Stonewall

Marie Cartier

LONDON AND NEW YORK

First published 2013 by Acumen

Published 2014 by Routledge
2 Park Square, Milton Park, Abingdon, Oxon OX14 4RN
711 Third Avenue, New York, NY 10017, USA

Routledge is an imprint of the Taylor & Francis Group, an informa business

ISBN: 978-1-84465-894-7 (paperback); 978-1-84465-649-3 (hardcover)

British Library Cataloguing-in-Publication Data
A catalogue record for this book is available from the British Library.

Typeset in Warnock Pro by JS Typesetting Ltd, Porthcawl, Mid Glamorgan.

To all of the gay women who came before me, cleared the path for me, and walked the path with me ... butch, femme, kiki, androgynous, lesbian, queer, and transgender ... who dared to walk into a gay women's bar and acknowledge themselves and their community and made a community for me ... to walk into.

To my mother—Joanne Marie (Curtin) Cartier—a woman who came of age in the 1950s.

To all of my informants, especially Rae Hamilton, who gave me so much support, as well as stories.

To those informants and friends, that I know of, who passed before this book was completed: Jo Duffy, Bobreta Franklin, Yolanda Retter, Mary Martinez, Lee Glaze, Mari Lamy ... and most especially to Virginia "Ginny" Borders, Heather Hamm, Stella Miller, Myrna Kurland and Elsie Solay.

May the "Last Dance" always be a sweet one.

May the stories collected herein encourage many more stories.

I've had butch women say to me,
"Baby, you are my church. You are my ... religion."
Marie Cartier, *Ballistic Femme*

Well, I had insomnia.
I used to phone up all the gay bars,
just to hear them answer the phone.
I would just hear the noise
and the laughter in the background.
I just wanted to be there.
Excerpt, *Myrna's Story*

CONTENTS

ACKNOWLEDGMENTS

Thank you to my informants, especially the Women of Forty Plus in Long Beach, California, founded by Heather Hamm, whose members welcomed me into their circle.

For helping me find informants—Marilyn Taylor, Toni Wallace, Deejay Rhonda, Carole Damoci-Reed, Pat Lamis, Darlene Boyar, Ginny Borders, Nancy Alperin, Rae Hamilton, Jeanne Cordova, Lisa Samson, Nancy Valverde, Kimberly Esslinger, Rorri Feinstein, Shirley Horowitz, Bill Huff, Ken Davis, Tanya Gilbert, Older Lesbians Organizing for Change, the Coalition of Older Lesbians in Los Angeles, Comunidad of St. Matthew's in Long Beach, California, and Anna Totta.

I thank especially my doctoral dissertation committee chair, Zayn Kassam—this could not have happened without her; and also Monica Coleman, Karen Jo Torjesen, and Alex Juhasz. Also thanks to Jack Coogan, Anne Taves, Laura Harris, Lillian Faderman, Jackie Huntzinger, Margo Goldsmith, Jackie Hughes Heacock, Emily Silverman, and Catherine Tuell.

For their support I thank Mary Duvall and Laura B. Hill, the community and baristas of Hot Java, and proprietor Ken Davis, my Claremont writing group Three Degrees of Separation, and Kahena Viale and also Lisa Samson. I especially thank Mary Sellars.

I thank the June Mazer Lesbian Archives, Los Angeles—especially Jeri Deitrich, Marcia Schwemer, and Angela Brinskele. I also deeply thank Joan Nestle and the Lesbian Herstory Archives, especially Maxine Wolf and the Archives Bar Project; also the GLBT Historical Society in San Francisco; the ONE National Gay and Lesbian Archives at the USC, as well as the Kinsey Institute.

I thank those who offered me an audience: Raedorah Stewart for the ONE; the Women of Forty Plus Group; the Laguna Beach Lavender Group; Jacob Hale and The Center for Sex and Gender; Alicia Gaspar de Alba, UCLA; Lucas Hildebrand, UCI; the Lesbian-Feminist Issues in Religion Group, American Academy of Religion; Lisa Isherwood and the feminist theology circle in the UK and Ireland; and my comrades in the western Queer Studies in Religion and the national Lesbian Feminist Studies in Religion sections.

I thank the transcribers of E-Lance around the globe who worked on transcribing the over 5,000 pages of the interviews, and many times sent personal emails of support along with the transcripts; and local transcribers: Katie Rouze, Angela Brinskele, Kristina Clemens, Althea Spencer Miller, and Ginger Conwell. For editing help—thanks to Tatevik Abrahamyan and Karen "Jade" Martner. For the cover photograph thank you to informant and friend Carolyn Weathers. For all work on permissions, photo reproduction, and chart creations and design, I thank my wife Kimberly Esslinger.

I thank my students for (almost) always being excited about my work. I thank the staff at both of the universities I teach at—especially Janaki Bowerman, Molly Nguyen of CSUN, and Vikki Duncan, Peter Chang, and Suzanne Wachman of UCI.

I want to also thank especially Janet Joyce at Equinox for holding faith with this book for so long; Katharine Greene, Tristan Palmer and Kate Williams at Acumen; Gina Mance and Hamish Ironside for their careful copyediting and proofreading; and Angus Barclay for indexing.

I have been helped in this project by the generous support of several institutions and individuals: Long Beach Lesbian and Gay Pride, Inc.; Jacqui Haschi, and Claremont Graduate University.

Some of the material in this book was first published in M. Cartier & B. Grossman, "'Oh My God, I'm Home': The Socioreligious Significance of Gay Older Women's Experiences of Women's Bars Before Stonewall," *Journal of Religion, Spirituality & Aging* 25(2) (2013); and my "A Theology of Corporeality Embodied in the Butch Femme Bar Culture of the 1950s and 1960s," *Feminist Theology: The Journal of the Britain and Ireland School of Feminist Theology* 12(2) (2004); and "Viewing 1950s Butch–Femme Sexual Practice as Possibly Religious Practice/Practicing Religion," *Theology and Sexuality: The Journal of the Centre for the Study of Christianity and Sexuality* 10(1) (2003). Other material originally appeared in "An Articulation of a Theology of the Body for Queer Theory," in *Women and Christianity*, C. Kirk-Duggan & K. J. Torjesen (eds) (Santa Barbara, CA: Praeger, 2010).

I thank all the butches and femmes, gay women, lesbian feminists, queer people in contemporary times and "back in the day" that created community despite the odds, and my personal communities of friends and lovers. For all the folks who said, "I can't wait to read it!" and to whom I responded "Me, too!" thank you for your continued interest. I thank the animals that grace me with their presence: Betty, Colette, Malibu, Luna, Neville, Oscar, and Felix—life *is* mainly about relationships—and love.

And to my wife: GK ... our favorite quote (by Erick Dillard), "Then we sat on the edge of the earth, with our feet dangling over the side, and marveled that we had found each other." ... 143.

PREFACE: MYRNA'S STORY

I would stay on the phone ... that was my lifeline.[1]

"I came out as gay in 1945—the year that the war ended," Myrna Kurland told me from her home high in the Hollywood Hills of California. "I was dating a softball player that I met at the gay bar. I met her at Mona's or else it was the Paper Pony. My first night in a gay bar was—freedom. I had a gay male friend and he took me there."

Myrna was in the gay bars for eight years. She showed me her "treasure from the 40s"—a gold softball on a necklace chain from her first lover—inscribed with the initials from the professional softball league to which women belonged while the men were in the war. "We went to the bar all the time. My entire social life was there—there was no other place." However, that night she first went to the bar—something else happened. Her father died that night. And she blamed herself, even though she knew that was irrational. She couldn't get over it. Also she told me that, "I'm Jewish and we lost so many people in the Holocaust. I felt it was my duty to have children. There was no other way to have children in the 1950s without getting married to a man. I married someone I disliked—that's what I felt I deserved because I was gay and I felt so guilty." She married a psychiatrist—someone to whom she would never be able to tell her secret. Her husband's practice was very involved in actively trying to change the sexuality/sexual deviancy of his clients—as would be almost any psychiatrist's practice at the time. If her sexual past and preference had been known to him in all likelihood she would have lost her children.

This brief story came as I was packing up my things, and although we had been speaking for about three hours, this was in response to my final question, "Is there any last thing you want to say about what the bars meant to

1. Interview, Myrna Kurland.

you?" I meant when she actually went to the bars in the 1940s—not knowing there was another story. She told me a story about when she did not actually *go to* the bars, but when she made sure the bars were still there—when she was married.

> INFORMANT: Well, I had insomnia. I used to phone up all the gay bars, just to hear them answer the phone ... Just to hear the noise, oh yes.
> INTERVIEWER: So you would call and just be on the phone?
> INFORMANT: No, I would just hear the noise and the laughter in the background. I just wanted to be there.
> INTERVIEWER: ... it helped you just to know it was out there?
> (Pause)
> INTERVIEWER: ... that's a really special story.
> INFORMANT: Yeah, oh God.

1. IT WAS THE ONLY PLACE

God does not live in a dogmatic scripture ... but instead abides very close to us indeed ... breathing right through our own hearts. I respond with gratitude to anyone who has ever voyaged to the center of that heart, and who has then returned ... with a report for the rest of us that God is an experience of supreme love.[1]

Baby ... you ... are my religion ...[2]

INTRODUCTION

Pre-Stonewall gay bars functioned as centers of communities, in the way that churches, as structures, function as the centers of many communities. For while many people do not go to church *per se*, if they belong to the religion the church symbolizes and houses, the structure of the church will also provide a structure to their own lives—for the occasional visit, for the identification it provides, for the knowledge of a community they could enter into—however they choose to do that, as well as for the list of attributes that we might assume religion provides—identity formation, community involvement, exploration of meaning, and a sense of something bigger than self. Religion is "the desire for depth ... the experience ... of the world imagined."[3] In religious studies we often call that "desire for depth," a sense of the sacred.

---

1. Elizabeth Gilbert, *Eat, Pray, Love: One Woman's Search for Everything across Italy, India and Indonesia* (London: Bloomsbury, 2006), 14.
2. Marie Cartier, *Ballistic Femme* (Los Angeles, CA: Performing Arts Collection, One Gay and Lesbian Archives, University of California, 1997). Comment made by a former lover (butch woman), also a line from this performance art play.
3. Lynda Sexson, *Ordinarily Sacred* (New York: Crossroad, 1982), 16.

I began writing this in a gay coffee shop in a gay neighborhood of California's fifth largest city, Long Beach. A city that has arguably one of the best Pride parades and festivals in the nation, maybe the world—at least that is what everyone says. The striking contrast between where I sat and the over one hundred stories I gathered haunts me. This feeling of being shadowed by a past I owe my present to and yet one I did not fully understand propelled this work.

Rae is an 84-year-old woman, with a great laugh. When I go to interview her, she has a picture for me of a dashing man in a suit with a brilliant smile, smoking a pipe. It is her at eighteen, the happiest years of her life, she says, when she was living in drag "24/7" and headlining as the star singer at Tess's Continental—a club in the 1940s on Santa Monica Boulevard in Hollywood managed by two gay women—Tess and Sylvia. She worked there one year and fell in love with a beautiful woman, a femme fatale, who didn't want to be with someone who dressed as a man. Rae showed me a picture with the dashing man on one side of the frame and on the other "his twin," Kay, a stunning blonde with polished nails in an evening dress.

"At first I thought I was in drag, until I got the hang of the make-up." Rae was never able to get another professional singing job and her girlfriend left after two years to be with a man and then came back to Rae, but not romantically.[4] Rae recorded an album of songs on vinyl when she was young in Hollywood during the time when you could walk in and press your record right there.[5] "Crazy About You," is about why Rae took back the girl who initially left her for a man. Rae says she was stupid in love; I say it's better to have loved and lost than never to have loved at all, that if she had one year that was the happiest of all her life, then that is more than many people have. She says K. D. Lang made it as a butch drag singer and implies she should have done that. I say K. D. Lang made it on the backs of people like you and she slowly nods. She's never considered this. She lives alone and her community is the friends she made in an older lesbian group—OLOC, Older Lesbians Organizing for Change. Before she connected with this group, she was alone for nine years. I want her to know that the success of butch drag communities is a historical evolution that became possible only through the struggles of previous butch drag communities.

This book is mainly about that previous culture, the bar culture that thrived for women between the years 1940–75. I call the period "pre-Stonewall" (even though Stonewall happened in 1969); this study covers those who were in the bars through the 1970s, because the effects of Stonewall did not reverberate through America until late into the 70s. For instance in Orange County, southern California, there was a popular butch-femme bar

4. Interview, Rae Hamilton.
5. This is how Elvis Presley recorded his first song.

called The Happy Hour that was regularly patrolled by police into the 1980s; and there was also police abuse in the bars of West Hollywood documented into the 1990s.[6]

This culture that provided four walls for people to have the happiest times of their lives, in some cases, and the worst times in others, was more than a bar. These bars served as cultural community centers or institutional foundations for gay women and were organized primarily by butch-femme individuals.

I am not the first to write about a bar as being more than a bar. Certainly many cultures have used the bar as a space for community. As an Irish citizen, I am very familiar with the use of the bar as a space for connection. *The Tender Bar*[7] and other publications are memoirs that explore this. The House of Blues, a popular blues bar, advertises, "If this is your religion, this is your church." So while my idea is not completely new, it is new to think of the bar *as* an actual church. And more unusual is to think of the gay women's bar and pre-Stonewall butch-femme community as religious.

One of my informants asked, "Marie, what is religious about this?" This has been the question asked more than any other. Sometimes the most vocal opponents have been the women themselves. For example, the famous memoirist and archivist, Joan Nestle, said to me, "I am nothing if not profane."[8] Religion has done very little for these women. They were kicked out of all traditional religions, and non-traditional religions would not gain prominence until "the dawning of the New Age" in the mid-1970s. The psychiatric community considered these women mentally ill. The police considered them sex offenders and felons; and the government considered them the nation's highest security risk. All of my pre-Stonewall informants were aware that they could be put into a mental institution where they might be subjected to electric shock, severe drugging and worse if they were not careful. All of them knew they could lose their jobs, especially if the job was a government one. All of them knew that they were considered criminals, and the spaces where they gathered were regularly raided and the participants arrested, and their names published. Often the only way to clear their names if this happened was to pay off unscrupulous lawyers. Many of them were arrested in the bars, and outside the bars. Many were harassed and raped by those same police and by straight men. Some of them were put in mental institutions, or in jail, or lost their jobs; many of them were in the military and were dishonorably discharged. In this environment there was one space

6. This later research was not documented in the long interviews cited in Appendix B, but in many shorter interviews—among them specifically for this reference: Lisa Hartouni, interview, March 18, 2010, Long Beach, CA.
7. J. R. Moehringer, *The Tender Bar: A Memoir* (New York: Hyperion, 2005).
8. Interview, Joan Nestle.

that was accepting—the gay bar, and over and over again I heard the words, "That was the only space."

The bar was the only space in which these women could actually *be*, in the most literal sense. For many of these women these four walls were the space in which they could actually have an identity that felt natural to them. This is interesting because so often they are accused of "role-playing," being masculine or feminine in the extreme (i.e., "butch" and "femme"), whereas they themselves would often say that the "roles" they were suspected of playing felt completely natural. In that rarified smoky air of the illicit bar, they were able to claim the roles or inhabit these identities for the first, and sometimes, the only time. In this space they were able to meet lovers, or rather find someone to love, have community, find themselves, have a sense of belonging, and, in general, find a structure in which they could create meaning for their lives. Isn't that what many of us credit religion with helping us to do?

What did these spaces mean? Even though they were regularly raided and their participants ridiculed, the women continued to go there, often at great risk. Joan Nestle told me about someone urinating through the door slot by the table she was sitting at, that suddenly a rain of urine fell on the floor next to the table where she was having a drink with a date.[9] Although the bar itself may have felt somewhat protected, people on the outside knew who was gathered inside, and felt free to comment on that, as did this person on the outside of the bar. For many women inside, their lives were secret from their biological families, their work partners, their friends outside "the life," often even husbands and boyfriends—but the women still came to the bar. Does this sound—religious? The early Christians felt this kind of ridicule and were not considered religious by the religion at large of the time.[10] Religions by definition have not provided safe or easy harbors for many of their participants. The difference between the gay women's bar/butch-femme communities and the early Christians is that we believe today that the early Christians were probably aware that they were practicing "religion" and the butch-femme community was not aware that they were practicing what could be called religion.[11] Religion has provided a space where you could find out *who* you are, *what* you are made of, *how* you wish to live, and for what or for whom you might die. This is what the butch-femme bars and surrounding communities gave to their participants.

9. Interview, Joan Nestle. See also Joan Nestle, "Butch-Femme Relationships: Sexual Courage in the 1950's." In *A Restricted Country* (San Francisco, CA: Cleis Press, 2003), 92–102.
10. With thanks for many insightful conversations to Dr. Lori Ann Ferrell, my mentor for the Preparing Future Faculty Fellowship Program, Claremont Graduate University, 2006–7.
11. But naming an entire community as sinners and divorcing them from the ability to name their actions as religious was not the issue for these Christians. It was the issue for the population which I studied.

In my one-woman show, *Ballistic Femme,*[12] I explored the butch-femme community of the late 1990s and I wrote, "I love this community—I would die for it."

And I also wrote, "I hate this community ... sometimes it is just really hard to sleep next to a soldier."[13]

The great lost and found department

Robert Short wrote that "The church is the great lost and found department."[14] A reason to live and a reason to die ... Isn't that what we think religion might be? To find a place where we can have a home inside of ourselves and with others? The names of these bars were instrumental—The Lost and Found (Chicago),[15] Tess's Continental, The Star Room, The If Club, The Oxwood Inn, The Happy Hour (Southern California), The Sea Colony (New York), and many others. Their names were spoken of wistfully, lovingly, angrily, or dismissively, but overall spoken with a deep longing for the community that existed there. All of these pre-Stonewall bars, like the infamous Chicago bar, The Lost and Found, were places where someone could be lost and then found. I see them as churches amid our mid-century landscape where a particular populace was able to often find solace, develop meaning, create home, and perhaps find someone to love. In many cases that person they found to love was themselves.

This community was a community with history and identity. However identity is not a static thing. There were numerous forces that contributed to identity formation such as oppression, individual and social repression, and social exclusion. The bar scene, despite its dangers, was often the safest place to question and form identity, and, I argue, was a religious community institution. The questions and desires of this gay women's/butch-femme community[16] were representative of perennial religious questions.

12. Cartier, *Ballistic Femme.*
13. *Ibid.*
14. Robert Short, *The Gospel According to Peanuts* (Atlanta, GA: J. Knox Press, 1965), 87.
15. The Lost and Found is also the name of one of the longest-running gay women's bars in the US, located in Chicago. The manager's story, Ava, is included in this study.
16. There have been, and continue to be, many arguments within the gay women's, lesbian and queer communities that begin with, "What is butch?" and "What is femme?" Let me clarify how I am using these terms. In regards to the history of the terms within these communities, there are four distinct time periods: the contested pre-Stonewall period, lesbian feminism, the sex wars and the opening of the lesbian leather culture period, and contemporary queer culture. I am discussing the butch-femme culture pre-Stonewall—a specificity to the gender question that is decidedly *historical.* During this period, *following* a butch woman was one of two identified ways to find your way to the *only* place of public gay community—the gay bar. (The other way was to ask a cab driver.) This reality cannot be taken out of historical context and discussed in

BABY, YOU ARE MY RELIGION …

In 1995, I was dating a butch woman who at one point said to me, "Baby, you are my religion," in response to my wanting her to go to Catholic Mass at Easter—being a "C. and E." (Christmas and Easter) Catholic myself.

In 1997, I premiered *Ballistic Femme*, about contemporary butch-femme communities at that time.[17] The comment went into a scene in which I washed off orange juice I had dripped over myself and then cut up more oranges, offering them to the audience in Communion. When I was washing off this "sacrament," I licked a cross I had around my neck and said, "I've had lovers say, 'Baby, you are my church; you are my religion.'"[18]

I came out in the lesbian feminist revolution of the late 1970s and 80s. As fervent members, we did not necessarily base our lesbian lives around sex lives as in sexuality, but around politics. With this one-woman show, I came out in a different way—basing my lesbian life on contested sexuality—that of butch-femme.

In the late 70s, WITCH[19] meant "Woman in Total Control of Herself," and "Women's International Terrorist Conspiracy from Hell". We questioned authority and realized "Women hold up half the sky." We had correct sex

---

ahistorical contemporary queer culture terms such as "fucking with gender," etc., which are contemporary millennial terms for gender deviance or *playing with* gender, without doing a disservice to the historical culture and its inhabitants. Lesbian feminism found butch-femme as role-playing, but, however, did discuss butch-femme as a historic reality for those gay women (not yet lesbians) who had come before them. The sex wars and the public birth of leather culture included many pre-Stonewall butches and femmes who found solace in the community of the new leather practitioners. Both butch-femme and leather embraced sexual outlaw status. These communities then bonded in much the same way that prostitutes and pre-Stonewall bar women did—forging a bond based on meeting on contested geographies.

A pre-Stonewall butch was a woman who often could be seen (especially if one was looking) as a biological woman—a woman who owned masculinity despite the culture's strict prerogative against it. And a femme was a decidedly feminine woman who openly valued this contested masculinity within a female biology. While I hope this project adds to our contemporary discussion of gender coding, it must be viewed as primarily adding to how we view the historical culture. There is a historical butch-femme culture and there is a contemporary butch-femme culture. The historic culture operated under a different set of strictures than does the contemporary culture. While gender transgression is still punished, and I in no way mean to detract from the courage it takes to live a gender transgressive life in any time period, today it is not necessarily illegal and does not *automatically* signify mental illness, felony, crime, sin, necessity for imprisonment, and the nation's highest security risk. These historical realities must be taken into consideration when discussing pre-Stonewall gender deviance, specifically butch-femme—otherwise we risk *playing* with the gender of our ancestors, when we are discussing a time period where gender deviance was anything *but* a game.

17. Cartier, *Ballistic Femme.*
18. *Ibid.*
19. Jo Freeman, "WITCH—Women's International Terrorist Conspiracy from Hell," www.jofreeman.com (accessed December 18, 2009).

lives that supposedly did not include penetration, if we could help it, nor butch-femme identities. As lesbian feminists, men and masculinity were out. If you can put one man on the moon, why not put them all there?

> Twentieth-century identity politics, linked closely to the lesbian feminist movement beginning in the early 1970s, dismissed butch-femme culture as politically incorrect. Many lesbians ... critiqued butch-femme as capitulation to oppressive patriarchal standards. Androgyny became the lesbian ideal. However, as ... Lillian Faderman points out in her seminal lesbian history *Odd Girls and Twilight Lovers*,[20] "androgyny" usually meant that *everyone* looked butch![21]

What was culturally outlawed was *femme* or women who looked like they were "tools of the patriarchy." When I wanted to wear lingerie that is what I was told, and I wondered where the patriarchy was exactly and could I join it—just for a night?

The second wave of feminism and radical feminism was a time where we smeared blood on our foreheads when we were menstruating and wore shirts that said, "I am woman. I can bleed for days and not die." We were an army, a women's liberation army, and when you draw that line in the sand, you need to know who is standing with you.

I saw this articulated in my interviews also. Who is standing with me as butch-femme? Lesbian feminist? Queer? What constitutes the community that steps across the line and stands with you, the rules of belonging, the benefits? The 1940s–70s bar culture has a history of being "dissed" as being about barflies and role-playing. I presented research from this project and an audience member asked me, "Don't you think feminism was important?", as if butch-femme and feminism are antithetical, and certainly they have been positioned that way in my own history, and in the history of actual events. Joan Nestle articulated this in *Restricted Country*,[22] writing that butch-femme prefigured and set the stage for feminist thought by privileging femme desire, and allowing a group of women to have femme or feminine agency, a place from which to be empowered, as Joan was.

After learning about butch-femme culture, after my sojourn in lesbian feminism, and my entrée into the sex wars that started in the 1980s and continued well into the 90s, I began to draft *Ballistic Femme*.[23] During a sold-out run at San Francisco's Lunacy Theater in 1998, while en route to the stage

---

20. Lillian Faderman, *Odd Girls and Twilight Lovers: A History of Lesbian Life in Twentieth-Century America* (New York: Columbia University Press, 1991).
21. Teresa Theophano, "Butch-Femme." In *glbtq:An Encyclopedia of Gay, Lesbian, Bisexual, Transgender, and Queer Culture*, ed. Claude J. Summers (Chicago, IL: glbtq, 2004) http://www.glbtq.com/social-sciences/butch_femme_ssh,2.html (accessed July 28, 2013).
22. Joan Nestle, *A Restricted Country* (Ithaca, NY: Firebrand Books, 1987).
23. Cartier, *Ballistic Femme*.

from the dressing room, I was approached by the lighting designer for the night, who leaned in as I was about to go on stage.

"You know, you should talk about butch-femme of the 1950s. You don't talk at all about butch-femme from the old days, the 50s," she said. I said, "And I'm not going to do it tonight." She had the script, and all my cues, and there was a sold-out house. We were most likely going to go on with the show—imminently. However, following that performance, for the remainder of the run in San Francisco and in other venues, I included a program insert, "Queen Ezmerelda" (a character from the show) says "Read More About It!" and exhorted that audiences read "more about" butch-femme, recommending *Stone Butch Blues*,[24] *Restricted Country*,[25] and *Boots of Leather, Slippers of Gold: The History of a Lesbian Community*.[26] I started reading these books and found out that the stage manager was right—there was a history there.

That led me to graduate school and to an exploration of "Baby, you are my religion," as I explored words like "religion," "theology," "corporal identity," "process thought," "community," and "identity." And also explored how the statement, "Baby, you are my religion," in the context in which it was spoken, fits into that discussion. As the stage manager's comment re-framed my gaze on what "butch-femme" meant, it is my hope to re-frame the gaze on what "religion" means, and how we see this period fitting into that discussion. In theology we talk about setting the table[27] so that more people may have a place at it. I want this project to set a place at the table for the habitués of pre-Stonewall bar culture.

PRE-STONEWALL ... NAMING MATTERS

Stonewall happened June 29, 1969, the day that gay icon Judy Garland died. It happened in New York City, at the Stonewall Inn, a popular gay dance bar. The following year, 1970, gay pride marches were held in New York City and in Los Angeles, and in LA also the first gay pride festival.

It has been described as "the hairpin drop heard round the world."[28] However, who heard it and what did they do about it?

Very few of the women I interviewed knew about Stonewall when it happened. Many did not know about it until the advent of lesbian feminism and their entrée into that arena. Many did not know about it until the emergence

24. Leslie Feinberg, *Stone Butch Blues: A Novel* (Ithaca, NY: Firebrand Books, 1993).
25. Nestle, *A Restricted Country*.
26. Elizabeth Lapovsky Kennedy & Madeline D. Davis, *Boots of Leather, Slippers of Gold: The History of a Lesbian Community* (New York: Routledge, 1993).
27. Kenneth D. Thurow, *A Place at the Table: Scripture, Sexuality, and Life in the Church* (Bloomington, IN: iUniverse.com, 2009).
28. David Carter, *Stonewall: The Riots That Sparked the Gay Revolution* (New York: St. Martin's Press, 2004).

of queer studies as a discipline and the use of the word Stonewall to describe everything from coffee clubs to a segment of the Democratic Party.

It is true that "Stonewall changed everything."[29] But Stonewall did not change everything by 1970. Women's bars were being raided as late as 1980 in southern California. The Huntress, a bar that specialized in serving a butch-femme crowd, often experienced police walk-ins, when women were forced to show IDs and threatened.[30]

Stonewall's history of women's participation is still mostly undocumented.[31,32] Also, the majority of the gay women's/lesbian community outside urban New York did not change immediately with Stonewall, because Stonewall's influence had not reached them yet.

Matthew Shepard,[33] the young man who was killed/crucified in Wyoming in 1998,[34] proves how urban-centered is the statement: "Stonewall changed everything." We are not speaking of just Wyoming when we speak of where Stonewall did not reach—immediately. We are also speaking of Orange Countrу—a half-hour from the urban center, Los Angeles, where a Gay Pride Parade was being held—which many of my participants simply did not know even happened.

Women who identified gay feelings and acted on them did not necessarily call that "being out," as we define that today (for example, married women who were "out" only in the bars, or never went to the bars). I interviewed participants who had gay identified lives from the period 1940–75, and later extended this to 1980 because of informants' particular histories with police harassment.[35]

Stonewall is a historical event, but also a political movement that did not change things for everyone upon its historical occurrence, but it did change things slowly, and it became an event whose repercussions took almost a decade to be felt outside of urban areas, and even the close suburbs of those urban areas.[36]

---

29. But not so quickly that we should not interview informants who identified gay feelings and acted on them after 1969—particularly between 1969 and 1980 and even later in different geographic regions.
30. Interview, Laura Hill.
31. Carter, *Stonewall: The Riots That Sparked the Gay Revolution.* This excellent history begins that documentation.
32. I begin to respond to this in the section on the 1960s. While the involvement of women at Stonewall is largely unwritten, it was beyond the scope of this project to cover it fully; I hope to explore this more in the future.
33. Moises Kaufman & Tectonic Theater Project, *The Laramie Project* (New York: Vintage Books, 2001). This play documents Matthew Shepard's impact on the gay and lesbian community.
34. The Matthew Shepard Foundation, "Our Story: The Matthew Shepard Foundation," www.matthewshepard.org.
35. Interview, Laura Hill. This is supported by this informant, among others.
36. Like the cell phone advertisement, "Can you hear me now?" the infamous "hairpin drop" had difficult reception. And in some places that hairpin is still questioning, "Can you

CLASS, RACE AND LOCATION … MATTER

Class

The black theorist bell hooks wrote *Where We Stand: Class Matters*.[37] She speaks of the necessity for working-class people to find community, despite racial differences. hooks also argues that perhaps working-class blacks have less in common with upper-class blacks than they might have with working-class whites, and she argues for coalitions based on class. She argues that—class matters.

The gay women's/butch-femme bar scene was primarily, but not exclusively, organized by working-class people. It was composed on any given night of a variety of classes—from upper to lower, but those who kept the space open were decidedly working class (except for the few upper-class bars—among them in Los Angeles were The Laurel Club and The Canyon Club, who counted several movie stars among their populations). The most commonly used phrase by the interviewees in regard to the bars was "that was the only place there was." So while the individual interviewee may have felt bad about this space in that it could be dismal and humiliating to be in a place raided and patrolled by police, where the population was primarily butch-femme/role-playing in the interviewee's mind—she still might have had a grudging respect for it. It existed. It was all there was. For many it was exciting remembering a place where there was a sense of belonging, and where identity was found, either in contrast to or in deep connection with, the bar. The bars were then crucial to a sense of community *for this* community. They were in fact "the only place."

The bartender and manager of the long-standing bar The Lost and Found in Chicago, Ava, put in at least half a century of service to the community. She stood behind the bar, pouring drinks and also performing a variety of surprising community services. She told me she "married people" in the 1950s.

She asked if I would like to see a copy of the service she used when she married people and added, "Who else was going to do it?"

As the captain of a ship is empowered as a legal choice for marriage because there is no one else, so is the gay woman bartender, she said. The bar

---

hear me now?" and is getting no response. For some geographic areas the answer is most likely, "Yes, I hear you." But there are many geographic areas that are still "pre-Stonewall." While the beginnings of a gay and lesbian revolution were heard round the world after Stonewall, it did take over a decade for most people to get in on the call. Matthew Shepard was murdered in 1999, two decades after Stonewall and that infamous hairpin drop.

37. bell hooks, *Where We Stand: Class Matters* (New York: Routledge, 2000). bell hooks traditionally uses initial lower case for her name in her publications—in honoring that choice I am using that here as well.

would be packed, and the people who were married often stayed together; there are couples still together for whom she officiated at the "wedding." Did the reception happen at the bar? "Honey," she said, "everything happened here. It was the only place."[38]

For some, the bars were places for sex and relationships were impossible. However, for this group of women in Chicago, who met there in the mid-twentieth century, relationships flourished and they still met regularly at the bar post-millennium. According to poet/theorist Judy Grahn, the gay women's bar could be a space where for the first time when a woman walks into it, she becomes her own person, sexually.[39] For many women it took enormous courage to enter these (often literally) underground spaces.

What then did the gay women's bar 1940–75 mean to gay women—working-, middle- and upper-class women?

Some middle-class women told me they did not go to the bar often—but not that they never went. There was only one woman I spoke to who said she had never been in a bar during the pre-Stonewall period, and she admitted that she was a "gay girl" only "Monday through Friday from 8:00 a.m. to 3:00 p.m., until the kids came home from school."[40] Only one person knew she had this secret life and that was the woman, also married, that she shared it with. When they broke up, no one knew. There was no one to talk to about the relationship existing or it ending.

Middle-class women were afraid to go to the bar—justifiably afraid of a raid. "I couldn't go—I had everything to lose," said one former academic, who went to a bar only twice in her life, saw very few people like her, was followed by a butch woman when she went to the bathroom and fled.[41] I had people tell me the bar was the place they went to get a girlfriend and that they would not return until they broke up and needed a new girlfriend. The bar for them served as a dating service, kept alive by others; the bar existed for this service—if needed. Middle-class women, particularly those in education, were correct in their assumption that they might lose their jobs and therefore their source of income, if the bar was raided.

However, a working-class factory worker and later career military woman that went to the bar all the time, every week-end, said, "I hate that, when they say 'we had everything to lose;' it's as if they are saying that I didn't—as if people like me had nothing to lose. The truth for me is that we all had everything to lose. It's not that I didn't have anything to lose. Everyone just has what they have, and everyone has everything to lose."[42] This woman was arrested in a bar raid and spent a night in jail.

38. Interview, Ava.
39. Paris Poirier (dir.), *Last Call at Maud's* (USA: Maud's Project/Frameline, 1993).
40. Interview, Sadie Smith*. An asterisk after an informant name means, throughout, that the name is a pseudonym.
41. Interview, Virginia "Ginny" Borders.
42. Interview, Carole S. Damoci-Reed.

One middle-class woman said, referring to those whose main community was the bar, and especially to butch-femme culture, "I got out. I don't see why they didn't."[43] The assumption in looking at this culture has been that it is too bad that the working class did not rise up and improve their situation. Many theorists, among them bell hooks, have argued that the reality of class is that it is extremely difficult to change your birth-assigned class station.[44] As of 2006, "Children from low-income families have only a one percent chance of reaching the top five percent of the income distribution, versus children of the rich who have about a 22 percent chance."[45]

Lillian Faderman, an academic who came from the working class, freely admits that if not for a lucky break in the form of a guidance counselor who "saw her," and recommended she focus on school and stop going to the bar, she might have followed an invitation to go away with, and to become, a prostitute. For she received the invitation from a woman, a prostitute, she fell in love with. If someone had not opened another door for her, she would have taken the door offered. As a working-class woman she did not see herself yet as having the ability to become an academic. The guidance counselor re-framed her gaze and she had enough cultural capital—good looks, and academic intelligence—to follow through on that re-framing.[46]

A lucky break combined with cultural capital is usually necessary for a person to change class positions from lower to upper. Not everyone gets lucky breaks. Not everyone has the ability/cultural capital or desire, combined with a lucky break, to become someone different to the person created by the station into which they were born. Rising up out of a working-class station always demands cultural capital. For gay women pre-Stonewall this might be traditional femininity, traditional attractiveness—enough so that a gay man would use her as a front, and she could use him. It might be that you knew such a circle of men—as opposed to the type of gay men who frequent and keep open a gay bar. Unlike middle- and upper-class men who went to the bars less frequently, in the bars men would often also be primarily working class. The necessary cultural capital might be intelligence in the academic sense and the ability to get into college. This is something that all the authors, but not all the informants I interviewed, did have. It might be a loving family, despite being gay. And finally it might be that a woman could hide her gayness when necessary—that she could pass.

The cultural capital an individual has correlates to economic status. For example, a Radclyffe Hall upper-class butch[47] would traverse social territory

43. Anonymous, personal conversation, 2006.
44. hooks, *Where We Stand: Class Matters*, 142–55.
45. Tom Hertz, "Understanding Mobility in America," (Center for American Progress, 2006), http://www.americanprogress.org/kf/hertz_mobility_analysis.pdf (accessed August 20, 2011)
46. Interview, Lillian Faderman.
47. Radclyffe Hall, *The Well of Loneliness* (Garden City, NY: Sun Dial Press, 1928).

easily compared to a working-class butch. For a working-class butch to make the transition to middle class *as a butch*, the question would be, how would she make a living? One way might be to join the military. This remained/remains a way for the working class to get educated, as some of my informants did.[48] If one was independently wealthy (as Hall was) then the presentation of self—while difficult in conventional society—was not economically impossible. However, the middle class was a difficult destination for a butch who presented as such in day to day life. It was limited in availability also to a femme woman. If a working-class femme was able to create an upwardly mobile path using different culturally available tools such as affiliations to gay men who had more cultural capital than she did, traditional looks, and the ability to negotiate the system, she might create a path to the middle class for herself and her butch. But this was simply not available for most women; most born in the working class would be destined to stay there, regardless of what they wanted. In light of this, it is important to look at the gay women's working class bar as having a different function than what we would normally assign a bar or even a community center. It was "the only place," a place with more agency than we assign any bar of any other population. While there were ways to get out of the bar culture, these ways were not available to everyone—nor did everyone desire to so change their identity. When a woman does get out of a culture, she is often not able to return and therefore she may choose, if she is able, to stay. For that culture is *family*.

Gloria Anzaldua, the Chicana lesbian theorist,[49] left her migrant farmer family to become an academic and in so doing left behind a part of herself. Who was she if she was so different from those she knew before school? Once an academic she no longer identified completely with her family back home, nor would she ever totally relate to her academic colleagues as family. Forced to make connections at "the borderlands," a place where fellow travelers met, she found home only in the liminal space of such borderlands.

In summary, to change class stations demands a certain amount of lucky breaks within the system of cultural capital and deficit in which we exist. Many gay women during this pre-Stonewall period, 1940–75, did not get them. For a butch—strong in presence, identity or looks—to rise up out of bar culture would be difficult because there was no place for such a differently-gendered person to exist outside of bar culture. A femme whose attraction was for a masculine woman would have a difficult time meeting that sexual need outside gay women's bar culture.[50] Falcon River, a passing woman of the 1960s and 70s from the South, said

48. Interview, Carol S. Damoci-Reed.
49. Gloria Anzaldúa, *Borderlands: The New Mestiza = La Frontera* (San Francisco, CA: Spinsters/Aunt Lute, 1987).
50. Interview, Linda Lack.

> There was not one other place that I could fit. That's why I went back after the police raped me. Over and over they raped me and over and over I went back. There was not one other place that I existed; or that my gay friends, the queens, could exist. It took all the courage I had to walk as a butch from the car to the bar. And it still is the most courageous thing I have seen—for a queen in Virginia at that time to walk from 'her' car to the bar. If anyone thinks we were not doing civil rights there—they were not *there*. That's all I can say.[51]

All classes of gay women depended on the gay bars as a recognizable public gathering space. Many frequented it often, some less frequently and others rarely—but as the *only* public space it provided the center for a diverse and otherwise invisible community. For the 1950s middle-class wife who wanted a lover and could let no one know about it, the bars provided a place.[52] For the butch factory worker, they provided a place.[53] For the femme woman who was attracted to the masculinity of the butch, they provided a place.[54] For the femme woman on the game, or prostitute who had found her economic path as a working girl in the oldest profession, they provided a place.[55] For the working-class lesbian without hope of rising to another station because she had no hope of further education, they provided a place.[56] For the woman who had no extra physical space and had to use the bar as her living room, they provided a place.[57] For the upper-class woman stifled in her upper-class society and needing a space for gay identity, they provided a place.[58] For all of these reasons and for all of these women, and more, the bars provided "the only place."

Race

Women of color used bar culture across class lines more than whites. Women of color did not see butch and femme as necessarily working class. In women of color communities, butch-femme has been, and is still, often the way gay women's/lesbian sexuality has been enacted. It was when women of color left their communities and dated outside, in white communities, that they found themselves faced with the directive that butch-femme

51. Interview, Falcon River.
52. Interview, June Loewy.
53. Interview, Carol S. Damoci-Reed.
54. Interview, Linda Lack.
55. Interview, Rory Devine*.
56. Interview, Delia Silva.
57. Interview, Nancy Valverde.
58. Interview, G.K.

was shameful and role-playing.[59] Within the communities themselves, the butch-femme couple was not considered this. According to Judie Jones, all black women were considered "bulldaggers" in the 1940s, whether or not they were strongly butch- or femme-identified.[60] Bulldagger is used almost exclusively for butch women among whites but among 1940s blacks it was a term used for any gay woman, butch or femme.

In southern California the primary ethnic group is Chicano/Chicana, or Mexican American. The Plush Pony and Redz were and are bars where Spanish is spoken almost exclusively. Bar culture in this community demands a strong sense of dress, and agency. The white class stratum does not apply here. For according to dominant standards, in this Spanish-speaking culture, all the people are working class. Within this culture however there are various class levels. Someone who can pull together an attractive butch or femme look has a place in the middle strata of not only gay but also straight culture within the Mexican society of east Los Angeles.[61]

Butch-femme identity had a solid place within women of color communities. This was not the optional way of being gay; it was *the* way to be gay. Amber Hollibaugh and Cherrie Moraga's essay, "What We're Rollin' Around in Bed With," defends butch and femme as a working-class and woman of color identity, and not a separate choice,[62] as deeply connected for black, Chicana and white working-class women in that it wove cultural capital and deficit together and could not be extricated one part from another.

Location

Dorothy Allison also defends butch-femme in *The Women Who Hate Me*[63] and *Trash.*[64] As a white Southern working-class woman, Allison writes how bars and butch-femme were part of not just her lesbianism but her class identity and of how impossible it is for her to not be working class. She cannot, nor wants to, give up that part of herself. She was and will always be working class, and she embraces this status.

---

59. Interview, B.F. (informal interview, does not appear in Appendix B). This censure of butch-femme refers to 1970s lesbian feminist coding of butch-femme as role-playing.
60. Interview, Ms. Judie Jones.
61. Interview, Nancy Valverde.
62. Amber L. Hollibaugh & Cherrie Moraga, "What We're Rollin' Around in Bed With." In *My Dangerous Desires: A Queer Girl Dreaming Her Way Home,* Amber L. Hollibaugh (Durham, NC: Duke University Press, 2000), 62–84. This essay has been printed in many publications. I use Hollibaugh's book as the reference here to highlight the title of her volume and its use of the word "home."
63. Dorothy Allison, *The Women Who Hate Me: Poetry, 1980–1990* (Ithaca, NY: Firebrand Books, 1991).
64. Dorothy Allison, *Trash: Stories* (Ithaca, NY: Firebrand Books, 1988).

The poet Nikki Giovanni wrote that of all the lenses that would be placed on her existence as a working-class black child none of them would see that she was also *happy*. "Black love is Black wealth and they'll probably talk about my hard childhood and never understand that all the while I was quite happy."[65]

Small Town Gay Bar, the 2006 documentary [66] about gay bars in contemporary Mississippi, shows that things are not a lot different there now than they were in the 1950s and 60s. The gay bar rises from the ashes again and again and has an illustrious history of activist owners who have demanded that gay people in the state—not just the city—have a place. People in the film state that they drive up to four hours to have a place to exist. Two young black men stand in front of a bar. One says about the other:

> You have to understand out here he is Lawrence. Just that. Inside he is Miss [finger snap!] Loretta. He doesn't really exist out here. He exists in there. We'll drive however far we have to, to get to be that. If the bar closes and we don't have any place to go, I'm not sure what will happen—I'm not sure where we will go to be ourselves.[67]

The gay bar is that transformative space. It allows/allowed a certain section, the queerest of the queer—the butches, high femmes and drag queens—the ability to *be*. It was the transformative nature of the space that made the severe police abuse that someone like Falcon River experienced to be transformed into something else. Falcon was Mr Roanoke. She won the drag king competition in 1973 and 1974. She was the butch to beat for other butches and also for the police.

"I wasn't going there because I was into suffering," Falcon says:

> I understand some of the books written about the period seem to indicate that. But that is not why I was going there. I was going there because, and you can quote me, pleasure was my consort. That's why I was going to the bar. It was the most fun I ever had when it was fun. And they [the police] were not going to take that away from me. No matter what they did to me—they could not take it away. And they hated that.[68]

65. Nikki Giovanni, "Nikki-Rosa." In *Black Feeling, Black Talk, Black Judgement* (New York: Harper Perennial, [1968] 1971). By Permission of Author. From "Nikki Rosa" © 1968. See also Carol Jago, *Nikki Giovanni in the Classroom: "The Same Ol Danger but a Brand New Pleasure"*, The NCTE High School Literature Series (Urbana, IL: National Council of Teachers of English, 1999).
66. Malcolm Ingram (dir.), *Small Town Gay Bar* (USA: Askew Productions, 2006).
67. *Ibid.*
68. Interview, Falcon River.

Someone like Falcon estimates that she was raped—vaginally, anally, or orally—at least once a month during the five years that she patronized the bars in and around Roanoke, Richmond, and Norfolk, Virginia. The type of abuse she experienced she also saw rained down on her friends who were queer, the queens and other butches, especially black butches. Falcon is mixed race, European American mix and Cherokee, but looks white. She is quick to say that as bad as she got it, "the queens especially got it worse than me."[69] The abuse was ongoing. Because the Mafia did not exist as a strong force in the South, as it did in the North[70] there was no one to protect bars in the South or pay off the police,[71] and thus the police were allowed to hate the homosexuals. And the police were the law.

Falcon reports that when a straight man and a gay man got in a fight in which both were injured, the police called an ambulance for the straight man and left the gay man. She remembers arrests where the butches and queens were handcuffed in the paddy wagon and remembers one drag queen raped face down on the floor of the paddy wagon in front of "all of us, and we were forced to watch. We couldn't do anything. We were cuffed."[72]

These stories were not shared among the bar participants; they "knew" what happened to each other, according to Falcon, and they went on without talking about it to each other. They were rarely booked, rarely charged, and when they were released they often met in an all-night diner. Here a local gay orthodontist, "the Doctor" of the group, was the one who sewed people up, as this population would not go to the hospital for fear of more ill treatment.[73]

The gay bar becomes then Mecca and worth fighting for. It was the cave the Christians met in, knowing they might be found out and thrown to the lions.[74] It meant more than a place to drink, more than a place to meet friends, more than an end to loneliness, more even than a place to meet others like you. It meant an end to the extreme loneliness and depression that came from not knowing, not others like you, but from not knowing you yourself. If the bar did not exist, there was no physical space where you existed as a queer person. To walk out of it forever would mean killing that part of yourself that could only exist in the bar.

The South, as well as other areas like Orange County, California, plays into the matrix of race and class of the gay bar. In the South, homophobia

69. *Ibid.*
70. Interview, Joan Nestle.
71. The bars in Los Angeles, and West Coast bars, according to several informants, paid off the police directly—whereas the bars on the East Coast paid off the Mafia.
72. Interview, Falcon River.
73. *Ibid.*
74. Stephen Benko & John J. O'Rourke, *The Catacombs and the Colosseum: The Roman Empire as the Setting of Primitive Christianity* (Valley Forge, PA: Judson Press, 1971).

transformed into hatred so strong that Falcon says without exaggeration, "They were trying to eradicate us. They hated us and wanted us dead."[75]

SIGNS OF THE TIMES ... PRE-STONEWALL

Prior to 1973 homosexuals were considered mentally ill by the psychiatric establishment and sinners by all religions in the US. In Martin Duberman's biography, *Cures: A Gay Man's Odyssey*,[76] he relates the different cures he undertook for over two decades to change his sexual orientation pre-Stonewall.[77]

New voices would speak but not until late into the 1960s. In the spring of 1967,

> a student homophile league—the first such group in the country—formed at Columbia University, and soon after, a group of Episcopal priests urged that homosexuality no longer be *automatically* regarded as sinful [but] it was also in 1967 that the Supreme Court sustained the constitutionality of an immigration law that barred aliens from entry or from citizenship if they were homosexual.[78]

Psychiatry created standards that were accepted by the entire dominant culture. If the individual homosexual did not believe he or she was mentally ill there was no official organization that could back that counter-belief. The idea that what psychiatry had to say could not be wrong is what led people like Duberman to seek treatment, even though he knew he could not be happy if he was not gay, and conversely wasn't allowed to be happy *and* gay. He received advice from a friend when he was struggling with therapy who said that she knew he couldn't choose to be happy, in other words "the climate of the day discouraged gay self-acceptance ... being happy wasn't in the nature of being gay."[79] Another after-effect of psychiatry's influence could be that a person might not believe she could possibly be gay—even though she knew she was. This conundrum was experienced by Starling Walter. In 1959 in Fayetteville, North Carolina, Starling took out three books from the library and they all said that lesbians were "crazy." She knew she was

75. Interview, Falcon River.
76. Martin B. Duberman, *Cures: A Gay Man's Odyssey* (New York: Dutton, 1991).
77. Martin B. Duberman, Martha Vicinus & George Chauncey, *Hidden from History: Reclaiming the Gay and Lesbian Past* (New York: Penguin, 1990). Post Stonewall he would go on to be an award-winning historian.
78. Duberman, *Cures: A Gay Man's Odyssey*, 124–5. Italics mine.
79. *Ibid.*

different but she was so sure that she was *not* crazy/mentally ill, that she figured she could not be a lesbian.[80]

When the American Psychiatric Association (APA) deleted homosexuality from its list of mental illnesses in 1973, homosexuals were no longer officially considered mentally ill. However, this did not mean that the changes that were in the initial work of the National Institute of Mental Health's (NIMH) Task Force on Homosexuality were implemented. This work was headed by Evelyn Hooker, who began groundbreaking research on homosexuality in 1954 (which played a significant role in the APA's change of heart). In 1969, the year of the Stonewall uprising, homosexuals were still incarcerated for homosexual sex and were considered mentally ill, and in need of treatment. In its 1969 final report, the Task Force was

> severely critical of therapeutic treatments of homosexuals and placed great emphasis on the alleviation and elimination of social discrimination through the implementation of a modern penal code, involving the repeal of sodomy laws, better public education on homosexuality and the establishment at NIMH of a center to study sexuality.
>
> These recommendations were never implemented.[81]

What made Hooker's 1957 research so groundbreaking was not only that it suggested that homosexuals were not mentally ill *a priori* but also that she was the first person to study the mental health of homosexuals by working with those who were not in therapy. This is how overarching the narratives were that regarded homosexuals as mentally ill, sinners, and deviant. Since homosexuals were considered mentally ill, all previous studies assumed mental illness because they were being done on those who were already in therapeutic models that labeled them mentally ill, and to some degree then these research subjects had accepted this narrative as they were already in treatment with those who believed the designation. Before Hooker no one had looked at a population that was not already proving the subtext of assumed illness. Because Hooker made friends with a group of gay men, her study of thirty men who were homosexual—and not in prison or therapy—was the first study to disrupt this assumed illness narrative, before coming to a conclusion regarding the subject.[82]

In terms of religion there was also a metanarrative during the period 1945–75 which cast homosexuals as sinners. As stated above, it was not

80. Interview, Starling Walter. One of the reasons cited by many informants for not using the word "lesbian" to describe themselves pre-Stonewall was that the word "lesbian" was seen and used almost exclusively in the medical sense, as in being one who was mentally ill.
81. Robert Aldrich & Garry Wotherspoon, *Who's Who in Contemporary Gay and Lesbian History: From World War II to the Present Day* (London: Routledge, 2001), 196.
82. *Ibid.*, 195.

until 1967 that a group of Episcopal priests advocated that homosexuals should not automatically be cast as sinners. Like the psychiatric designation of mental illness, the designation of sinner was considered *a priori*. Homosexuals, by virtue of living in a culture that embraced this metanarrative, did not get to choose to not be sinners or mentally ill—they were already so designated. However, while the psychiatric community had standards and an official governing board that could be approached, as it was by Hooker's team, there was/is no such official board that governs the entire metanarrative that controls the concept of sin and the homosexual's designation within that.[83] While every major denomination has a governing board that sets creed regarding sin and homosexuality, the millennium religious discussion can be examined through the California gay marriage debates that happened in spring 2008.

Homosexuals were cast as sinners by the religious right, and the left tried to side-step religious definitions by attempting to center the discussion on civil marriage and cast religious marriage as a different argument—which it is. In a November 2008 episode of the talk show *Dr Phil*, the host showcased gay marriage by bringing on six experts—pro and con. The experts who were pro gay marriage were Gavin Newsom, the mayor of San Francisco who in 2004 authorized San Francisco's City Hall to legally perform gay marriages; Gloria Allred, the Los Angeles lawyer who successfully defended Robin Tyler and Dianne Olsen, the couple who were part of the lawsuit that won the right to marry throughout California in May 2008; and Joe Solmonese, then president of the Human Rights Campaign, a gay rights advocacy group. None of these people were by definition arbiters of religion. On the con side were Jim Garlow, pastor of Skyline Church in San Diego County; the president of the National Organization for Marriage, Margaret Gallagher; and the co-campaign manager of the "Yes on 8" campaign, Jeff Flint. Pastor Garlow's primary reason for being against gay marriage was that, "as a follower of Jesus Christ, I believe the Bible clearly states it begins with a marriage and ends with a wedding, so consequently, as a Christian, I feel strongly, and almost everywhere, all the world religions hold the same view."[84] The pro side did not take up the religious argument by, for instance, arguing from *What the Bible Really Says about Homosexuality*,[85] but asserted that gays and lesbians deserve equal rights, and that marriage is not about religion but about civil rights. Marriage *is* about civil rights,[86] but the arguments surrounding gay marriage were and are *very much about religion*.

83. And there still is not as of this writing (2013). Nor am I advocating for such.
84. *Dr Phil*, episode aired November 21, 2008, www.drphil.com (accessed December 19, 2008)
85. Daniel A. Helminiak, *What the Bible Really Says About Homosexuality* (Tajique, NM: Alamo Square Press, 2000).
86. My wife and I got married during this short legal window, June 16 to November 5, 2008, because of love *and* a desire for our civil rights. We were legally married in Long

It is crucial to examine the identity construction that pre-Stonewall homosexuals were placed in regarding religion. To say that the bar denizens were without religion is false. There is a difference between being cast as a sinner and being cast as an atheist. An atheist does not believe in God. A sinner has disparaged God in such a way as to be cast out of God's favor. An atheist, while not popular with faith communities, is not necessarily a sinner, and his or her arguments may be engaged. Not so the designated sinner, whose actions are evil and whose reasons for those actions are not to be engaged. Within all religions of the period pre-Stonewall, homosexuals were already cast into a category—sinner. Who did it benefit for gay people pre-Stonewall to be cast as sinners? Certainly, as suggested, not the gay person.

"An Inuit hunter asked the local missionary priest: 'If I did not know about God and sin, would I go to hell?' 'No,' said the priest, 'not if you did not know.' 'Then why,' asked the Inuit earnestly, 'did you tell me?'"[87]

Approximately 91 percent of the population identified as Christian in the 1940s; and still 82 percent of Americans in 2007 told Gallup interviewers that they identified with a Christian religion. That includes 51 percent who said they were Protestant, 5 percent who were "other Christian," 23 percent Roman Catholic, and 3 percent who named another Christian faith, including 2 percent Mormon. Because 11 percent said they had no religious identity at all, and another 2 percent didn't answer, these results suggest that more than nine out of ten Americans who identify with a religion were Christian in one way or another in 2007. In the 1937 Gallup Poll, 73 percent said they were also church members. That number stayed in the 70 percent range in polls conducted in the 1940s, 1950s, and 1960s. Since 2002, self-reported church membership has been between 63 percent and 65 percent.[88]

America was Christian during the pre-Stonewall period (and still is primarily), and considered homosexuals as sinners, so cast by Christian faith. One of the reasons why the gay bar was "the only place" to socialize was that it was the only place where, when one was known to be a homosexual, one was not automatically cast as evil/a sinner. Beverly told me that the gay women's bar was the only place where she was "seen" by anyone. Beverly ("Bev"), the chief librarian for the Department of Transportation created the library that educated the builders of California's first freeway system, was a woman in a high-level job in the 1940s, and had certainly been seen

Beach, California, on the Queen Mary, by the captain of the ship, October 29, 2008. Less than a week later, gay marriages were outlawed in California by Proposition 8; as of this writing (2013), the 18,000 couples who were married during this window are allowed to stay married in California, and as of July 1, 2013, gay couples could once again marry in California, for the US Supreme Court struck down Proposition 8.

87. Annie Dillard, *Pilgrim at Tinker Creek* (New York: Harper's Magazine Press, 1974), 123.
88. Frank Newport, "Questions and Answers About Americans' Religions" (2007), http://www.gallup.com/poll/103459/questions-answers-about-americans-religion.aspx (accessed December 26, 2008).

by people, among them her employers. Even though it was unusual for a woman during this time to be seen in this way by her employers, it was only in the gay bar that Bev herself felt seen. The bar she said was the only place she personally felt seen or safe. Did the class difference in the bar bother her? Obviously she was more highly educated than many women, and certainly this would include the working-class butch-femme community that populated most mid-century gay women's bars. The level of education did not matter to her, she said; she did not go to the bar for that—she went for community, as she said "to be seen," and to be without secrets.[89]

The most unpardonable sin in society

Emma Goldman wrote that "The most unpardonable sin in society is independence of thought."[90] The gay bars served as an alternative place to the dominant space, which offered no real *place* for homosexuals, and therefore the bar *was* also a religious space and therefore *created* religious place for mid-century gays. It does not follow that the homosexuals who entered the bar were not religious. They were cast as sinners and were very aware of the fact that their birth religions had cast them out. If asked, almost all informants who identified gay feelings prior to 1970 had an identifiable birth religion as an identity marker. Homosexuals, like everyone else, were religious people with an identity marker, but they were religious people who had been categorically and as an entire group cast out of their birth religions. They entered the gay bar as that identity, sinner, and were either troubled by it, or ignored it. But they were all *aware* of it. The gay bar was *accepting*—it was a place where one could "be seen" in Beverly's words, maybe be at home, and it replaced the outside of the bar world with an inside of the bar world. The inside of the bar world was however *surrounded* by the outside dominant religious community—any identity developed inside the bar was informed by resisting that outside dominant culture.

Troy Perry who founded the now world-wide Metropolitan Community Church (MCC) did so in response to activism he saw in the gay bar. When Lee Glaze, owner of Los Angeles' The Patch, stood up to arresting officers in 1968 and demanded that the remaining patrons go and get all the flower bouquets they could from all "the queens in the city who are florists" and then led a march down to the station to bail out "the queens in the way a

89. Interview, Beverly "Bev" Hickock.

90. Emma Goldman, *Red Emma Speaks: An Emma Goldman Reader*, ed. Alix Kates Shulman (Amherst, NY: Humanity Books, 1972), 15.

queen should be treated,"[91] with bouquets of flowers, Perry was so inspired by Glaze's action of standing up to the police that he began the MCC.[92]

On March 2, 2000 when California passed Proposition 22 that designated marriage as a legal union only between a man and a woman I was at a large rally at the Los Angeles Gay and Lesbian Center. When the results confirming the passage of the proposition were announced, there was an immediate reaction. Many people spontaneously shouted, "God made us, too!"

In the 1970 documentary *It's a Gay, Gay, Gay World*, Pat Rocco[93] documents the first gay pride rally in Hollywood. There was a marcher with a placard, "The Lord is my Shepherd and He Knows I'm Gay."[94] On November 4, 2008, Proposition 8[95] was passed in California, invalidating the Supreme Court decision of May 2008 that allowed homosexual marriages. In the massive statewide protests that followed the November decision, many of which I attended in Southern California, one of the most popular placards read, "America is NOT a religion." The passage of Proposition 8 confirms how strongly Church and State have always been intertwined in the United States. The Church of Jesus Christ of Latter-day Saints, the Mormon Church, gave an estimated 77 percent of donations to support California's marriage ban. Californians Against Hate released figures showing that $17.67 million was contributed by 59,000 Mormon families to groups like Yes on 8; contributions in support of Proposition 8 totaled $22.88 million. Additionally, the group reports that the Mormons contributed $6.9 million to pass a similar law, Proposition 102, in Arizona.[96]

One could not escape religion as an American, as the placard from the 2008 rally tried to make clear. America is not supposed to be a religion, but recent elections have shown how deeply religion affects election outcomes. How does this metanarrative of predominantly Christian faith affect the general populace, and how did it affect the homosexuals of pre-Stonewall? The gay bars of the period provided an alternative religion to the traditional church/metanarrative of contemporary Christian culture. While each religion has a governing board and some religious movements such as Unitarian Universalism, Universal Life, Reformed Judaism, and others have

91. Interview, Lee Glaze.
92. Troy D. Perry & Charles L. Lucas, *The Lord Is My Shepherd and He Knows I'm Gay: The Autobiography of the Rev. Troy D. Perry, as Told to Charles L. Lucas* (Los Angeles, CA: Nash Publications, 1972). MCC started with twelve members and now has 43,000 members.
93. Pat Rocco (dir.), *It's a Gay, Gay, Gay World* (archived at One Gay and Lesbian Archives: Performing Arts Collection, University of Southern California, Los Angeles, CA, 1970).
94. Perry & Lucas, *The Lord Is My Shepherd and He Knows I'm Gay*.
95. Proposition 8 text: "Only marriage between a man and a woman is valid or recognized in California."
96. Michelle Garcia, "Mormons Bankroll Anti–Gay Marriage Amendments in California, Arizona," *The Advocate.Com*, October 22, 2008.

through the very recent decades declared that homosexuality is not a sin, there is nothing uniformly equivalent for mainstream religious reform as there was for psychiatric reform. So there has been no universal moment when homosexuals became people who deserved civil rights within the church, rather than people who were not only actively sinning (which would imply actions with points that stop and start) but were also, because of the way they lived, sinners; that is, they were nouns instead of verbs. They were identified as embodying the action of sin, and today in most of the world's religions, they still are.

How did this definition of sinner from the dominant paradigm affect the homosexual population? I interviewed ninety-three women, eight men, and one "transgender individual" (self-identified as such), who, sometime during 1945–80, were living lives that were either privately or publicly gay. Overwhelmingly they said that the gay bars of their various periods were "the only place" to go, literally. Not the only "good" place, but the *only* public place. The gay women's bars of mid-century America then functioned for their participants in the same way as a church would have, since there was no major or minor religion that accepted gay people. Also, the bar culture itself was imbued with, and lent itself to, an inherent theology that *today* we most likely would label liberation theology, but for which I created the word "theelogy."

Looking at a historic culture and calling it something other than what it was called in its actual time period utilizes Jennifer Terry's "Theorizing Deviant Historiography."[97] When we look at a culture that was once considered deviant, as all homosexual communities were prior to 1973 when the American Psychological Association rescinded its designation of homosexuality as a mental illness—in order to correctly interpret that culture today—we must utilize "deviant historiography." Can we say that gay women pre-Stonewall were not deviant, using the lens of queer theory, feminist ethics, and other post-Stonewall methodologies, even though during their own time they were considered deviant? We can look at a culture that was considered not only irreligious, but evil, and reconsider whether it was also a base for religious community and lived theology. Deviant historiography demands that we not be ahistorical, while at the same time it allows for contemporary analyses to re-interpret the historical material. For example, David Johnson documents that the McCarthy era witch hunts had as much or more to do with identifying homosexuals as with identifying communists, and did in fact result in:

97. Jennifer Terry, "Theorizing Deviant Historiography: Feminist Theoretical Lineages of Deviant Historiography: A Retrospective Preface." In *Feminists (Re)Vision History*, ed. Ann-Louise Shapiro (New Brunswick, NJ: Rutgers University Press, 1994), 276.

> wholesale firings of thousands of government workers on grounds of "moral turpitude" ... containment of sexuality was as central to 1950s America as containing Communism. With the nation on "moral alert" because of the Cold War, stable, monogamous, heterosexual marriages were seen as a key weapon in the arsenal against degeneracy and internal Communist subversion.[98]

In addition, the charge was harder to beat; if one became a communist, one could *un*become that. However, being labeled a homosexual meant that you were inherently corruptible and *always* would be:

> In the troika of sinners routinely listed as security risks—the alcoholic, the loquacious and the pervert—only the pervert was always a security risk. The other two categories involved qualifications—not all those who talk, but those who talk too much; not all those who drink, but those who drink too much. But even one homosexual encounter qualified someone as a security risk, making it perhaps the easiest such offense to prove. It was the only one of the three to be illegal, thereby automatically enlisting every police force in the nation in its enforcement ... the only one that warranted a full scale congressional investigation, the one requiring specialized security officers, the only category about which government departments kept specific records. In most statistics about security risks, *homosexuals composed the single largest contingent.*[99]

John Garcia has owned Ripples, a gay bar in Long Beach, California, for over thirty years. The bar Ripples was also a gay bar for decades before John took it over in 1974. Garcia started out his career working at Douglas Aircraft in 1962 in southern California. He was at the point in his career there where he needed special clearance in order to advance in his position. At that point he was propositioned by a man at work. He met up with this person later at a motel. Following this, he was approached by the management of the company and shown photos of his sexual interlude. He never saw the man he had sex with again. He was told to admit he was a homosexual and resign or the information would be turned over to the authorities. He did not admit he was a homosexual.

"I didn't have to be homosexual to have been there once," he explained. He was terrified of the interrogation, and the pictures they had. He was sent to work in a unit where people had been informed he might be homosexual

98. David K. Johnson, *The Lavender Scare: The Cold War Persecution of Gays and Lesbians in the Federal Government* (Chicago, IL: University of Chicago Press, 2004), 10–11. Italics mine.
99. *Ibid.*, 8.

and he was harassed. He voluntarily quit six months later. When he walked into his first gay bar, it was the first time he felt safe. It was like he entered "a safe haven," even though he was aware an arrest could happen; he felt safe knowing that he was with others like himself finally.[100]

Such charges translate into contemporary, not just historical, reality for people accused of homosexuality in the 1940s through the 1960s. A women's studies student in the late 1990s told me that when he was on duty as a police officer an elderly man came in to register as a sex offender. He asked the man what kind of crime he had committed. The man said he was arrested for homosexuality in the 1950s. Deviant historiography allows double vision; we see the original picture and the one informed by recent knowledge.

Butch-femme bar culture is not necessarily considered deviant today, and sometimes it is even seen as exemplary. In queer theory, texts such as Judith Butler's landmark *Gender Trouble*[101] hold up the butch woman and the butch-femme relationship and its ability to destabilize gender categories as creative gender performances available in contemporary culture. This view gives validity to a form of gender expression that was not available to pre-Stonewall butch-femme women. However, this analysis does not refer specifically to pre-Stonewall butch women, who may have been seen as creative by the inhabitants of the gay bar, but were also generally reviled in the greater world. Queer theory itself has re-defined gender deviancy as gender creativity and is an example of deviant historiography. Gender studies employ terms such as "gender fucking" and represent people once considered gender deviant as now fucking *with* gender, and with the metanarrative that deems gender as biologically mandated.

When the American Psychological Association deemed in 1973 that homosexuals were no longer mentally ill, there was born a generation of homosexuals, for which being considered mentally ill, had never been their reality. They were preceded by generations whom society had considered mentally ill. Homosexuals then held both realities—their lived historical experience considered mentally ill, and a new definition that said the culture in which they lived had wrongly categorized them.

As this 1973 study of psychology ultimately did for homosexuals, I want to begin to show that homosexuals were not necessarily irreligious when they congregated in bars, but that the bars themselves became akin to churches for a new urban community, that of the homosexual. The focus of my interviews was almost exclusively women[102] who today would be called lesbians; in their coming out period they mostly called themselves gay women.[103]

100. Interview, John Garcia.
101. Judith Butler, *Gender Trouble: Feminism and the Subversion of Identity* (New York: Routledge, 1990), 156–7.
102. I also interviewed gay men and one transgender person.
103. See Appendix A: Demographics.

For women during this period the predominant way to organize was that of butch-femme. The butch-femme bar culture provided the framework in its gendering and community and public urban spaces, the gay women's bars, for a religious experience. This community then, mid-century butch-femme culture, should be added to the conversation of contemporary theology.

What if, for some, human affection is akin to religion?

> We can live without religion and meditation,
> But we cannot survive without human affection.[104]

That butch-femme bar culture community may add to theological discussion is not completely new. Joan Nestle's "Butch-Femme Relationships: Sexual Courage in the 1950s" was included in the anthology *Que(e)rying Religion.*[105] The editors wrote that Nestle's article considered an "unspecified connection between religion and homosexuality, as she makes no overt religious claims." However she "does articulate a strong belief statement about communal lesbian survival and uses such terms as 'erotic independence,' 'essential pleasure,' 'celebration,' and 'erotic heritage' that suggest religious language and lend themselves to religious categorization."[106]

However *Library Journal*'s review of the same book while recommending the volume, in particular singled out Nestle's article as having "no obvious religious elements" and stated that it did not "support the theme." However the review suggested that since religion and homosexuality seem to work in opposition, the volume furthered ways "in which they may be intertwined."[107] Why did the reviewer single out butch-femme relationships as being outside the theme of "que(e)rying religion?" Especially when the text explored other traditionally suspect areas for religious introspection such as "the sacrality of male beauty and homosex," "radical relatedness and feminist separatism," "lesbian mythology," and even "a spirituality of creative marginality"—why critically pull out butch-femme relationships as *especially* without credence for religious conversation?[108]

---

104. Dalai Lama, "Spirituality and Nature," Middlebury College, Middlebury, VT, September 14, 1990. http://www.dalailama.com/messages/environment/spirituality-and-nature (accessed July 7, 2013).
105. Gary David Comstock & Susan E. Henking, *Que(e)rying Religion: A Critical Anthology* (New York: Continuum, 1997), 323–9.
106. *Ibid.*, 282–4.
107. Debra Moore, "Book Review: Que(e)rying Religion: A Critical Anthology," *The Library Journal* (1997), http://www.amazon.com/Querying-Religion-Critical-Anthology/dp/product-description/0826409245/ref=dp_proddesc_0?ie=UTF8&n=283155&s=books (accessed April 13, 2010).
108. Comstock & Henking, *Que(e)rying Religion*, 5–8.

The editors did include Nestle's piece because of its language. The language of religion lends itself to the discussion of gay women's/butch-femme relationships and their places of congregation, the bars. It is an illuminative, transcendent language that looks at things differently, as is suggested by the inclusion of Nestle's essay, as well as the other essays which do not immediately speak to "religion."

Nestle's is the most significant, but not the only work, where butch-femme community and sacrality intersect.[109] Despite the *Library Journal* reviewer's protestations, Comstock and Henking are not the only writers to suggest that the stories provided by Nestle and others that chronicle butch-femme culture evidence a connection between butch-femme community and sacrality and/or religiosity. Kathleen Rudy in *Sex and the Church*[110] analyzes the contributions Kennedy and Davis made in *Boots of Leather, Slippers of Gold: History of a Lesbian Community*[111] in terms of erotic community. She explores what "our sexuality has to do with loving God and being church," and suggests it is time we ask how having sex affects "one's relationship with God and with the Christian community" rather than, for instance, whether homosexuals can marry.[112] She points to practices and ways of being with the gay and lesbian community as places where the heterosexual culture *may learn from*, rather than *criticize*. She cites many religious thinkers, from Saint Benedict to Dorothy Day, who have criticized Christians who prioritize their individual relationships over communal relations and suggests heterosexuals could learn from gay men, who might offer them a model for caring within community.[113] Christine Gudorf's *Body, Sex and Pleasure*

109. Christine E. Gudorf, *Body, Sex, and Pleasure: Reconstructing Christian Sexual Ethics*, (Cleveland, OH: Pilgrim Press, 1995).

110. Kathy Rudy, *Sex and the Church: Gender, Homosexuality, and the Transformation of Christian Ethics* (Boston, MA: Beacon Press, 1997).

111. Kennedy & Davis, *Boots of Leather, Slippers of Gold: The History of a Lesbian Community.*

112. Rudy, *Sex and the Church: Gender, Homosexuality, and the Transformation of Christian Ethics*, 103–7.

113. However, Rudy's book is also problematic. She praises the idea that heterosexuals and others can learn from gay male sexual communities in terms of how what happens in sexual communities is not anonymous, promiscuous, or non-relational, but "communal." (*ibid.*, 77) She then goes on to criticize butch-femme communities as "sexual activity rather than emotionality." There is no source for her quoting the "self-defined mannish lesbian" and her "lipstick lesbian partner" except to say in the footnote that butch and femme were more connected to male communities and therefore "coalition under the sign of queer is thus made much easier" (*ibid.*, 151). She sees butch and femme public roles as performative and having no relation to emotionality or domesticity. Lesbianism in "no longer defined by spiritual connections or caretaking but rather by public sexual roles." She privileges male sex communities as having public sexual roles that are worthy for spiritual discussion but not butch and femme public roles. In speaking of erotic communities, in which she includes butch-femme bar culture, she has used the same language to praise the creativity of gay men, but blames butch-femme for not being defined by spiritual connection precisely because it has a public face, just as gay men do. Not only does this privilege male sexuality as creative and transformative but it damns

also analyzes the benefits of integrating sexuality into Christian sexual ethics.[114] This book was published in 1994, along with a whole body of work that theorizes body and sexual theology, suggesting that merely integrating the two is insufficient. Since homosexuals were and are defined *by* their sexual practice as being different from the norm and as being necessary, this served to set them apart as sinners. If integrating sexuality and religion is a millennium concept, then placing homosexuals, who are different and centered on sexual practice, at the table of religious discourse itself is essential. Homosexuals have not had a seat at the proverbial table, as they have been those who were talked *about* rather than those who were talked *with*. Heterosexuals, then, can learn from homosexuals—not only because homosexuals have been ostracized on account of their sexual practice but because they have persevered in terms of creating community and developing sexual practices that differ from those of heterosexuals. What can be learned from this community if it is looked at without prejudice? Gudorf suggests examining Kinsey's 1953 findings that gay women report higher rates of orgasm than heterosexual women.[115] This is significant because 50 percent of women cannot reach orgasm through intercourse.

> Inability to have an orgasm, discontent with the quality of orgasms, and the ability to have orgasms only with one type of stimulation are common sexual complaints among women. Some studies have found that about half of all women experience some orgasmic difficulties ... About 50% of women experience orgasm through direct clitoral stimulation but not during intercourse ... About 10% of women never experience an orgasm, regardless of the situation or stimulation.[116]

Since procreation has not been the stated goal of sexuality within lesbian communities in contrast to the pursuit of sexual pleasure/orgasm, there may

---

female queer sexuality in favor of female domesticity; it also does not read into butch-femme community its domesticity and connection. However, the value of the work lies in bringing queer erotic communities into the discussion of Christianity and its necessary transformation. The book *Boots of Leather, Slippers of Gold* is not as much about public sex roles as it is, as its subtitle announces, "the history of a lesbian community". After all, Kennedy and Davis interview subjects who were involved in their community for a period of thirty years. Also, Kennedy and Davis themselves do not identify as queer scholars but as lesbian scholars—hence their subtitle. Thus, although Rudy identifies gay erotic communities as being useful to Christian ethics, she particularly disavows butch-femme from the discussion. What I propose to do is firmly insert butch-femme bar culture into that discussion.

114. Gudorf, *Body, Sex, and Pleasure: Reconstructing Christian Sexual Ethics.*

115. Alfred Kinsey *et al.*, *Sexual Behavior in the Human Female* (Philadelphia, PA: W. B. Saunders Company, 1953), Chapter 11, 446–501.

116. "Female Orgasmic Disorder," in *Encyclopedia of Mental Disorders* (2010), http://www.minddisorders.com/Del-Fi/Female-orgasmic-disorder.html (accessed April 12, 2010).

be much to learn from lesbian praxis if including sexual pleasure is part of Christian ethics.

> If the Christian community can ... experience more egalitarian, intimate marriages, ... the validation of sexual pleasure, the ability to choose parenthood for the sake of loving children, and the appreciation—neither oppression nor mere tolerance—of gays and lesbians ... then the people of God may discover that sexuality theology radically revises many central Christian doctrines, often in ways that none of us now perceive.[117]

Female sexuality, and the idea that females *have* sex, has been contested quite publicly in the US since Kinsey's dual volumes. While Kinsey was praised for the male volume published in 1948,[118] he was damned for even asking women these questions in his female volume published in 1953. A repeated theme in the publicity surrounding the female volume was that the type of woman who would respond to questions about sexuality could not represent the norm, and so statistics based on talking to women about sex could not be believed because only questionable women would talk about sex—therefore anything gathered by talking to such women was questionable.[119] Gay women's/lesbian bar culture is worthy of theological consideration on the grounds that sexual ethics reform might start with lessons from communities who defined themselves through sexuality even to the point that they were ostracized.

THE ORDINARILY SACRED

A place can define you because you take up space in that place. Philip Sheldrake's *Spaces for the Sacred*[120] insisted, *à la* Martin Heidegger, that "place is the house of being." He also quoted from Walter Brueggemann's, *The Land: Place as Gift, Promise and Challenge in Biblical Faith*:

> Place is space in which important words have been spoken which have established identity, defined vocation, and envisioned destiny ... vows have been exchanged, promises have been made and demands have

117. Gudorf, *Body, Sex, and Pleasure: Reconstructing Christian Sexual Ethics*, 25.
118. Alfred C. Kinsey *et al.*, *Sexual Behavior in the Human Male* (Philadelphia, PA: W. B. Saunders Company, 1948).
119. Kinsey Archives, "Publicity Files, 1953 Volume," ed. Kinsey Institute of Sex Research (Bloomington, IN: Indiana University). Personal research August 2008.
120. Philip Sheldrake, *Spaces for the Sacred: Place, Memory, and Identity* (Baltimore, MD: Johns Hopkins University Press, 2001).

> been issued. Place is ... a declaration that our humanness cannot be found in escape, detachment, absence of commitment, and undefined freedom ... a yearning for place is a decision to enter history with an identifiable people in an identifiable pilgrimage.[121]

Sheldrake suggests that place and the sacred are also just as likely to cause division as provoke consensus and harmony. For example, Jerusalem/the Holy Land is a place in which three major groups and several sub-groups contest the meaning of sacred sites.[122]

The same arguments swirl around the gay women's/butch-femme gay bar and its habitués. While I could have called this volume "the only place," because it was the phrase that almost all of my informants used *on their own* at some point in the interviews, the idea that this "only place" could somehow be a sacred place to some of these inhabitants is hotly contested. Butch-femme culture has appeared marginal to some rather than as a place where a group of people decided to, *à la* Sheldrake, "enter history with an identifiable people in an identifiable pilgrimage," however that is exactly what the butches and femmes and other bar attendees of the period *were* doing.

We cannot, as investigators and articulators of religious thought, decide that "place" is different from "space" and then ignore the words from a diverse and large group of people who claim a particular space was "the only place" and then say that that place had no theological significance. If in fact the city has a particular theological resonance, *à la* Augustine's *The City of God*,[123] then the urban mid-century gay women's bars created environments where we "cannot separate functional, ethical and spiritual questions."[124] For a place to be sacred, places must "affirm the sacredness of people, community and the human capacity for transcendence."[125] For the gay bar, with its Mafia owners and police raids, its prostitutes and drug runners, its butches and femmes *role-playing*,[126] its bad neighborhoods, working-class inhabitants, alcoholics, mix of straight people going to gawk at gay women in the back room, its cross dressing men—drag queens and queer youth without the money for full drag (who David Carter credits for the majority of street activism at Stonewall[127])—what could possibly be sacred about all of that? If

121. *Ibid.*, 7.
122. *Ibid.*, 6–7.
123. Saint Augustine, *The City of God*, trans. Marcus Dods (Peabody, MA: Hendrickson Publishers, 2009).
124. Sheldrake, *Spaces for the Sacred: Place, Memory, and Identity*, 153.
125. *Ibid.*
126. This is in italics because there is performative value in all of our roles. As discussed earlier in reference to Judith Butler's *Gender Trouble* (156–7), butch women, and butch-femme couplings, may embody the perfect destabilized gender performance and the ability to "perform" creatively lived lives.
127. Carter, *Stonewall: The Riots That Sparked the Gay Revolution*, dedication.

place is sacred, then it cannot be this place, correct? However, if this place *is* "the only place"—what kind of place is it?

The only place at which most of my informants could feel things that place is supposed to give—community, affirmation of people's sacredness, and human capacity for transcendence—was at the gay women's bar; so we must examine that for them this place was sacred space as we who discourse have agreed space and place are religiously categorized. It is a given that the gay bar was the only space where a *place* was established for gay community. Within the four walls of the gay bar was the only secure space where gay women could know for sure that they had encountered other gay women—thereby creating a place where they could meet someone like themselves. This latter statement affirms the sacredness of the people within the walls, because there was no other place where gay people could even be acknowledged.

People sometimes question the existence of God by asking, "Where was God in the Holocaust?" or other traumatic incident. A process thinker might say "God was in those who fought back."[128] Where was God in the gay women's bars of mid-century? God was in those who established community, who looked at a newcomer and made her feel, as many informants told me, "at home" for the first time or "seen."

> Augustine's city was a community of believers—the "City of God." Within the human city, this community could be seen as set apart from the stream of the everyday (the Church) ... it was hidden entirely given that the human Church contained those who might not make it into the Kingdom and that many people would by God's grace make it into the Kingdom without the benefit of clergy.[129]

If in fact the gay bar was the only place and it fulfilled the conditions of "place" as opposed to "space" by giving a group of people community and affirming their sacredness by first affirming their identity, then we must reconsider the function of the gay women's gay bar prior to the event Stonewall as religious.

128. Marjorie Suchocki, "Backgrounds in Contemporary Theology," unpublished lecture notes taken by Marie Cartier (Claremont, CA: Claremont School of Theology, 1998, fall).
129. Sheldrake, *Spaces for the Sacred: Place, Memory, and Identity*, 158.

2. THE 1940s "THANK GOD THE JAPANESE SURRENDERED."

Figure 2.1 "We Can Do It!", Rosie the Riveter (1942–45). Poster produced by Westinghouse for the War Production, created by J. Howard Miller. (Image courtesy of the US National Archives and Records Administration.)

> The most successful advertising war recruitment campaign in American history utilized Rosie the Riveter, a fictional character immortalized by posters supporting the war effort. [It] recruited more than two million women into the workforce [in] war production plants and necessary civilian services ... millions of American women had never worked outside their homes. ... the ads led to tremendous change in relations between women and the workplace ... employment outside of home became socially acceptable.[1]

OVERVIEW

> Thank God the Japanese surrendered ...[2]

Ginny was attracted to a female summer camp counselor and felt confused and frightened by her feelings, not knowing what they meant. On the night the Japanese surrendered, thus ending World War II in 1945, the only thing they had to celebrate with at the summer camp was coffee. Ginny drank so much coffee, and got so jittery, that the counselor/source of her nervousness wrapped a blanket around her. In her jittery state Ginny finally asked the question that was on her mind: "Do you have a penis under there? Because why else would I feel the way I do?" Her friend said, "If you really feel this way come to my house and we'll talk." So after camp Ginny did, and the woman, Corinne, read to her for twenty minutes from the groundbreaking novel, *Well of Loneliness* by Radclyffe Hall, and "we were together for 47 years. I didn't need permission. All I needed was an explanation."[3] *The Well of Loneliness*[4] was the only thing in print in the forties that suggested gay women existed. "And Stephen answered: 'I know that I love you, and that nothing else matters in the world' ... Then Stephen took Angela into her arms, and she kissed her full on the lips, as a lover."[5] That one scene from the novel was the world of information Ginny needed to know that such feelings were *possible*.

How important is it to have the knowledge that you are not the only one who feels attracted to a member of the same sex? The play *Body of Faith* was based on interviews with LGBT people; one story was of an elementary

1. War Information and War Manpower Commission & J. Walter Thompson, Volunteer Agency – Historic Campaigns, "Women in War Jobs – Rosie the Riveter (1942–45)," http://www.adcouncil.org/default.aspx?id=128. Image used by the War Advertising Council's Women in War Jobs campaign (accessed July 3, 2009).
2. Interview, Virginia "Ginny" Borders.
3. *Ibid.*
4. Hall, *The Well of Loneliness*. Gay women were called inverts in the book.
5. *Ibid.*, 145–6.

school student in the 1980s Midwest who found the word "homosexual" in the school dictionary. He was so excited to see himself described somewhere that he rushed to tell his teacher. When he went to look up his special word again, it had been firmly blacked out and he could not read it anymore.[6]

In the 1940s a woman might identify that she was a homosexual if she was serving in the Armed Forces,[7] or working in a factory,[8] or reading *The Well of Loneliness*, or by finding her way to the gay women's bar,[9] which was not easy, but was far less dangerous than it would be in the next decade. As Allan Bérubé states in *Coming Out Under Fire*, World War II needed and recruited women and men, many of whom turned out to be gay.[10] A populace emerged that had not existed before. This new tribe freed from traditional communities was on the loose in urban America. You could walk into a gay women's bar in Washington, DC, as did informant Jane Scott, and see service women in uniform. In fact, it was mandated that if you went out in public, you went out in uniform.[11] However going to a gay bar was not grounds for dismissal from the military. The psychiatric coding that would erupt in the late 1940s in order to ultimately remove homosexual elements from the military was not yet in place. This language would position homosexuals, or those that demonstrated homosexual behavior—masculinity in women and femininity in men—in league with criminals, because in the late 1940s and 1950s homosexual acts became criminal.[12] In the early 1940s in some military enclaves, female homosexuals were still often just called *gay girls*.

This change in attitude varied in different sections of the city and often depended on the class and race of the woman involved. Rae Hamilton could sing in a dinner club for her supper as a butch drag singer in the early 1940s in Los Angeles,[13] but towards the end of the decade, and a few miles further, in East LA, Nancy Valverde was arrested for "masquerading."[14] These changes were due to changing mores and a diminishing tolerance for gay women now that the war was over. They were also due to the fact that Rae lived in a gay section, was a white woman/drag performer who lived

6. Luis Alfaro, *Body of Faith, A Drama* (Woodstock, IL: Dramatic Publishing Company, 2007). *Body of Faith* premiered in 2003 at the Los Angeles Gay and Lesbian Center, California, produced by the Cornerstone Theater. Cornerstone Theater generates scripts from interviews with real people.
7. Allan Bérubé, *Coming Out Under Fire: The History of Gay Men and Women in World War Two* (New York: Free Press, 1990).
8. Interview, Jane Scott*.
9. Interview, Shirley Horowitz. Shirley told me that when she came out in the 1940s there were two ways to find a gay bar—ask a cab driver or follow a butch woman.
10. Bérubé, *Coming Out Under Fire: The History of Gay Men and Women in World War Two.*
11. Interview, Jane Scott*.
12. Johnson, *The Lavender Scare: The Cold War Persecution of Gays and Lesbians in the Federal Government.*
13. Interview, Rae Hamilton.
14. Interview, Nancy Valverde.

full-time in butch drag, and did so for a full year. Nancy, on the other hand, lived in butch drag, was not a performer, was Mexican and was the only butch she knew. When she was getting arrested—which she estimates happened two to five times a month for five years, she did not have the support of a gay city section around her. Why was one arrested and one not? Nancy never left Lincoln Heights where she grew up, and where everyone knew that she was a woman, so when she began dressing more as a man she was still *known* as woman and she opened a business that competed with male businesses—a barber shop. Rae on the other hand moved far from her origins before she began dressing in drag. She was not *known* as a woman, and so often passed as a man, and she sang in a gay establishment and was not competing against male businesses.

In the early 1940s then, when America was still at war, the attitude toward homosexuals was more tolerant, certainly more so than it would be after the war. Because the military needed the young workforce, among them gay men and women, this new population also needed to find a temporary community space. The bars of America catered to that need, and thus often became new homes for this population.[15]

Many of these bars were more clubs than bars, such as Tess's Continental in Hollywood on Santa Monica Boulevard where Rae sang. It resembled more the Tropicana of *I Love Lucy* fame than the seedy bars described in gay women's pulps of the next decade. Rae made her primary living singing at that club where she was supported by a small back-up band and where there were tables and a light dinner was served.[16]

"That was the happiest time of my life," Rae said, remembering a somewhat classy club, run by gay women, that brought in enough money to pay her and the small band that accompanied her and that did not have obvious Mob ties. Rae was paid above the table, and has pay stubs that show a regular employee who paid taxes as a butch drag singer in a gay girl club.[17]

However, making your homosexuality part of a wage-earning way of life was not an option for most women. If they were lucky enough to find the gay bar, it did not necessarily mean they had given up the option of marriage to a man. When Jane Scott fell in love with a woman in the Army it was not too surprising, albeit disappointing, that the woman she fell in love with decided to not stay with her, but to get married in order to have children.[18] The decision to marry was often prompted by the desire for children.

15. Martin Meeker, *Contacts Desired: Gay and Lesbian Communications and Community, 1940s–1970s* (Chicago, IL: University of Chicago Press, 2006).
16. Interview, Rae Hamilton.
17. *Ibid*. As far as I or Rae knows she did not have a license to cross-dress; however she did get official pay checks from Tess's Continental as a singer/entertainer and still retains those pay stubs.
18. Interview, Jane Scott*.

Jane got married herself for this reason,[19] but continued to see women and eventually wrote a book about a relationship with another wife, *Wives Who Love Women. The Love of Good Women* also explores this from the point of view of factory women, who gained enough economic independence to force similar choices in their marriages. One left her husband to live with a woman. Another convinced her husband that they should all live together—he would have a wife who still took care of the home, but no longer slept with him.[20] Jane Scott also made this choice.[21] The threat of a woman actually leaving her husband and living alone or with another woman was still, however, rare and so homosexuality interfering with heterosexual marriage relationships was not deemed as significant as it would be in later decades. In the 1950s the condemnation of butch as predator luring women away from men was drawn sharply by psychiatry, underscored in lesbian pulps and invoked by the McCarthy era as evil.[22]

Rae Hamilton was able to live in drag without police harassment in Hollywood in the 1940s and she made a living as a butch drag singer. However she fell in love with a "femme fatale" who convinced her it would be easier to exist dressed in women's clothing. Rae quit the bar, and never went back as she was too afraid to face Tess and Sylvia, the owners. Her love relationship lasted a few years, and then the woman went back to men, although in later years they lived together for over a decade in a platonic way and are still connected as primary chosen family.[23]

So *if* you found your way to the 1940s gay women's bar your experience *might* be a pleasant cocktail club, or a mixed bar with service men and women in uniform. Since bars were often set up to facilitate service women and the urban set, your chances of finding this type of bar in the 1940s were better than finding it in the 1950s. In the 50s you became the rebel *with* the cause to keep the bar open, and often looked the part,[24] as the biker dude did from the gang that James Dean wanted to join in *Rebel Without a Cause.*[25] However in the early 1940s the bar might also be where a woman could exclaim, *à la* Auntie Mame in the 1950s, "Life is a banquet! And most poor suckers are starving to death!"[26] But by the late 1940s, Auntie Mame might have said something different on entering the gay bar. Choosing between

19. Jane Scott, *Wives Who Love Women* (New York: Walker & Company, 1978).
20. Isabel Miller, *The Love of Good Women* (Tallahassee, FL: Naiad Press, 1986).
21. Interview, Jane Scott*.
22. Johnson, *The Lavender Scare: The Cold War Persecution of Gays and Lesbians in the Federal Government.*
23. Interview, Rae Hamilton.
24. Nicholas Ray (dir.), *Rebel Without a Cause,* (USA: Warner Bros. Pictures, 1955).
25. Douglas L. Rathgeb, *The Making of Rebel without a Cause* (Jefferson, NC: McFarland, 2004).
26. Morton DaCosta (dir.), *Auntie Mame,* (USA: Warner Bros. Pictures, 1958).

illicit community life in the bar, or isolated life outside the bar made many women exclaim, like James Dean in *Rebel*, "You're tearing me apart!"[27]

The most significant issue facing the gay women of the 1940s was that for the first time they could en masse be employed and therefore choose to, or choose not to, get married. While this had been primarily a privilege of women who went to women's colleges, this was not a given choice for other classes. In the 1940s a woman could join the military, or work in a factory or other employment and bring home a pay check. Public bars and dinner houses sprang up in urban areas to serve this new economically independent and youthful population. Before the war's end gay women served in the different branches of the military. Military medical employee Chris Schumacher, naval officer and head of a recreational facility for 1,000 women, remembers that "the gay ones" made the better military personnel; they were tougher. The women who went off the edge and had to "be put in straight jackets" were usually the straight women. She theorizes gay women's ability to better withstand rigors of war was a strong support system.[28]

In the 1940s for the first time women could disconnect from their families of origin, establish economic independence and create community. As Chris observed, gay military women better withstood the rigors of the war because they had stronger community than did straight women.[29]

Rae said the life in the bar was the "happiest time of my life."[30] Jane found the bars in California "very friendly,"[31] and June found "her head opened up" when she found a gay bar.[32] Among other limited spaces the bars were where one could find a community of women. College girls had this experience throughout the decade, but by the late 1940s the preference for female companionship, whether in a girls' college, factory, or military life, would become suspect as military and government agencies tried to rout out homosexuals,[33] factories sought to restore jobs held by women to men,[34] and the female homosexual became synonymous not only with the independent woman, but with the supposed damage such women were doing to America.

27. Stewart Stern, *Rebel Without a Cause*, screenplay (Los Angeles, CA: Performing Arts Collection, University of California, 1955). Stern was the writer for the movie, and Ray the director. The movie opened in 1955, with Dean as its lead. Stern did extensive interviewing in juvenile facilities and based his characterizations on the people he found there—most likely including homosexuals.
28. Interview, Chris Schumacher.
29. *Ibid.*
30. Interview, Rae Hamilton.
31. Interview, Jane Scott*.
32. Interview, June Loewy.
33. Johnson, *The Lavender Scare: The Cold War Persecution of Gays and Lesbians in the Federal Government.*
34. Penny Colman, *Rosie the Riveter: Women Working on the Home Front in World War Two* (New York: Crown Publishers, 1995), 95–103, chapter 9, "Peace": "The men had been promised their jobs when they came back."

> As they lived their lives after World War II, many women war workers did not talk about their experience. For some women it was too painful to remember how quickly their careers as welders, riveters, and crane operators had ended. Other women who were working hard just to survive did not have time to reminisce. Many women felt that people were not interested in their stories, especially during the 1950s when there was an escalating trend toward blaming working women for problems ranging from juvenile delinquency to divorce.[35]

The importance of community escalated during this period (the late 1940s), and the one community that remained, if not the only one that flourished, for gay women was the gay women's bar.[36] While during the war bar attendance could be assumed by military personnel,[37] by the end of the decade bar attendance became grounds for military dismissal. This changed the face of the masculine woman, the "Rosie," from hero to anti-hero.[38] And while bars at the beginning of the decade ranged from seedy to somewhat respectable "clubs," by the decade's end, one would be hard pressed to find the latter outside of wealthy enclaves.[39]

RELIGIOUS AND THEOLOGICAL IMPLICATIONS

> Love doesn't make the world go round. Love is what makes the ride worthwhile.[40]

If being part of a community is a tenet of identity then those denied community in traditional settings will set up alternatives. Community, or ecclesiology, is part of church identity that one can contribute to. Disconnection

35. *Ibid.*, 102–3.
36. Kennedy & Davis, *Boots of Leather, Slippers of Gold: The History of a Lesbian Community*. This book documents over thirty years of history of a community centered around the butch-femme dynamic and bar culture and shows how central the bar culture was in forming "the only place" where any such community could be found post World War Two. Although this entire study focuses on Buffalo, NY, the study is considered emblematic of what might be happening in the rest of the US in terms of female homosexual community formation. I would add that of course there is a big difference between bar attendance in a smaller city such as Buffalo, NY and in New York City, or Los Angeles, and certainly these are in turn all very different to bar life, especially in terms of level of danger, in cities anywhere in the South.
37. Interview, Jane Scott*. For example, Scott remembers meeting some of the base officers in a gay bar and they "pulled rank" on her and her friend—saying that they could make them dance on the table if they wanted, and that they had to go out in uniform if they were to go out in public.
38. Bérubé, *Coming Out Under Fire: The History of Gay Men and Women in World War Two.*
39. Interview, June Loewy.
40. Quote attributed to Franklin P. Jones. See www.answers.com/topic/franklin-p-jones.

from community, from the ability to be part of something bigger than self, disconnects people from their selves.[41] Theology has to account for the lemon sellers, Marcella Althaus-Reid writes in *Indecent Theology*.[42] For the lemon sellers in her native Argentina, who wear skirts in order to squat to urinate, are absolutely essential to her theology. To urinate is a human and humble act and liberation theology must take it into account. Her theology asserts liberation theology must take into account that woman selling lemons because she cannot go far from her fruit stand and there is no public restroom provided for her.[43]

Theology must also take into account gay bar culture—the pre-Stonewall people with no public space provided for them, other than the bar. The 1940s necessitated the creation of two gay communities, one in the war years of the early 40s, and one in the later 40s at the war's end. During the war years, the masculine woman was celebrated *à la* Rosie the Riveter. Whether or not she was actually homosexual was not necessarily celebrated, however, such a woman was not routinely kicked out of the military, even when she outed herself. Legend has it that Johnnie Phelps, Eisenhower's secretary, when asked by the general to take a message citing that all female homosexuals would be routed out of the military famously responded with, "Then my name will be first on the list." The consequence of this response was that the general rescinded the order.[44]

At the end of the decade, the psychiatric position on homosexuals changed. Codes were developed to cleanse the military of them.[45] And by the 1950s homosexuals would be asked, then forced to leave government jobs.[46] The religious implications for gay bars were that they then went from being *meeting places* for gay women, to the *only places* that *tolerated* gay women.

It would not be until the late 1950s that alternative spirituality, such as Eastern religions or body-based sects—yoga or meditation—would be introduced to the US. The emergence of this was marked by the publication of Eliade's *Yoga: Immortality and Freedom*,[47] followed by *The Sacred*

---

41. See, for example, Mircea Eliade, *The Sacred and the Profane: The Nature of Religion* (New York: Harcourt Brace Jovanovich, 1959).
42. Marcella Althaus-Reid, *Indecent Theology: Theological Perversions in Sex, Gender and Politics* (London: Routledge, 2000), 1–2. In fact her introduction is entitled "The Fragrance of Women's Liberation Theology: Odours of Sex and Lemons on the Streets of Buenos Aires."
43. *Ibid*.
44. Greta Schiller & Robert Rosenberg (dirs), *Before Stonewall* (USA: Before Stonewall, 1985).
45. Bérubé, *Coming Out Under Fire: The History of Gay Men and Women in World War Two*.
46. Johnson, *The Lavender Scare: The Cold War Persecution of Gays and Lesbians in the Federal Government*.
47. Mircea Eliade, *Yoga: Immortality and Freedom*, Bollingen Series 56 (New York: Pantheon Books, 1958).

and the Profane.[48] But it would not be until the mid-1970s that there would be acceptance of the idea that one could *create* spirituality. While some of these ideas existed before in limited spaces such as in pockets in the Harlem Renaissance with its creation and love of jazz as a kind of life-force,[49] or the beginning of communities that practiced body-based ideas such as Tantra, on the whole religions were fixed sects with rules that were decided upon by religious authorities. Certainly by the end of the 1940s with the emergence of the Cold War and McCarthyism, the less radical an individual was, the better, as America re-made itself.

In the creation of mass urban bar culture for gay men and women what was needed was conformism. As authors Kennedy and Davis have observed, bar culture and specifically butch and femme "roles" operated as an organizational system that centered the burgeoning lesbian community.[50] In the rabid fear of the 1950s the roles for both masculine and feminine women developed strongly—at least as seen from the outside.

What however emerged from my interviews was that it was very possible that, once one gained entry to the scene, one could manipulate the role one had originally assumed. The bars functioned to give people community and a cover, but also functioned as a place to stretch the gender role that the biological sexes were assigned within the larger community. Not only did this flexibility give gay women community, but it also gave them growth within that community. If they did not exercise the option of joining a bar culture community, then many of them would have been forced to live in isolation. While individuals can create their identity individually, if one does not belong to a larger group, that individuality is not recognized as such, but is seen as an outcast identity. Outcast (by definition more severe than outside the law or outlaw) identity is far removed from individual identity in that it carries the weight of being cast out and ostracized. In this respect, the bars gave gay women, especially at the end of this decade, *the option of being individuals*, albeit different from the mainstream, *rather than outcasts*.

For culture to address the outcasts, the lemon sellers, and incorporate them as individuals with specific needs rather than outcasts, is what *liberation* theology reminds us to do. Janet Jakobsen and Ann Pellegrini, in *Love the Sin*, write this about butch-femme relationships in the mid-twentieth century:

> historically there have not been the same opportunities for lesbians to develop the sort of public and quasi-public sexual institutions that characterize gay male sexual culture. Nonetheless, despite and perhaps

48. Eliade, *The Sacred and the Profane: The Nature of Religion.*
49. Geneviève Fabre & Michel Feith (eds), *Temples for Tomorrow: Looking Back at the Harlem Renaissance* (Bloomington, IN: Indiana University Press, 2001).
50. Kennedy & Davis, *Boots of Leather, Slippers of Gold: The History of a Lesbian Community.*

> in some sense because of material constraints on their public assembly lesbians have forged fresh possibilities for doing intimacies, sexual and otherwise. For example, social historians Elizabeth Lapovsky Kennedy and Madeleine D. Davis have documented the rich communities that lesbians developed in the working-class culture of 1950s Buffalo, New York. The histories of such communities are complicated. But the accounts offered by Kennedy and Davis ... show us that these communities produced alternative practices of sex and gender that offered some safety and support in the face of oppressive gender, sexual, racial and class norms.[51]

This is in the chapter "Valuing Sex," at the end of which they advocate:

> the alternative values developed in lesbian and gay sexual communities offer all of us a deeply ethical vision of the work sex can do to open up new horizons of possibility between people. What is at stake here is nothing less than what kind of social world, what kind of America, we wish to create. Sexual relations are part of this re-imagination of the possible.[52]

Sheldrake's model of "space and place"[53] can show how this community created *a place* out of *general space* (and how they found their place *in* space) where a communal identity could be birthed that *then* could struggle for liberation in specific ways. But solid community itself was indeed rare. Unlike other communities that would struggle for liberation, the gay community did not coalesce or recognize each other as community easily—their meeting spaces were fragile places that were interrupted by raids, and so on. Despite this, in the 1940s, during and after the War, it began to be possible to see yourself in community and not as the only one—even if, as the decade moved towards the 1950s, you were in the only place that those others could be in with you. But first a sense of community had to be established. By the end of the 1940s most homosexuals were just realizing that there might indeed be others like themselves.

By specifying historic butch-femme bar culture as a place where we as a culture can begin to re-imagine our world, Pellegrini and Jackobsen are among those who begin the argument that I extend. This historic culture was doing something that was revelatory, the "deeply ethical vision of the work sex can do." They look not just at historic but also at contemporary queer culture to assess how we can re-imagine sexual relations, and posit

51. Janet R. Jakobsen & Ann Pellegrini, *Love the Sin: Sexual Regulation and the Limits of Religious Tolerance* (New York: New York University Press, 2003), 146–7.
52. *Ibid.*, 147.
53. Sheldrake, *Spaces for the Sacred: Place, Memory, and Identity.*

butch-femme bar culture as a primary example, not just of how we re-imagine sexual relations, but our very world.

In the 1940s, although bars were primary to almost all gay women's sense of identity, they were not the only place to find community. The bars were democratic; they were available to all. For some women, women's colleges or the military served a similar function for the *time that they were able to stay* in those *time limited* environments. However, a queer community that existed in several places—such as the military, women's colleges, *and* the gay women's bars—was replaced in the 1950s with the reality that the bars *became and were* "the only place" for most gay women.

DEMOGRAPHIC HIGHLIGHTS

I interviewed in my friendship circle, and widened that out to friends from my circle.[54] I interviewed any woman who identified as gay, or lived a gay lifestyle, in whatever way she managed to make that happen, during 1945–75.[55] I did not look specifically for bar culture gay women/lesbians, butches or femmes, or anyone who fit a profile of someone who found bar culture important. What I found was that bar culture was the central organizing principles of gay women's culture pre-Stonewall, and it functioned to give a sense of order and cohesion to an otherwise despised community. I located women of different ethnicities, religions, ages, and class backgrounds to ensure diversity, but I did not necessarily identify informants prior to the interviews as bar culture habitués.

For the 1940s I wanted to find women who had identified gay feelings and/or had had relationships with women during the 1940s, or who identified that they were "in the life" during the 1940s. Such women were likely to be over eighty years old, and so women of that age were specifically sought. Of the thirteen women[56] *who identified gay feelings in the 1940s and acted on them* four were World War II veterans. One of these was discharged without

54. In this section I reference that which is important to deduce but difficult to do so from demographics cited elsewhere. I have chosen not to cite material which would unnecessarily expose identity. All the demographic statements in this section are from personal interviews I conducted.

55. I interviewed women who had secret relationships with other wives, as well as women who were an active part of bar culture. I did not know the details of the woman's homosexual life prior to the interview, except that she had some kind of relationship with gay feelings and with another woman during the period 1945–75, and self-identified as gay during that period.

56. There are fourteen informants listed, but they actually represent thirteen—one informant gave a second interview, with a particular story, that she wished to have labeled Anonymous.

honor for being gay,[57] and one was a pilot in the fledgling World War II female pilots program.[58]

At one time one informant spent three months in Juvenile Hall specifically for cross-dressing or "masquerading" and eight days in solitary confinement, because she was caught kissing a girl.[59] Another also dressed 24/7 in butch drag for a few years, and primarily frequented the predominantly gay enclaves of Hollywood.[60]

Three were married (to men) and all of them have children from those marriages. One of those was a "Rosie the Riveter" and worked putting rivets in jets and later joined the military. For her, the bars were a place to congregate in uniform, as she was required by military rules to be in uniform if she went out. In the early 1940s when she went to bars in Washington, she would see male officers as well as female military personnel and it was common and not illegal for them to frequent gay bars.[61] Another married woman found the bars by accident. She was riding a bus which stopped across from the If Club in Los Angles. She saw masculine women for the first time and felt like "the top of my head came off" and she knew what she was missing. She proceeded to put the children to bed, sneak out of the house on her husband, and go to the bar. She never dared to have a "much longer than one night" relationship with any of the women because she was afraid of losing her children.[62] One woman, who would later marry, had a long-term relationship with one of the pro-women softball players from the leagues that were set up during the war. She married in the 1950s in order to have children and was terrified her psychiatrist husband would discover her past and she would lose her children. She connected with the bars during her marriage purely through phone calls to make sure the bars still existed.[63]

One informant was a Pacific Islander and she reported that there was no gathering in bars when she lived on the Hawaiian Islands. All the gay community happenings occurred in private homes.[64] One was a teacher who was totally closeted, and only went to a gay bar once. The only friends she had were those of her girlfriend who taught in college. Since she taught high school, she did not dare to be out to her co-workers. In fact, even the close friends that she had with her lover of forty-seven years were never told directly—it was assumed *but not discussed*—that the couple they had drinks with every Friday were gay.[65]

57. Interview, Chris Schumacher.
58. Interview, Mari Lamy.
59. Interview, Nancy Valverde.
60. Interview, Rae Hamilton.
61. Interview Jane Scott*.
62. Interview, June Loewy.
63. Interview, Myrna Kurland.
64. Interview, O.K.
65. Interview, Virginia "Ginny" Borders.

One of the veterans, one of the very first female engineers, was also a butch escort for traveling saleswomen for a large department store and was recruited from the gay bar by an employee of the store. She reports that only once did a woman want "additional action" other than just escort service. She refused.[66]

Among one informant's many jobs was that of a driver for prostitutes. She was fourteen. She went on to be a female barber who won a case against the city of Los Angeles for masquerading in male clothes and won the right to wear clothes suited to her profession.[67] One was an upper-class librarian who only felt in community in the bars.[68] Two were taxi drivers and reported that there were only two ways to find a gay bar (and therefore community), "Follow a butch woman. Or ask a taxi driver."[69]

Three of the women I met through Older Lesbians Organizing for Change, an activist organization for lesbians over sixty. Five I met through the Coalition of Older Lesbians. One was not involved in groups but was at one point heavily involved and it was where she met her girlfriends. Three women I met through the Forty Plus Group in Long Beach, California, a social organization for women over forty. Most of their members are now primarily over sixty, even though it is open to women over forty. Other groups are closed to women under sixty, other than invited visitors. Six self-identified as butch, one as femme, one self-identified as kiki but did not identify as kiki during the period, and the remaining self-identified as androgynous. One of the androgynous women was a veteran and said the uniform prevented butch or femme identification, so someone would approach the bar table where military women were sitting and ask, "OK, who's butch and who's femme here?" She would identify as femme in that instance.[70] Two were not heavily in bar culture and did not identify with "the roles" of bar culture, but both identified as "more butch" than femme.

All but one of these women was in her mid to late eighties. At the time of the interviews, all lived independently, and eight owned their homes. Two lived together in a condo and one lives in the first ever historic Gay Elder Housing[71] opened in Los Angeles in 2007, Triangle Square, about which a film was recently made for which she was the poster girl.[72] Two women were completely isolated before they found these current social groups, and one is a woman who only went to a gay bar once. When her lover died she became an alcoholic. She quit drinking and become sober only after she joined a gay

66. Interview, Hazel "Ev" Everette.
67. Interview, Nancy Valverde.
68. Interview, Beverly "Bev" Hickock.
69. Interviews, Shirley Horowitz, and Marie McPherson.
70. Interview, Jane Scott*.
71. Interview, Nancy Valverde.
72. Carolyn Coal (dir.), *A Place to Live: The Story of Triangle Square* (USA: NoCo Media Group, 2008).

women's social network that was created as an alternative to the bar in the 1980s by another informant who was part of the pre-Stonewall gay community. This woman, Heather Hamm, saw that the community needed an alternative because she originally went to the bars.[73] The other gave up bar life to please her femme girlfriend and when that girlfriend left she found herself increasingly, and then completely, isolated until she chanced upon an older lesbians meeting.[74]

They are all proud of being gay and/or lesbian and don't believe they could be "any other way." They all felt that the bar, whether they liked it or hated it, was "the only place" for any kind of public gathering. For instance, the teacher hated the bar and had very small gatherings at which homosexuality was not discussed; the Pacific Islander only attended house parties, and the other women had varying degrees of connection to the bar, but for all it was a central place—whether or not they attended regularly.

VOICES FROM THE 1940s

Many women who literally *informed* my work had been silenced for so long. As theologian Nelle Morton encouraged, I wanted their voices to be "heard into speech."[75]

Hearing women into speech

The biographical narratives in each section are organized according to age, with the eldest informant (at time of interview) listed first. If informants were the same age at the time of interview, then they are organized alphabetically by first name (or an initial system). The exception is any interview labeled "Anonymous"—it would go after named informants, in its age category.

All informants' names are actual names, unless noted. Identifiers represent: age of informant at time of first interview, race, butch/femme or other gender identification, and religious identification in childhood.

73. Interview, Virginia "Ginny" Borders. While it is true that this woman had a drinking problem because of the severe isolation she faced after her lover's death, it is also true that many women in bar culture also became alcoholic due to the nature of bar culture itself.

74. Interview, Rae Hamilton.

75. Nelle Katherine Morton, "Hearing to Speech: A Sermon," Kresge Chapel Sermon (Claremont, CA: Claremont School of Theology, April 27, 1977). Published in Nelle Morton, *The Journey is Home* (Boston, MA: Beacon Press, 1985), 201.

***Beverly Hickock**, 88, Caucasian, butch, Presbyterian*: Beverly, Dr Hickock, created the information library that informed the builders of the California Freeway System. She found her way to the gay bar as part of a school research project—and then went back on her own. Even though she was a professional woman, she never felt "seen" except by the other bar clientele.[76]

***Marie McPherson**, 86, Caucasian, gay, Catholic*: Marie was terrified to be gay and fought it, then she met Shirley Horowitz and at the time of the interview they had been together for over fifty years. They met in New York City through their siblings who were in theater together. Marie and Shirley committed to lives of adventure—working to get travel money, then traveling until it was gone. They worked as cab drivers in the 1950s in Miami and often picked up gay men who cruised the beaches. If a man got in a cab on time he could avoid arrest—one could only walk on the beach for a certain number of hours before they legally had to get off the street. Marie and Shirley found their first gay bar by following a butch woman. The popular wisdom was that way was the only way to find one—other than asking a cab driver.[77]

***Mari Lamy**, 85, Caucasian, butch, Christian (agnostic)*: One of the women pilots in the fledging female Air Corps in World War II. She enjoyed the bars as a place to go with other women, but did not go often. After the Air Force let go its women pilots, she received a PhD in Education and became a teacher. Dr Lamy was afraid of losing her job if she was found in a gay bar.[78]

***O.K.**,[79] approximate age 85[80], Pacific Islander, gay, unknown religious identity*: O.K. originally agreed to longer participation in this project, but once the interview began, found it too painful to remember the details from her early gay life and terminated the interview. She did not go to bars—that was not available on the Island—only house parties. Today she is in an elder lesbian social group.[81]

***Shirley Horowitz**, 85, Caucasian, gay, Jewish.*[82] See entry for Marie McPherson.[83]

76. Interview, Beverly "Bev" Hickock.
77. Interview, Marie McPherson.
78. Interview, Mari Lamy.
79. If an informant wished anonymity, but did not provide a pseudonym, initials are used (which do not correspond directly to their real names).
80. Age is approximated—based on information made available the informant was in her mid-80s.
81. Interview, O.K.
82. Interview, Shirley Horowitz.
83. Their interview was conducted together.

***Anonymous**, 85, Caucasian, gay, unknown religious identity*: Anonymous's (A's) lover was raped when she stopped at an underpass to urinate going to the airport to pick up A. She had a bladder problem and there were no public restrooms. She did not tell anyone—including A that she had been raped. She found out when they both found out that the lover was pregnant from the rape. Sure that her lover would lose her teaching job if found pregnant, they went away and the lover had the baby in an unwed mothers' home. A spent many nights in the field outside the home. They gave the baby to the lover's brother; the child was never to know who her mother was and A and her lover did not talk more about it.[84] As a rule, they very rarely went to gay bars.[85]

***Rae Hamilton**, 84, Caucasian, butch, Christian Scientist*: Made her living as a butch drag singer at The Continental, a gay female nightclub in Hollywood run by two gay women in the 1940s—Tess and Sylvia.[86]

***Virginia "Ginny" Borders**, 83, Caucasian, androgynous, Methodist*: Ginny was with her partner Corinne for over forty-seven years. They got together the night the Japanese surrendered. Both teachers, they did not go to gay bars. Their social circle was limited to Corinne's friends, who they played cards with, and all assumed possible homosexuality or tolerance for homosexuality, but did not discuss it.[87]

***Jane Scott (pseudonym)**, 82, Caucasian, lesbian, Catholic (Buddhist/Religious Science)*:[88] Although Jane was an actual "Rosie" (the Riveter), working in a defense plant, she longed to be part of the Army, where popular wisdom had it that at least 50 percent of the women were gay. She was too young to enlist so stole her sister's ID and entered as her sister. She remembers having to go out in uniform—even when going to a gay bar. Eventually she did marry a man and her husband agreed to her relationships with women;[89] see her *Wives Who Love Women*.[90]

---

84. Other identifiers have been left out. This story is from a much later interview from a previous informant who wanted to reveal more of her story, but wanted this kept anonymous.
85. Anonymous story. This source gave two interviews—this part of her story must remain anonymous. This is the only interview in the study for which this particular scenario occurred.
86. Interview, Rae Hamilton.
87. Interview, Virginia "Ginny" Borders.
88. If an informant's religious affiliation changed from their birth or childhood religion, it is indicated in parentheses after the original religious identification.
89. Interview, Jane Scott*.
90. Scott, *Wives Who Love Women*.

***June Loewy**, 82, Caucasian, femme, Jewish*: Afraid of losing her daughter if her gayness came out, June did not dare to have a long term relationship, even though she wanted one. (This is what she had at the time of our interview, with informant Mari Lamy.) She snuck out at night after her husband was asleep, to go to the bars, for over a decade.[91]

***Chris Schumacher**, 81, Caucasian, butch, Christian*: A 2nd Lieutenant in the Army when her gayness was discovered because of a security check, Chris was dishonorably discharged because a college professor was pressured to "out" her. Although she liked bar culture, once discharged she became a teacher and could no longer go to the bars for fear of losing her job.[92]

***Myrna Kurland**, 81, Caucasian, kiki,*[93] *Jewish*: During the war Myrna dated one of the pro-women's softball players who played on one of the teams organized to keep baseball alive, while the men were away. But as a Jewish woman she felt pressured to marry after the war. During her fourteen-year unhappy marriage she would call the bars after her husband was asleep, just to hear the voices in the background. Her husband, a psychiatrist who believed homosexuality was an illness, Myrna thinks may himself also have been gay. She was very afraid he would put her away and that she would lose her children if her sexuality was revealed.[94]

***Hazel "Ev" Everette**, 80, Caucasian/Spanish, butch, Catholic*: Ev was approached to be an escort for female buyers in Los Angeles for a large department store—Bloomingdale's. She agreed and was employed as a butch escort for female buyers, for approximately twenty-five dollars a night. Later, she joined the military and was one of the first female engineers.[95]

***Nancy Valverde**, 76, Mexican, butch, Catholic*: Nancy has been featured in several documentaries, among them *A Place to Live*[96] and *On These Shoulders We Stand*,[97] as well as an experimental opera.[98] She is the second woman to fight the LAPD's masquerading charges and win. She was arrested throughout the 1940s and 50s. She helped create the still-operating gay

91. Interview, June Loewy.
92. Interview, Chris Schumacher.
93. "Kiki"—a term used in pre-Stonewall butch-femme bar culture to refer to someone who did not identify specifically as butch or femme.
94. Interview, Myrna Kurland.
95. Interview, Hazel "Ev" Everette.
96. Coal, *A Place to Live: The Story of Triangle Square*.
97. Glenne McElhinney (dir.), *On These Shoulders We Stand*, (USA: Impact Stories, 2009).
98. Butchlalis de Panotchtitlan, *The Barber of East L.A.* (Los Angeles, CA: One Gay and Lesbian Archives, Performing Arts Collection, University of Southern California, 2008).

women's bar, Redz, in east LA When the management hired "one of our own," a gay woman bartender, Nancy and her friends decided "they gave us an inch; so we took a mile." They stood on the street denying men entrance saying it was only for women "a private party." She has helped raise children and still cuts hair.[99]

99. Interview, Nancy Valverde.

3. THE 1950s
"I SHOULD HAVE MADE A LIST OF MY GIRLFRIENDS!"

Figure 3.1 "Lemme stay. I wanna watch." Mercedes McCambridge in an unaccredited role as a butch gang leader in *Touch of Evil* (dir. Orson Welles, 1958). She is the figure on the far right. (Feature Film, publicity still with Mercedes McCambridge, Courtesy of Universal Studios Licensing LLC ©1958 Universal Pictures Company, Inc.)

OVERVIEW

I should have made a list of my girlfriends![1]

The 1950s held conflicting realities for gay women,[2] many of which were media-stoked and known to gay women that lived the life. Such conflicts are embodied in the roles of gay icon Mercedes McCambridge, famous for playing tough talking dames of the period,[3] and also of the period's future.[4] In the 1958 *Touch of Evil* she is the butch gang leader who wants to watch the rape of naïve Janet Leigh; an unlikely role or request from a real butch living on the mean streets of the urban US.

Stella said, "I should have made a list of my girlfriends," when we met and unraveled her history;[5] she is emblematic of many gay women—butch and femme—from that period. Many had girlfriends, and plenty of sex. I did not meet, nor heard of, any butch that "watched," much less wanted to watch a rape. I did hear from women forced to watch a rape that was perpetrated as punishment for being gay. Many informants talked of such an experience and in one case that experience has been dramatized.[6] Butches during this period, although biologically female, were characterized by the media as the butch gang leader type character above with a masculinity that designated them not only as queer, but as predatory, inhabiting a maleness coalesced in a female form so perverted that it could wreak havoc on normal society. Such depictions took place despite the Freudian doctrine of the previous decades that proclaimed the true invert, the butch or drag queen, as having little chance of rehabilitation. The best the true invert could hope for was to adjust to his or her lifestyle as best one could as the abnormal person within normal society that had no place for him or her.

In a famous letter to an American mother in 1935, Freud wrote:

> Homosexuality is assuredly no advantage, but it is nothing to be ashamed of, no vice, no degradation, it cannot be classified as an illness;

1. Interview, Stella Miller.
2. I do not use "lesbian" to describe women who did not use that term to describe themselves. I use "gay women" as this was what most called themselves prior to the rise of lesbian feminism in the 1970s.
3. Nicholas Ray (dir.), *Johnny Guitar* (USA: Republic Pictures, 1954). McCambridge plays against Joan Crawford who wants to run her out of town. They are the real cowboys—while the male cowboys sit back and watch.
4. William Friedkin (dir.), *The Exorcist* (USA: Hoya Productions, 1973). This was another unaccredited role for McCambridge, and one for which she had to fight to receive credit and royalities. Her role was the famous demonic voice.
5. Interview, Stella Miller.
6. Panotchtitlan, *The Barber of East L.A.* This performance opera was partially based on the real life story of Nancy Valverde, the real barber of East LA and the opera centers around the story of a rape of a femme, which a butch must watch.

we consider it to be a variation of the sexual function produced by a certain arrest of sexual development. Many highly respectable individuals of ancient and modern times have been homosexuals, several of the greatest men among them (Plato, Michelangelo, Leonardo da Vinci, etc.). It is a great injustice to persecute homosexuality as a crime, and cruelty too ... If [your son] is unhappy, neurotic, torn by conflicts, inhibited in his social life, analysis may bring him harmony, peace of mind, full efficiency whether he remains a homosexual or gets changed ...[7]

Despite this 1935 writing, homosexuals continued to be prosecuted in the *name of justice*. Many butch women were considered "true inverts" and, according to Freud, could not be rehabilitated. However, this did not prevent psychiatry from prescribing treatments such as electric shock that would try to change sexual orientation. At least a third of those interviewed knew someone intimately who had been institutionalized for being gay. One informant's lover was mentally crippled by the experience and never recovered. *Every woman* was aware she could be institutionalized, and knew she was considered mentally ill. "Ev" Everette volunteered "one of our own even had a lobotomy, right?"[8] She then said she was speaking of the actress Frances Farmer.[9]

There were also many women able in psychological terms, but unwilling, to be rehabilitated. This was the feminine woman or femme (as opposed to the masculine, "invert" or butch) who also populated bars and created the butch-femme culture that organized gay female relations.[10] Butch Stella then

---

7. Freud, Sigmund Freud, "A Letter from Freud," *American Journal of Psychiatry*, April 1951, p. 786. Although this was reported in significant journals, such as *American Journal of Psychiatry* in 1951, Freud's 1935 proclamation did not affect the field that considered homosexuality a mental illness until 1973, when homosexuality was removed from the diagnostic manual of mental illnesses.
8. Interview, Hazel "Ev" Everette.
9. William Arnold, *Frances Farmer, Shadowland* (New York: Berkley Books, 1982). This book, made into a movie by the same name, documents the inhuman treatment culminating in a lobotomy experienced by Frances Farmer—an independent woman/actress imprisoned in several mental hospitals because of that independence. Many, among them informant Ev, have said this independence was actually her homosexuality. Farmer was in Kimball Sanatorium in La Crescenta, CA, an unincorporated part of Los Angeles County. Her place of work, Hollywood, and her location for part of her incarceration/treatment suggest that this geographic connection could situate her as one of "our own" as Ev suggests, in terms of her being part of the Hollywood gay women's crowd during the 1940s.
10. Nestle, *A Restricted Country*. This memoir documenting the bars of New York City is still the most important source for showing what the bars meant to urban women in terms of creating community and one in which butch-femme relationships flourished providing a measure of safety for a completely disenfranchised people. However, this New York

could recount her adventures and lament that she wished she "had made a list," in order to remember all of her past lovers!

While the two images of butch monster/predator and butch lover/prideful of sexual technique are in conflict, one thing was certain—the butch could bring a woman to orgasm—which in an age of sexual misinformation, the straight man often could not.

> In 1953, Alfred Kinsey noted that 78% of lesbians achieved orgasm in most of their sexual encounters, compared to 55% of heterosexual women. Reportedly, 15% of women have experienced multiple orgasms at some point, but studies suggest that lesbians have them more often. ... it has been shown that unlike heterosexual sex, lesbian activity is geared toward partner gratification—specifically by taking more time and varying positions so that both partners achieve orgasm. Studies consistently show that lesbians in long-term relationships have more gratifying sex than do straight women.[11]

While research on lesbians' multiple orgasms is recent, research that indicated gay women achieved orgasm more frequently than straight women was published in the Kinsey Report on women in 1953—and was widely read.[12] Because the gay woman herself *was* a woman, she had privileged information about the female body. Many butch women considered themselves good lovers, and it was in this area that they competed with men, and flaunted their knowledge.[13] For many considered the non-orgasmic woman a challenge, one they frequently overcame.

Cultural contradictions abounded. For example Sandra Tignor, an African American self-identified kiki[14] fell in love with a white woman while they were students at Bellevue Nursing School. They carried on a torrid affair sneaking around to meet each other.[15] Bellevue Nursing School was on the same property as the infamous Bellevue Psychiatric Facility. Flo, in her seventies, said that in the 1930s through 1950s a bounty was put on the heads of homosexuals. She still went to the bar despite the danger. "They

experience can not be generalized to ascertain what was happening throughout the US, particularly in more rural areas, and throughout the South.

11. Dr. Frank Spinelli, "The Advocates: Spry in the Sky—Sisters Doin' It for Themselves," *The Advocate*, August 2009, theadvocate.com (accessed August 14, 2009).
12. Kinsey *et al.*, *Sexual Behavior in the Human Male.*
13. During the course of the research I was told a joke, reportedly told first by Lilly Tomlin, about how she loved that butch women would walk around the old school gay bar holding their beers by *hooking their thumbs in them*, thus signifying sexual prowess.
14. Urban Dictionary (February 20, 2009), http://www.urbandictionary.com/define.php?term=kiki&defid=426508 (accessed August 19, 2009). Pronounced "kye-kye" ("i" as in"why"), kiki signified a woman who did not identify as butch or femme.
15. Interview, Sandra Tignor.

were offering twenty-five dollars if you turned in a homosexual to Bellevue. They had seventy-two hours then to try him out, and then they could keep you. Anyone could turn someone in. It was really cheesy. But it was the only place you could go [the bar] and feel like you were part of a family."[16]

"During much of the 20th century, electroshock, radiation, castration, and even lobotomy were common medical 'treatments' for homosexuality. One doctor, Walter J. Freeman, would lobotomize gays and lesbians at public events, as many as 25 a day, often with an unsterilized ice pick."[17] Treatment deemed as "therapy" to "repair" homosexuality, in fact most "therapy" itself, has a very long, dark, *and yet* legal and culturally acceptable history.[18] These so-called treatments also included cold water immersion, severe drugging, as well as "talk" therapy. However, New York was also the site of the Village bar scene that included bars like The Sea Colony, the epicenter of butch-femme bar community.[19] Carol remembers going to The Sea Colony across the bridge from New Jersey. "I would put on a tie that I kept hanging over the rear view mirror of my car and I would not come back until Monday!"[20]

Despite "the only place" moniker the gay bar receives, there were selected other places. Nursing was a profession where gay women who became nurses met each other, according to S.E., a nurse on one of the first open coronary by-pass teams in the nation. She met "a lot of my girlfriends ... [and that] includes my long term partner" in the operating room.[21] It was possible to meet women while in the military in college, or while employed in a field such as nursing, teaching or other female centered profession. One could also meet women in an all female environment—such as the convent. However, these were limited worlds and not available to everyone. Not everyone could get in to worlds such as the military, college or the convent—and once in those worlds one would often have to leave by default as would happen to college women, or would be asked to leave as happened to military and convent women.[22] As for meeting in the professions, one had to

16. Interview, Reverend Flo Fleischman. See also David Mixner, "LGBT History: The Decade of Lobotomies, Castration and Institutions." *Live from Hell's Kitchen*, July 28, 2010. http://www.davidmixner.com/2010/07/lgbt-history-the-decade-of-lobotomies-castration-and-institutions.html (accessed July 7, 2013).
17. Diva, "Interesting Sex Facts," www.chud.com/forum/archive.
18. Karen Ocamb, "California to LGBT Youth: No More 'Ex-Gay'—You're Officially OK!" *Frontiers LA.com*, October 1, 2012. http://www.frontiersla.com/News/Context/Story.aspx?ID=1783388 (accessed July 20, 2013).
19. Nestle, *A Restricted Country*. This bar is memorialized in this memoir.
20. Interview, Carol S. Damoci-Reed.
21. Interview, S.E.
22. Interviews, G.J., Bronco Alda Moonwater and Jeanne Cordova. Although I did not interview anyone from the 1950s who was asked to leave the convent, I did interview several women who were asked to leave in other decades. At the time they were not told why, and they did not find out why until later. Both G.J. in the 1960s and Bronco in the 1970s were asked to leave by their Mother Superior and had no idea why until much

be careful exposing to another *as a gay woman* in the workplace. The truth was that for most women the only way to meet women *who were known to be gay* and to ascertain that they were safe to expose one's own gayness to, would be to meet them at the gay bar.

At the end of the war the government's questioning of deviants (i.e. homosexuals) increased along with strict codes of conduct distinguishing between straight and homosexual behavior. These unwritten codes were what Adrienne Rich would call "compulsory heterosexuality" in the lesbian feminist 1980s,[23] writing that gender boundaries are created by biological determinism, enforced by compulsory heterosexuality and a gender police. In the 1950s the punishments included being fired, discharged without honor, incarcerated in a mental institution, among others. Whereas in the 1930s and 1940s a man portrayed as a filmic swish/fairy might be portrayed as fun-loving and debonair, à la Fred Astaire in *Top Hat,*[24] or a woman/filmic butch as cross-dressing Kate Hepburn in *Sylvia Scarlett.*[25] In the 1950s, however, such portrayals would be *queer.* Rosie the Riveter, the butch 1940s call to action to resist gender stereotypes and work in a male factory job, was supplanted by the happy homemaker of the 1950s, portrayed most effectively by girl-next-door Doris Day in *Pillow Talk* playing against Rock Hudson, now known to have been gay.[26] Day was also supposedly a gay girl.[27] This is best illustrated in *Calamity Jane*, where it appears she might love another woman until the end where she loves a man, and from which sprung the theme song of the period's gay women's bars, "Secret Love."[28] So, although queer people acted in and submerged themes in 1950s films, the 1940s *gender deviancy* was no longer positively portrayed—men became strong and masculine *men*, and women became soft and feminine *women*.

Although the image of Rosie the Riveter has been used to promote strong women from its inception to its use in the 2008 Hillary Clinton Presidential campaign[29] and beyond, its edginess—the promotion of butchness or masculinity/strength in women—has never become so commonplace that it

---

later. Jean voluntarily left because she came out in the convent and did not want to live a closeted life within its walls.

23. Adrienne Rich, "Compulsory Heterosexuality and Lesbian Existence," *Signs* 5(4) (1980): 631–60.
24. Mark Sandrich (dir.), *Top Hat* (USA: RKO Home Video, 1935).
25. George Cukor (dir.), *Sylvia Scarlett* (USA: RKO Radio Pictures, 1936).
26. Michael Gordon (dir.), *Pillow Talk* (USA: Arwin Productions, 1959).
27. Andrew Davies & Andre Schafer (dirs), *What a Difference a Day Made: Doris Day Superstar* (USA: Florianfilm, 2009). This documentary explored Day's long rumored homosexuality. Day hereself has never actually "come out," but many works, among them this film, explore her possible gayness. The song she sang, "Secret Love," was one of the most popular songs in gay bars of the 1950s.
28. David Butler (dir.), *Calamity Jane* (USA: Warner Bros, 1953).
29. Hillary for President, "Hillary Clinton for President '08 Campaign Store," www.demstore.com (accessed August 17, 2009) .

lost its edge. It is still radical for a woman to be masculine and still useful to society as Rosie originally depicted. However in the 1950s, any Rosie should let a man have her job, as her job was to raise a heterosexual family.[30]

Women who refused the seduction of the *Feminine Mystique*, which Betty Friedan unmasked in 1957 in early chapters and which exploded into the US consciousness in the book edition in 1963,[31] were seen as freaks/deviants or at best spinsters/old maids until the feminist movement of a decade later.

> She (Friedan) knew that what she was writing was revolutionary, since the genesis of the book, the results from a questionnaire to her fellow alumni, had produced such a negative reaction from various women's magazines when she tried to sell the results as an article in 1957. As Friedan notes in her introduction to the tenth anniversary edition of *The Feminine Mystique*, "the then male publisher of *Mc Call's* ... turned the piece down in horror"[32]

The 1946 classic *It's a Wonderful Life*[33] foreshadows this transformation by casting Donna Reed as the happy housewife in the film's real time. In a fantasy/nightmare sequence she is the harrowed spinster librarian, having not married Jimmy Stewart. That she had a career at all coded her as unmarriageable and perhaps then gay. In other words, it was not "a wonderful life" if you remained unmarried.

The 1950s was also the rise of Senator Joe McCarthy's House on Un-American Affairs Committee, and the Cold War, where people lost careers and went to jail if they were labeled homosexual.[34] As Joan Nestle said, there was a reason "why they called us pinko Commie fag."[35] So the question asked at McCarthy hearings, "Are you now, or have you ever been, a Communist?" was actually often asked in back rooms as, "Are you now, or have you ever been, a homosexual?" In the hearings the term homosexual would not routinely be used, but Communist could be used as a code word for it. This is visualized in *Good Night, Good Luck*, which dramatizes the on-air feud between radio and television journalist Edward R. Murrow and Senator

30. Colman, *Rosie the Riveter: Women Working on the Home Front in World War Two*. The last third of this book documents how women who were sought out in the 1940s for factory jobs were then asked, forced, encouraged, and finally shamed into leaving those same jobs in the 1950s.
31. Betty Friedan, *The Feminine Mystique* (New York: Norton, 1963).
32. Ryan D. Poquette, "The Feminine Mystique: Female Repression," in *Nonfiction Classics for Students*, ed. Marie Rose Napierskowski (Detroit, MI: Gale, 1998). See www.enotes.com/feminine-mystique/female-repression, January 2006 (accessed August 19, 2009).
33. Frank Capra (dir.), *It's a Wonderful Life* (USA: Liberty Films (II), 1946).
34. Johnson, *The Lavender Scare: The Cold War Persecution of Gays and Lesbians in the Federal Government.*
35. Interview, Joan Nestle.

McCarthy, in particular when the CBS journalist Don Hollenbeck commits suicide because he is accused in the press of being a "pinko."[36] Homosexuals might be, like Joan Nestle, people on the edge who had attended a Socialist meeting and therefore easily labeled "Commie." Or they might not be Communist, but their real crime, and one that they could not negate, was the crime of being a "fag."[37] They would agree to the Communist accusation, because the love spoken of at Oscar Wilde's 1895 English homosexuality trial that "dared not speak its name" would still not speak half a century later, and those accused would be found guilty as charged.

The 1950s gay woman lived between a rock and hard place, hounded to give up her job and get married. If not possible because of her class, she should feel ashamed and strive to be able to quit her job. If she had a government job—educational, medical, or social—she lived under the shadow of McCarthy era fear. If married with children, she lived in fear of losing them, as did June waiting until her husband was asleep, then sneaking out to the gay bar,[38] or Myrna who called gay bars in the middle of the night just to hear the voices in the background.[39] The phrase "there was no other place" was more true in the 1950s than in any other decade; gay bars existed as an oasis of four walls in which the rock and the hard place eased literally to create a pocket of breathing room.

The factors that determined where a young gay woman would end up after coming out in the 1950s were luck, and a complicated matrix of social or cultural capital. Such capital is amassed from traits considered worthy within the dominant paradigm, as opposed to the non-dominant section of society.[40] The gay bar functioned as a place where gayness had currency. Gayness had no currency in this period otherwise. It was not just deviant *outside* the dominant culture, if known, but completely *isolated the gay person from the entire culture* itself—except for the gay bar.

However, even the gay bar needed some capital—that is, you have to have money to buy drinks. But, capital could also be the ability to pass as straight or traditionally feminine. The beautiful acclaimed historian Lillian Faderman was a pin-up girl of the 1950s who supported her lover with work in

36. George Clooney (dir.), *Good Night, and Good Luck* (USA: Warner Independent Pictures, 2005). The actor Ray Wise portrayed the journalist Hollenbeck and it is clear from his performance that something shattering has happend to his reputation—we are led to believe that it might actually be homosexuality that he is accused of, rather than "simply" being a "pinko."

37. Interview, John Garcia. John was up for a security clearance and was set up. He was asked out by a fellow male employee and taken to a motel for sexual relations, where, unknown to him, pictures were taken.

38. Interview, June Loewy.

39. Interviw, Myrna Kurland.

40. Pierre Bourdieu, *Distinction: A Social Critique of the Judgment of Taste* (published in French as *La Distinction*) (Boston, MA: Harvard University Press, 1984), 66.

the pin-up sex industry,[41] was also in love with a prostitute and was offered the job of a prostitute. She said that if not for a guidance counselor who saw her potential as a scholar (she went on to be an eminent historian) she might have "followed her and become a prostitute" herself.[42] As a working-class and recognizably ethnic (Jewish) woman, her resourcefulness in rising up out of the bar culture was based not only on her own enterprising spirit, but also her cultural capital, which included the luck of being born with superior intelligence as well as drop-dead good looks and the luck of having very supportive female relatives who were insistent upon her getting an education. She was able to move into the Hollywood scene later where beautiful, feminine gay women resided (not necessarily femmes attached to butches) and, as she put it, "I ran from the butch-femme bar scene as soon as I could."[43] But she still went to and worked at a gay bar—the Laurel Club, a club known for its Hollywood actress clientele and its headliner, the Marlene Deitrich-esque Beverly Shaw. But this was not before Lillian found her sexuality in the If Club, where she acknowledges she went specifically to "have sex" and discover herself as a gay woman. It was on the streets of Hollywood, near the butch-femme bars that she met Frankie,[44] her first butch lover, and it was at the If Club where she fell so in love with a prostitute that she almost traveled across the country and joined her in that profession.

This same woman entered UCLA and was afraid to check out a book on sex variance with the unsexy title *Sex Variant Women in Literature: A Historical and Quantitative Survey*,[45] the groundbreaking self-published 1956 work. Faderman took it surreptitiously from the shelf and read it in different crannies within the library and returned it to its place without checking it out before she herself left the library. Why? Because she was afraid of being labeled a deviant by the university; she could not out herself by checking out an academic book about sex variant women, or even be seen reading it.[46] That a woman of Faderman's intelligence would have this hard a time being out in the rarified academic world of UCLA illustrates how difficult it might be for a gay woman not in school to make her way "out."

41. Lillian Faderman, *Naked in the Promised Land* (Boston, MA: Houghton Mifflin, 2003).
42. Interview, Lillian Faderman.
43. *Ibid.*
44. Frankie Hucklenbroich, *A Crystal Diary: A Novel* (Ithaca, NY: Firebrand Books, 1997).
45. Jeannette H. Foster, *Sex Variant Women in Literature: A Historical and Quantitative Survey* (New York: Vantage Press, 1956).
46. Joanne Ellen Passet, *Sex Variant Woman: The Life of Jeannette Howard Foster* (Cambridge, MA: Da Capo Press, 2008). Faderman relates this story in her introduction to this biography of Foster, who she never met in person—only through her work. Foster was rare herself; she was interviewed by Kinsey for his research and then asked and became Kinsey's librarian. She left the Kinsey Institute for many reasons, one of which was to write her own book.

Upon hearing the above story, a friend told me that she herself worked in a library in urban academic southern California in the early 1980s and was also afraid to check out books on homosexuality. This was before she herself came out two years later, and a few months after that she graduated with her girlfriend watching. By this time, she had visited a gay bar, and later would be a DJ in one, the butch-femme Huntress in Mid-Way City from 1989 to mid-1990. But she would remain closeted in various degrees. Her first teaching job was at a Catholic school with teenagers; she continues to teach but is still fairly closeted in academia. She says that even today she might not check out lesbian books from that library because she works there, today as a professor. During that period her girlfriend was looking into the highway patrol as a profession. If there was a line outside the bar her girlfriend needed to leave because her background was being checked and she couldn't be seen standing in front of the bar. They could go in if there was no line, but they could not loiter. When her girlfriend was in the force, the girlfriend gave my friend a T-shirt emblazoned with "California Highway Patrol" (CHP) on the front and told my friend that she could not wear it in any gay space or at any gay event. My friend told me that otherwise her girlfriend was not skittish about her sexuality, but did have a deep understanding of "the hell her life could have become if the CHP knew she was gay in the 80s. It's not that she ever told me; you never got any impression from her that she was worried. It was just the way it was—you weren't 'out' as a police officer, period."[47]

Another friend said that as an out butch firefighter in urban Los Angeles in the 1990s, she worried that no one would "watch her back" in a fire in which she might get trapped or otherwise need assistance. She was a firefighter for the city but was aware of deep homophobia around her. Her femme girlfriend worried for her safety on a daily basis.[48]

There is research now, however, that suggests that, due to the Iraqi War and the desperate conditions for its infantry, young service people returned and have said that they do not mind serving next to a known homosexual.

> a 2006 Zogby International poll, commissioned by the Michael Palm Center of US combat veterans from the Iraq and Afghanistan wars ... 75% of soldiers were comfortable working with gays and lesbians, and 68% either knew for certain or suspected there were homosexual members of their own unit. Yet clearly the combat readiness of our military has not suffered with the known presence of gay troops.[49]

---

47. Interview, Mary. Although this informant preferred to use her entire real name, she declined in the end for fear that her ex-lover would still be under scrutiny for her sexuality and could be identified in some way if she did so.
48. Interview, Bren*, 1998.
49. Log Cabin Republicans, "Issue: Gays in the Military," www.logcabin.org/lcr.chicago/gays-military (accessed August 19, 2009). On September 20, 2011, the U.S. repealed the "Don't Ask, Don't Tell" doctrine, finally allowing gays to serve openly in the military.

It remains to be seen if these attitudes will affect our cities' homosexual civil servants. In California from June 2008 to November 2008 homosexuals could legally marry within the state, per a California Supreme Court ruling.[50] That ruling, which allowed homosexuals full civil rights for the first time, was revoked at the ballot with the passage of Proposition 8, November 4, 2008. Many organizations rose in order to fight Proposition 8 and the fight for marriage equality in California was documented around the world.[51]

We often hear about the people who make (or in Faderman's case write) history because they had lucky breaks.[52] We don't hear about those without cultural capital that would allow them to rise up and what was remarkable about their lives is that they *did* survive, despite the odds. H.C. runs a rubber stamp store, and works a second job. She can't go to the older lesbian social meeting held in Long Beach because, at sixty-five, she must still work day and night. Her story is very familiar. She was accosted by the police for cross-dressing in Long Beach, hid during several bar raids, had a factory job, fell in and out of love with straight women, and is astounded by contemporary queer culture. She attended her first elder lesbian social, after which everyone gathered at the local gay coffee shop. She was shocked because she had never in her life been in a public space—other than a gay bar—as an out lesbian.[53]

As the 1950s wore into the 1960s and beyond, some women left bar culture for other gay lives. Joan Nestle left bar culture for a political life in Gay Liberation.[54] This was also true of Carolyn Weathers who came out butch-femme in Texas, moved to California where she became a hippie and joined the West Coast Gay Liberation Front (GLF).[55] For them, bar culture was the *entrée* into gay culture, and they took different paths out, or deeper into, that culture. The 1950s culture provided the birthing place for their sexuality. And it would stay that way deep into the 1960s, when activism emerged and things began to change.

---

50. However, during this time military could not marry because of the "don't ask, don't tell" rule. Gay marriage during this period was legal in certain states, among them California. US gay military could not get married without "outing" themselves at the federal level, and so military men and women were told that even though it was legal to marry in California during that window, it was not legal *for them*.
51. The Courage Campaign, "Prop 8 Upheld: Be Fearless in Response," www.couragecampaign.org (accessed September 17, 2009). Many organizations sprung up to fight against Proposition 8. The Courage Campaign was the organization with which I, with our own Long Beach Equality group, was most closely aligned in California. As of this writing, the prohibition against gay marriage has been declared unconstitutional. In June 2013 the Supreme Court struck down Propostion 8.
52. Interview, Lillian Faderman. Faderman is the first to acknowledge she did receive such breaks, citing in particular her guidance counselor.
53. Interview, H.C.
54. Interview, Joan Nestle.
55. Interview, Carolyn Weathers.

"ONCE I HAD A SECRET LOVE"

Figure 3.2 "Once I had a secret love/That lived within the heart of me/All too soon my secret love/Became impatient to be free .../At last my heart's an open door/And my secret love's no secret anymore" ("Secret Love", from *Calamity Jane*, © 1953 [Renewed], WB Music Corp, used by permission). Doris Day in *Calamity Jane* (dir. David Butler, 1953), singing the hit "Secret Love" (Ed Clark/Time & Life Pictures/Getty Images). "Secret Love" was written specifically for Doris Day for the film. It became an immediate hit.

The most significant issue for 1950s gay women was that they were not just called but actually *were* in the eyes of the law deviants, inverts, sinners, criminals, felons, *and* mentally ill. There was *no* religion, major or minor, that housed them. Alternative religious movements did not gain currency in the US until the 1970s. Consequently your job was in danger if you were outed, unless you were someone like Carole who worked for Juju Fruits Candy and, although arrested, did not lose her job because she had five brothers and her family knew Mafia members.[56]

Several women felt the Mafia protected them, and felt comfort from them. Joan Nestle, although ambivalent about the bouncer at the Sea Colony, said "Vinnie protected us, but he also made jokes about us ... it was confusing. We were all outlaws and that also bonded us."[57] While bar culture spread in the 1960s to include the South, this did not necessarily come with Mafia protection, and some women felt the police had the agency "to kill us."[58] The

56. Interview, Carol S. Damoci-Reed. She still exclusively eats only this candy.
57. Interview, Joan Nestle.
58. Interview, Falcon River.

Mafia watered down drinks, regularly scheduled raids with the police, but also paid off the police so the entire bar would not be shut down—at least not for long. The police were receiving "gayola/payola"[59] as well as providing police presence. On the East Coast the bars paid off the Mafia, who paid off police. On the West police were often paid by the bars through services, such as prostitute services.[60]

Senator Joe McCarthy and the House on Un-American Affairs Committee broadcasted live into American homes. Communists and those who were different were all suspect, especially homosexuals. As noted, Joan said, "There was a reason they called us Commie pinko fags. We were all lumped together—many of us were red diaper babies, we came of age in a home where that was discussed."[61] The idea that a psychiatrist could spot a homosexual was attractive to the fear-filled 1950s, for the homosexual's secret world easily merged with this secret Communist world in people's minds, and was cemented by McCarthy. The Cold War's agents were the medical, religious, and psychiatric establishments and, as in any war, spies are rewarded for turning in enemies.

If you named names of suspected Communists, and those who were homosexual, you were rewarded if only by being without a sentence yourself. So, when Chris Schumacher was accused of homosexuality in the 1940s because of the testimony of a former lover,[62] or when John Garcia was accused of being homosexual in the 1960s because of the testimony of a man he was propositioned by, had sex with, and was photographed with without his knowledge[63]—they were not able to question those who had made the allegations. The fact that the allegations had been made was *supposed* to be all that was required to lose a job. Both of these individuals tried to fight and hold on to their jobs, but were both unsuccessful. If you were accused, the *societal* charge was so great that it was almost impossible to escape unscathed—or even alive. *The Children's Hour*, Lillian Hellman's play[64] based on a true story,[65] documented this. The 1930s filmed version was without homosexual content;[66] the 1950s film was packaged with

59. When Mafia paid off police it was called "payola;" when Mafia paid off police to keep gay bars open it was called "gayola."
60. Interview, Barbara Kalaish.
61. Interview, Joan Nestle.
62. Interview, Chris Schumacher.
63. Interview, John Garcia.
64. Lillian Hellman, *The Children's Hour* (New York: Dramatists Play Service, 1934; Acting edition 1953). It premiered in 1934 at Maxine Eliot's Theatre, New York, where it ran for two years.
65. Lillian Faderman, *Scotch Verdict: Miss Pirie and Miss Woods V. Dame Cumming Gordon* (New York: Quill, 1983). This is the true story of two headmistresses, accused of being homosexual by one of their students, on which Lillian Hellman based her play.
66. William Wyler (dir.), *These Three* (USA: Samuel Goldwyn Company, 1936).

homosexuality intact and released in 1961.[67] Two schoolmistresses, Martha and Karen (Shirley MacLaine and Audrey Hepburn), are accused in whispers we never hear of being gay and the Martha character ultimately kills herself because she can't stand the pressure of the charge—for *it doesn't matter if they beat the charge*, which they do. It doesn't matter if they know the charge was untrue, for we are led to believe the charge was *not true*—the only truth to the charge was that *once accused*, Martha, acknowledges that yes, she *may have had* romantic love feelings for Karen—feelings which were not acted upon. Even so, Martha screams to Karen at the end, "Don't you see? *It's in me*." And then she kills herself.[68] There was no place to *be*.

Bars provided then a place *to be*—even for significant events, such as the weddings Ava performed at the Lost and Found in Chicago. She considered herself empowered as the captain of a ship is so empowered in the absence of anyone else.[69] The ceremony she used solemnized unions with the biblical, "these three remain: faith, hope, and love. But the greatest of these is love."[70] However, whereas the area inside the bar *might* be *somewhat* protected due to Mafia "gayola", the area around the bar was without protection—in any area of the country, North or South. Falcon from the South reported that in the late 1960s the walk to and from the bar could be the most dangerous part of the evening. "Seeing a drag queen walk from her car to the bar was and is still the most courageous thing I have ever seen."[71] Nestle from New York City reported sitting at a table and the mail slot in the door flipping open and urine streaming near her and her date.[72] The 1950s woman was aware that hostility permeated the world of the bar, but surrounded it as well.

Barbara tended the bar and lived behind The Star Room in Los Angeles and remembers police coming into the bar and being paid off with prostitute service. She was never officially informed of how this worked by the owners, but surmised how the pay off happened as she observed from behind the bar.[73] Falcon also reports that later in the ensuing decade police would break the law—physically assaulting, even raping, homosexuals that they pulled from Southern bars, but did not actually arrest, so there was no record of the assault. She also saw many times a femme drop to her knees to "do" a judge or policeman so that her butch lover would be released. Falcon genuinely asked "So, who had it worse—me or them? It was bad for all of us."[74] The novel *Stone Butch Blues* dramatizes this type of 1950s bar culture—a butch goes to jail, is raped by police (as was Falcon), her femme girlfriend comes

67. William Wyler (dir.), *The Children's Hour* (USA: The Mirisch Corporation, 1961).
68. *Ibid.*
69. Interview, Ava.
70. 1 Corinthians 13:13
71. Interview, Falcon River.
72. Interview, Joan Nestle.
73. Interview, Barbara Kalaish.
74. Interview, Falcon River.

to bail her out (as did Falcon's), and the butch makes no noise, for fear her femme lover would hear the cries.[75]

Perhaps because she had ties to the Mafia community Carole did not experience police harassment, other than verbal abuse when she was arrested at The Sea Colony and jailed.[76] Nestle however remembers police taking a butch woman from the same bar and feeling her up and down because "they could ... We would all crowd around—but that wouldn't stop them from doing what they wanted to do ... to show that *they could*. We as gay women couldn't stop them—we had no power really other than to witness it."[77]

This is the play pool, slick your hair in a duck tail, smoke a cigarette a certain way, or wear a poodle skirt, beehive and red lipstick era. In *Restricted Country*[78] Nestle writes that these unique roles for men and women were also unique to butch-femme bar culture. Kennedy and Davis's respondents' confirm this in *Boots of Leather, Slippers of Gold* writing that female *as femme* desire had a unique *place* in this culture.[79] A femme woman like Joan, or Madeline, or Lillian, when she first entered bar culture, could go to a gay bar because she wanted to have sex and not feel "dirty" about that. The outside culture and the walk to the bar might feel dirty and try to make her feel her desire was wrong, but in the bar, her *actual desire* to have sex was prized. This was radical as during the 1950s any woman's sexual desire was suspect, hetero or homosexual.

Informants were prostitutes, were asked to become prostitutes, saw police paid through prostitute services, and were harassed. By going to the bar a woman admitted she was sexual and would take risks for it. But she also acknowledged desire and exhibited her intentions. Judy Grahn entered bars in the 1960s and said, "It took enormous courage for a woman to walk through the door. The gay women's bar was the underground."[80]

This decade symbolized butch-femme and bar culture more than any other. The title of the history of lesbian life *Odd Girls and Twilight Lovers* combines two lesbian pulp titles of the period.[81] This is how the 1950s saw gay women—as "odd" girls and "twilight" lovers. In fact, they *were* twilight lovers for they had very little reality in daylight. Most did not know each other's real names, only bar names, and many informants confirmed this.

It is no coincidence then that much vampire fiction has been written about lesbians, as both must live only in the night and be asleep through the

75. Feinberg, *Stone Butch Blues: A Novel*.
76. Interview, Carol S. Damoci-Reed.
77. Interview, Joan Nestle.
78. Nestle, *A Restricted Country*.
79. Kennedy and Davis, *Boots of Leather, Slippers of Gold: The History of a Lesbian Community*.
80. Interview, Judy Grahn.
81. Faderman, *Odd Girls and Twilight Lovers: A History of Lesbian Life in Twentieth-Century America*.

day.[82] The only place to be alive as a gay woman was the bar. So much so that the *de rigueur* ritual when seeing someone outside the bar, as all respondents reported, was to not acknowledge each other if either person was with someone *not* seen also in the bar. No one wanted to out a person one had met in a gay bar by acknowledging them outside of it. The power in the bar seemed limited—to flirt, play a game of pool with friends, light another's cigarette—but actually it was immense because it was a place where one existed. The butch-femme romantic world organized female homosexual life in the 1950s and it took place in the twilight world—but it did *take place.* Gay women birthed themselves into very different sexual selves from what the dominant culture asked.[83] However, in the daytime world, this twilight world was undercover as deeply as Alice's rabbit hole.

However, connections were made with others. Nestle reports walking through the Lower East Side to the bar and running into a "fellow outlaw," "a fellow traveler." He was passed out in the street. She moved him, a big man, by herself. Why? She did it because she felt a sense of community with him as "fellow outlaws."[84] When talking with butch informant Flo, I expressed surprise that so many drug dealers, prostitutes, and pimps were her friends. She said, "Honey that is *the only people* we could hang out with."[85] The walls of the bar were not a jail because one could enter and hopefully exit freely, but they were *actually* four walls. Therefore the bar community was criminal for those who would criminalize it, and akin to heaven for many others.

RELIGIOUS AND THEOLOGICAL IMPLICATIONS

Hells Kitchen theologian, Walter Rauschenbusch creates theology, much as Altheus-Reid does with the lemon sellers,[86] except he speaks of alcoholics.[87] Many gay women did become alcoholics. More than one said, "This is what

82. Jewelle Gomez, *The Gilda Stories: A Novel* (Ithaca, NY: Firebrand Books, 1991). This is unique as it is a lesbian vampire fantasy by a *lesbian* author. The publication also prefigured much of the vampire literature published after the millennium, which as a rule showcases ambiguous sexuality.
83. Friedan, *The Feminine Mystique*. This book would expose the culture's demands for women for what they were—a mystique that made most women depressed, many clinically so, because it could never be reached—the supposed happiness that was "the happy homemaker." However, this was about heterosexual women. While homosexual women lived in danger, and many were depressed and alcoholic because of the shame and danger in which they lived, they were not under a misconception that this was supposed to make them happy. There was a reality to gay women's lives in the fifties, that was not true for straight women.
84. Interview, Joan Nestle.
85. Interview, Flo Fleischman.
86. Althaus-Reid, *Indecent Theology: Theological Perversions in Sex, Gender and Politics*.
87. Walter Rauschenbusch, *A Theology for the Social Gospel* (New York: Macmillan, 1917).

we had to do—drink—so of course people became alcoholic."[88] Rauschenbusch's theology should reach these people. However theology did not reach the homosexual women of the 1950s. In fact, even Alcoholics Anonymous (AA), founded in 1935, would not necessarily have been open to a gay alcoholic before the 1970s. Rauschenbusch is insistent that theology must reach out even to those in Hell's Kitchen, New York City. Alcoholics Anonymous did respond to this call, but *not* necessarily for gay alcoholics. Although AA is not a religion, it does recognize a "higher power," and therefore uses "God language." However, it was not assumed that the gay alcoholic was not a sinner first (because she was gay) and an alcoholic second. While private gay meetings were available to those *in the know* as early as the 1950s, a publicized gay friendly meeting did not happen until the late 1960s.[89] Attending these private and limited gay AA meetings where one could find comfort in a higher power meant that one would lose the comfort of gay bar society, the only semi-large culture a homosexual had; difficult as it is to imagine one's life encased in a bar, it is even harder to imagine one's life in a meeting.

Being sober is challenging even with support, and in the 1950s staying sober without the bar culture (only place) was exceedingly hard.[90] In Borden's *The History of Gay People in Alcoholics Anonymous* one informant reports being at a "gathering of physicians and other alcoholism professionals in New York in the early 1950s and hearing someone say, 'Many people can recover from alcoholism, except, of course, the homosexuals.'"[91]

Since Alcoholics Anonymous meetings are mandated open to all alcoholics it is not allowed by the by-laws to have a meeting that is *closed* to non-gay members (although there are women-only meetings). However since the 1970s there have been meetings specifically advertised as gay-friendly, and by 1980 this presence was solidified at the July 1980, national conference. "Gay AAs have their own program at the 40th AA Anniversary in New Orleans."[92] Prior to this, a gay alcoholic would have had to come out as gay *and* alcoholic in order to get help, assuming that he or she was even made to feel welcome. In the 1950s gayness was closeted in meetings, and through

88. Interview, Rory Devine*.
89. Audrey Borden, *History of Gay People in Alcoholics Anonymous: From the Beginning*, Haworth Series in Family and Consumer Issues in Health (London: Haworth Press, 2006), 77. Borden identifies that the first group that would fit the definition of a modern gay group would be the San Francisco Fell Street Group, established in early 1968. In order to be considered a gay group, the group should have three criteria: started by gay alcoholics, for gay alcoholics; held in a public venue, rather than a private home; and publicized as a gay meeting inside and outside of AA. This group also appeared in the World Directory of AA meetings in 1975.
90. *Ibid.*, chapter 4, "Five Views of Sober Gay Life in the 1950s and 1960s," 37–67.
91. *Ibid.*, 51.
92. Alcoholics Anonymous—Alcoholism Recovery, "Important Dates in AA History," http://www.cyberrecovery.net/forums/showthread.php?t=629 (accessed July 28, 2013).

the 1960s to the 1980s many gay alcoholics who revealed their gayness were harassed.

> In the 1960s, 70s and 80s, gay AA groups and their members were subjected to surveillance, harassment, and other forms of intimidation by some of the more homophobic members of AA. Parking lots outside gay meetings were monitored ... Gay members' automobiles were identified. Meetings were invaded in an attempt to shut them down. George M. who volunteered at the New York General Service Office for many years, reported hearing of a gay AA group in Australia whose members were told that unless they disbanded, their full names and addresses would appear in the local paper ... members of gay groups were vulnerable to such attacks ... and their sobriety, their jobs, their homes, families, and physical safety were at stake.[93]

It was very difficult for a homosexual to receive help in the 1950s for alcoholism when they were also declared a national security risk and prosecuted as such. People felt it was patriotic to inform on anyone who was a security risk, and high on the list were homosexuals. To alert other gay alcoholics who wanted help in finding a gay-friendly meeting or at least a meeting where other gays would be present even if they did not make their presence known to the general meeting, was to "place certain words, phrases, acronyms, and references in their group names that gay alcoholics would recognize, but straight alcoholics would not—such as naming a group a 'Live and Let Live' group."[94]

> Gay and lesbian alcoholics in recovery often face unique challenges. Professional assistance may be sometimes tainted by the prejudices ... limitations may become more pronounced when one seeks assistance from mainstream sobriety self-help groups, where prejudices and lack of knowledge can be more glaring ... For those living outside of metropolitan areas where there is a large gay and lesbian population, the feelings of isolation and lack of social acceptance that many gay people experience can be intensified. ... worsened by the further isolation of dealing with addiction to alcohol, and getting sober itself can be hampered by imposing a social barrier to the interpersonal support that is widely regarded as so important to recovery. ... contact with sober gay men and sober lesbians can be vital to those seeking recovery.[95]

93. Borden, *History of Gay People in Alcoholics Anonymous: From the Beginning*, 72–3.
94. *Ibid.*, 74.
95. Gay and Lesbian Alcoholics, "Alcoholic Recovery in the Gay & Lesbian Community," www.gayalcoholics.com (accessed September 21, 2009).

This information is written for alcoholics *in 2009*; one can imagine the struggle to get the "interpersonal support" AA cautions is vital to recovery in the 1950s, when the only interpersonal support a gay person could count on receiving was in a bar. Carolyn Weathers relates how her sister Brenda became alcoholic, as many women did, due to the nature of the double life she led as a homosexual, and that she could not find help in the straight Alcoholics Anonymous groups. She went on to found the Alcoholism Center for Women in LA in 1974, the first facility of its kind on the West Coast.[96]

The 1950s did not start the rumblings of liberation theology. But they showcased its need. What happened in the 1950s that did affect some of the urban gay women's experiences was the early beat generation,[97] the introduction very slowly of the counter-culture, and of yoga and body-based worship[98] alongside the extreme conformism that rocked the nation.

It was also the birth of the teenager, specifically because of the film *Rebel Without a Cause*.[99] Since many of these women were teenagers, the rebellion of youth was attractive:

> during the Second World War, legions of women, for the first time, could legitimately be employed, this economic freedom facilitated a freedom to create a new kind of masculinity—that of the butch. These butches dated femmes, a new kind of woman. This type of coupling was apparent in urban culture, but was not presented on film ... James Dean, an admitted homosexual, acted in *Rebel Without a Cause*, as a butch woman, cloaked in the guise of his fictional heterosexuality. This gave heterosexual men the permission to learn the new masculinity that had been created during the war—by butch women. Dean is the perfect butch for Judy (played by Natalie Wood), except he is male—or is he? Is it a coincidence that Hilary Swank's Oscar-winning role in *Boys Don't Cry* was frequently compared to "a young James Dean?" What are the implications of Dean's gender bending? Was Dean a new kind of man—or woman?[100]

Butch-femme and their innovative gender creations provided major contributions we have not fully considered, one of them to create a significant

96. Interview, Carolyn Weathers. This facility is still in operation today.
97. Regina Marler, *Queer Beats: How the Beats Turned America on to Sex* (San Francisco, CA: Cleis Press 2004).
98. Eliade, *Yoga: Immortality and Freedom*; Eliade *The Sacred and the Profane: The Nature of Religion*.
99. Ray (dir.), *Rebel Without a Cause*.
100. Marie Cartier, "The Butch Woman Inside James Dean or 'What Kind of Person Do You Think a Girl Wants?'" *Sexualities* 6(3–4) (2003): 443–58. In this extended study I write of James Dean's masculinity and the contributions butch women made to it—specifically from this generation.

foundation for what we today call queer theory. The invention of the teenager as espoused in this period where a transient youth population sprung up in the wake of the war, meant a new breed of person had been born. The teenager symbolized rebellion even in this age of overarching conservatism. The period's ability to coalesce an outlawed population owes a debt to this creation. Process thought is the many becoming one. In the 1950s many disillusioned teenagers, many of them gay, found a community that became in a sense, one.

DEMOGRAPHIC HIGHLIGHTS

Lillian Faderman has said that the "fifties were the worst decade for lesbians."[101] Gay women were perceived as having no redeeming societal value—no Rosie the Riveter image as has been stated. As sinners and lacking God's help in changing that sin, the culture turned to psychiatry and its cures, among them shock therapy and excessive drugs as cures of the homosexual disease. Although one informant was forced to undergo an exorcism to rid her of homosexuality, the threat of psychiatry as a way to rid homosexuals of themselves hung over everyone.

I interviewed twenty-one women who identified gay feelings and acted on them in the 1950s.[102] Three of them are African American, one is Mexican, one was mixed Mexican/Native American,[103] and sixteen are Caucasian. One has a daughter that is half Native American.[104] Five are Jewish, one "Holy Roller,"[105] two Baptist, and four are Catholic. One Catholic had Puerto Rican parents and had the exorcism mentioned performed on her to rid her of her gayness. It failed.[106] Two informants are Christian, one Greek Orthodox, one Methodist, one Unitarian, one Protestant and two are unknown to me in their religious identity.

Two were ex-military, one was dishonorably discharged,[107] four were involved in bar culture as their means of employment, one a bar owner,[108] one a bartender[109] (both butch), and one an erotic bar performer (in a

101. Lillian Faderman, "Lecture Presentation," paper presented at Another World is Possible: The Los Angeles Social Forum, June 28 2008, Los Angeles, CA.
102. All the demographic statements about informants are from personal interviews.
103. Stella Miller died in 2009. I performed her last rites because at the Catholic hospital where she was, there was no one else available to do a pagan ceremony.
104. Interview, Theresa Blackwell.
105. Interview, Judie Jones.
106. Interview, Mary Martinez.
107. Interview, Stella Miller.
108. Interview, Jewel Thais-Williams.
109. Interview, Barbara Kalaish.

straight bar) and one waitress (in a gay women's bar).[110] The erotic bar performer dated several butch women in the 1950s; and freely admits she went to the bar "to have sex," as three other femme informants also said. Four were/are academics, four nurses, one a Vegas and New York dancer,[111] one a talent agent and someone who knew gay Hollywood celebrities,[112] one an accountant, one a mortgage broker by day and at night "dated prostitutes and roller derby girls ... and dressed as a butch,"[113] one a factory worker,[114] one bred dogs and told no one about her life. "I cried into a lot of dog fur."[115]

Three were arrested, two spent time in jail—for being gay.[116] One frequented The Sea Colony, made famous by Nestle's essays,[117] one had problems with the military and one had problems with the police as she tried to run a gay bar, and they raided her bar until the AIDS epidemic when they told her they were afraid to enter her bar, for fear of contracting the disease.[118] Six were butch, seven femme, one "kiki," one a"bulldagger." "All of the gay women were called bulldaggers in Harlem, didn't matter if you were butch or femme."[119] Two were closeted except to their lovers and had no concept of butch-femme. One femme acted femme upon coming out, then moved into an androgynous community, and one rarely went to bars as she was a nurse and did not strongly identify with the "roles" butch and femme.[120]

Seven were married and all had children, one was in a lavender marriage, a marriage to a gay man.[121] Only one had never gone to a gay bar.[122] One was a nurse who rarely went to gay bars.[123] For the rest, bar culture was significant whether or not they liked the bars for they all went to bars at a certain period as their main social outlet. I met the women through the social clubs mentioned in Chapter 2 and also through a woman who hosted a party at which she brought together women from her retirement community.[124] It was the first time some of these women had met each other and been at

110. Interview, Lillian Faderman.
111. Interview, Judie Jones.
112. Interview, Selma "Sunne" Mahovel.
113. Interview, Andy.
114. Interview, Carole S. Damoci-Reed.
115. Interview, Sadie Smith*.
116. Interview, Carole S. Damoci-Reed.
117. Nestle, *A Restricted Country*.
118. Interview, Jewel Thais-Williams.
119. Interview, Judie Jones.
120. Interview, S.E.
121. Interview, Lillian Faderman. Her child is one of the first born using artificial insemination when she was no longer married to a man, but permanently partnered to a woman.
122. Interview Sadie Smith*.
123. Interview, S.E.
124. Interview, Marilyn Taylor.

a gay function. One was from a local gay coffee shop and is cared for by a younger woman I had also interviewed,[125] one was a former professor,[126] one a woman she referred me to, one a woman who I ran into at a conference for gay historians,[127] one was someone whose work I had admired and we became email friends and she granted two extensive interviews.[128] Three were African American women who I connected with through friendship networks.

I met women though the Women of Forty Plus Group in Long Beach,[129] an older lesbian social group which I attended for a year before I was allowed to seriously interview anyone within it. By that time I was not a visitor but a member and have remained so. Seven informants were in their 70s, fourteen in their 60s and all lived independently; half own homes or condos, one lives in her own apartment with other gay members who care for her, and two had Alzheimer's.[130] All are proud to be lesbian and are out. Two informants founded gay/lesbian historical societies,[131] three write gay/lesbian history,[132] and two founded lesbian social clubs: one for older lesbians and one for African American lesbians.[133] One works for GLBT rights,[134] and four have published GLBT books.[135]

One still runs a gay bar.[136]

VOICES FROM THE 1950s

Theologian Nelle Morton encouraged creating a theology that would hear women into speech.[137] I hope that the theology that I am constructing will be useful to these women themselves, the lemon sellers of their period.

125. Interview, Mary Martinez.
126. Interview, Lillian Faderman.
127. Interview, Madeline Davis.
128. Interview, Joan Nestle.
129. The "Forty Plus" group is in Long Beach, CA and was founded by informant Heather Hamm as an alternative to the bars in the late 1980s, when its members were primarily over 40. Today its members are mainly over 60.
130. One I interviewed before she contracted Alzheimer's, the other already had the disease at the time of the interview. At the time of this writing, the one being cared for by her partner has passed away.
131. Interviews, Madeline Davis, Joan Nestle.
132. Interviews, Madeline Davis. Lillian Faderman, Joan Nestle.
133. Interviews, Heather Hamm, Sandra Tignor.
134. Interview, G.K..
135. Interview, Jane Scott*. This is in addition to the three women who have been cited previously as having published books on LGBT history.
136. Interview, Jewel Thais-Williams.
137. Morton, "Hearing to Speech: A Sermon."

Hearing women into speech

Biographies are organized according to age. The biographies are presented to document the emergent gay female bar culture community in the US after the war.

***Barbara Kalaish**, 78, Caucasian, butch, Jewish:*[138] Barbara, a bartender at the Star Room, witnessed police being paid with prostitute service. She took to being butch quickly once she found it. Barbara "came out"[139] in the mid-1950s, and before that was married with children.[140] She remembers making and selling dildos in the backroom of the Star Room. They made them from mattress stuffing and electrical tape!

***S.E.**, 75, Caucasian, gay, Catholic*: S.E. was a surgical nurse and met her lover in the operating room (she was part of one of the first coronary bypass teams in the nation). You could meet women in the operating room because so many nurses were gay. She "came out to herself" at 13 but didn't go to gay bars until she moved to Long Beach, CA at age 25.[141]

***Sandra Tignor**, 74, African American, kiki, Baptist (Science of Mind)*: Sandra met her first lover, Edie, a white woman and they snuck into each other's rooms at Bellevue Hospital—the same hospital that in the 1950s did electric shock treatment on homosexuals.[142]

> I came out without the benefit of the bar. I had married a man in 1957, but it didn't last long. [My girlfriend] found out the names of the bars in the Village ... they were integrated ... .primarily white. And that was the thing that disconnected me from the bars ... there were no mirrors for me. But I did go because there was nowhere else to go as a couple.

---

138. In these excerpts I have kept a woman's story together—informants in each decade talk about successive decades. For example, Barbara's story happens in the 1960s, but she identified gay feelings and acted on them in the 1950s.
139. There are varying definitions of coming out, such as to one's self, or in a gay bar to people in one's life. For people pre-Stonewall coming out, if they used that term at all, meant acknowledging one's love for the same sex to one's self, and then entering gay bar culture. By coming out here Barbara entered gay bar culture, and since Barbara entered lesbian feminism in the 1970s, she uses this phrase for herself and talks about when she "came out" in the 1950s, using a term she became comfortable with in the 1970s, but which wouldn't have been used in the 1950s.
140. Interview, Barbara Kalaish.
141. Interview, S.E.
142. Interview, Gypsy Powers. Her story documents severe abuse within mental institutions of homosexuals. Gypsy's friend was kidnapped by her parents and forcibly placed in a mental institution in New York during the 1960s.

> The Daughters of Bilitis[143] came into existence in New York City. And Edie did go to a couple of their meetings. I wasn't interested ... I didn't ... feel that I needed a lot of support ... I knew my family would not be happy with me hanging out, particularly, with a white woman. And not just hanging out, but being lovers ... but I also was clear that that would be their problem not mine.[144]

***Theresa Blackwell**, 73, Caucasian, femme, Catholic (Church of Religious Science)*: Theresa ran away with her Mexican girlfriend and worked in a migrant farm camp and her Native American husband found her and knocked her out cold. Her lover ran because her husband would have killed her. Later her husband tried to take her daughter. He said that his wife was a homosexual. When the cops approached her, Theresa said she was gay and that her daughter would be better off with her, not with him, and she managed to keep her daughter.[145]

***Madeline Davis**, 70, Caucasian, femme, Jewish*: Madeline co-wrote *Boots of Leather, Slippers of Gold: The History of a Lesbian Community* because, like Nestle, who founded the Lesbian Herstory Archives, she felt the stories of butch and femme had not been told.[146] Madeline was part of the beat scene; she did not view her homosexuality as terrifying because she was already non-conformist.[147] "I went into the bars for the first time in 1957. They were in Buffalo, New York." She cannot imagine what her life would have been like without the Buffalo bars The Carousel and The Midtown.

> I wonder if I would have come out if that had not been a wonderful world ... I can't visualize who I would have been ... that was the world I knew ... the other world wouldn't exist for another ten years ... feminism would have evolved independent of bar culture but the melding of that with those working-class women was very important towards the evolution of the liberation that we know now.[148]

***Stella Miller**, 70, Mexican/ Native American/Irish, butch, Native American: Creed of White Buffalo*: She was discharged from the military as undesirable but still "loved every minute in the Army" because she was with other gay women. She wished she "had made a list" of all her girlfriends. She was a nurse for fifty years and in a fifteen year relationship with a prostitute.

---

143. Marcia M. Gallo, *Different Daughters: A History of the Daughters of Bilitis and the Rise of the Lesbian Rights Movement* (New York: Carroll & Graf, 2006).
144. Interview, Sandra Tignor.
145. Interview, Theresa Blackwell.
146. Joyce Warshow (dir.), *Hand on the Pulse* (USA: Frameline, 2002).
147. Marler, *Queer Beats: How the Beats Turned America on to Sex.*
148. Interview, Madeline Davis.

She was on drugs. But she was basically a good person. When I first met her, she had ... hot pants on, and her hair done up and all this stuff. She said some of the men ... all they wanted to do was talk. So she was willing to talk about anything. I learned some stuff from her. She was married. She had a little girl. Her husband died of cancer and he used to hit her and stuff like that ... anyway. Life goes on."[149]

***Selma "Sunne" Mahovel**, in 70s, Caucasian, butch, Jewish*: Sunne hob-nobbed with Hollywood celebrities during her bar days. The Hollywood scene played out mainly in private parties, but it did overflow into select bars—in the Valley and the Canyons around Los Angeles. However, she came into gay life in New York City, "I called up friends and said 'I went to a gay club. Would you like to go and see what it's like?' And they would pile into my car. But unbeknownst to them I was fascinated. And I wanted to have a woman make love to me. In the 1950s I was at the Bagatelle, it was the only bar I ever went to." Later in California she said,

> I knew the woman who ran the bar, Joani Presents,[150] I knew her very well ... and she was in the movie *Some Like It Hot*.[151] She had her own little band. One of my hooker friends had a big affair with Lana Turner. I knew quite a few that Suzanne Pleshette played games with. Tyron Power's wife, she was. It's not that they were gay; they were bisexual. A lot of these women played both sides of the field.[152]

***Andy**, 69, Caucasian, butch, unknown religious identity*: Andy hung out at the If Club. She was there when a prostitute was run over by a car. She could not believe the callousness of the police—because the woman was known to be a prostitute and gay. She talked about how hard it was to stay off drugs and alcohol in the bar culture—as there was nowhere else to go, and she loved the people who went there. They were her people, even "if they became alcoholic ... and so on".[153]

***G.K.**, 69, Caucasian, butch, Christian*: G.K. found release from upper-class roots in bar culture. She also found and escaped from an abusive marriage and fell in love with a go-go dancer from Miami and brought her back to California to live with her; love was found in the bar, not just sex.[154]

---

149. Interview, Stella Miller.
150. Dan Luckenbill, "Los Angeles," in *glbtq: An Encyclopedia of Gay, Lesbian, Transgender, and Queer Culture*, ed. Claude J. Summers (Chicago, IL: glbtq, 2006). www.glbtq.com/social-sciences/los_angeles.html (accessed January 15, 2010). The bar, named Joani Presents, is placed in historical context in this article.
151. Billy Wilder (dir.), *Some Like It Hot* (USA: Ashton Productions, 1959).
152. Interview, Selma "Sunne" Mahovel.
153. Interview, Andy.
154. Interview, G.K.

***Jewel Thais-Williams**, 68, African American, butch, Southern Baptist*: Jewel experienced police harassment when she opened her second bar—the first gay Black disco in the US in the 1970s, still in operation today, The Catch One.[155]

***Carole S. Damoci-Reed**, 67, Caucasian, butch, Methodist*: Carole had a man's tie hung over her rearview mirror; every Friday she put it on and she took it off Monday on her way back to the candy factory where she worked. She didn't know where she would stay in the Village but "there was always a girl I ended up staying with—I wasn't worried." She was arrested and spent the night in jail. She was friendly with the Mafia and was also in the Army serving as an officer for eight years.[156]

***Judie Jones/"Miss Judie,"** 67, African American, bull dagger, Holiness Sanctified Church: "Holy Roller" (Unity Fellowship)*: Judie got the "Holy Roller" treatment when her parents found out she liked girls; she was sent to a juvenile school. However, it was an all girls' school and so, "It was pretty much a great place to be." In Harlem in the 1950s all gay women were called "bull daggers ... whether or not they were butch or femme."[157]

***Lillian Faderman**, 67, Caucasian, femme (lesbian), Jewish*:[158] Lillian Faderman is a well-known historian of gay and lesbian life and a college professor.[159] Her high-school guidance counselor told her she had to quit going to the bar. She had fallen in love with a prostitute and almost moved away with her. She was seventeen and going to the If Club in Los Angeles with a fake ID "in order to have sex."[160]

155. Interview, Jewel Thais-Williams.
156. Interview, Carol S. Damoci-Reed.
157. Interview, Judie Jones.
158. If an informant identified as gay female or lesbian (such as butch, femme, kiki, etc.) and then switched later in life I have indicated that later category in parentheses. In Lillian's case she entered bar culture identifying as "femme," but upon exiting bar culture identified as "lesbian."
159. Lillian Faderman, *Surpassing the Love of Men: Romantic Friendship and Love between Women, from the Renaissance to the Present*, (New York: Morrow, 1981); *Scotch Verdict: Miss Pirie and Miss Woods V. Dame Cumming Gordon* (New York: Quill, 1983); *Odd Girls and Twilight Lovers: A History of Lesbian Life in Twentieth-Century America; To Believe in Women: What Lesbians Have Done for America—A History* (Boston, MA: Houghton Mifflin, 1999); *Naked in the Promised Land;* Lillian Faderman and Stuart Timmons, *Gay LA: A History of Sexual Outlaws, Power Politics, and Lipstick Lesbians* (New York: Basic Books, 2006). I personally met Dr Faderman in the 1990s when she was teaching "Lesbian Literature" at UCLA—an institution where she was enrolled in the 1950s, and was afraid to check out a book about lesbian literature and so read it between the stacks.
160. Interview, Lillian Faderman.

Sadie Smith*, *67, Caucasian, gay, Christian*: Sadie knew she was gay at fifteen but still married the first man she went out with—who ended up being verbally abusive. She had children with him, stayed with him until he died and she was in her sixties. During the marriage she had a closeted relationship with a woman for over a decade. The husband found out and threatened to take away her children; the woman stayed married. Sadie spoke to no one about the relationship for seventeen years until, when she was in prescribed counseling for her husband's death, what surfaced was grief over her lost female lover—for the first time.[161]

Heather Hamm*, 66, Caucasian, femme (gay), Catholic*: Heather cared deeply about the women she came out with—loved the women, didn't love bars, but knew about these women because of the bars. She created the Women of Forty Plus[162] in her forties in 1988 as an alternative. Over two decades later it is still one of the most active lesbian elder groups in the nation, meeting once a week. In 2009 their float for the Long Beach Lesbian and Gay Pride Parade won for "Best Use of the Rainbow Colors."[163]

Joan Nestle*, 66, Caucasian, femme, Jewish*: Joan is a chronicler of gay life pre- and post-Stonewall, and founder of the Lesbian Herstory Archives in New York City.[164] Joan knew she had arrived as a gay woman when she was in a diner in the Village and a butch looked at her and asked, "So, how are things at the Colony these days?" referring to The Sea Colony. Joan was so proud to be identified as a "femme" or "gay," and felt that she had "arrived."[165]

Marj Johnson*, 66, Caucasian, androgynous, Protestant (agnostic)*: Marj was so afraid of being gay and of what her father and the nuns would think that although she had deep feelings for women she rarely acted on them until middle age. She went to a gay bar in her youth, was approached by a butch woman in the rest room, and felt so alienated by the woman's approach and class that she never went back.[166]

161. Interview, Sadie Smith*.
162. "Heather H. Hamm—Obituary," *Long Beach Press-Telegram*, December 19, 2009.
163. Interview, Heather Hamm.
164. Nestle, *A Restricted Country; The Persistent Desire: A Femme-Butch Reader* (Boston, MA: Alyson Publications, 1992); *A Fragile Union: New and Selected Writings* (San Francisco, CA: Cleis Press, 1998); Joan Nestle and Naomi Holoch (eds), *Women on Women: An Anthology of American Lesbian Short Fiction* (New York: Plume, 1990); *Women on Women 3: An Anthology of American Lesbian Short Fiction* (New York: Plume, 1996); Joan Nestle, Clare Howell, & Riki Anne Wilchins, *Genderqueer: Voices from Beyond the Sexual Binary* (Los Angeles, CA: Alyson Books, 2002); Joan Nestle & John Preston, *Sister & Brother: Lesbians & Gay Men Write About Their Lives Together* (San Francisco, CA: HarperSanFrancisco, 1994).
165. Interview, Joan Nestle.
166. Interview, Marj Johnson.

***Mary Martinez**, 65, Mexican, femme, Catholic*: Mary's Puerto Rican parents had a Catholic priest perform an exorcism on her to rid her of homosexuality. It did not work.[167]

***Starling Walter**, 65, Caucasian, gay, unknown religious identity*: Starling knew she was different and looked up "homosexual" in the school library as a teen. When she saw it meant mentally ill, she assumed she could not be homosexual or "lesbian," because she knew she was not mentally ill. It took her years to find out that she could be homosexual or "lesbian" and not be mentally ill.[168]

***Kate Flaherty**, 63, Caucasian, femme, Unitarian (Spiritual)*: Kate was in her teens and her lover had an apartment while Kate was still living with her folks. Her lover died tragically in a car accident. Because they were totally closeted, Kate did not know what had happened to her lover until she came to the building and saw her lover's father packing her things. She deduced what had happened by hanging around the building—her lover had died and was never coming home. She had no one to talk to. Finally she found the gay bars and the southern California music scene of the early 1960s.[169] Kate feels it was "the music of the time" that saved her.[170]

***H.M.**, in her 60s, Caucasian, femme, Greek Orthodox (Presbyterian)*: H.M. was a college student and professional woman—but "everyone went to the bar. I preferred the If Club, although it was pretty sleazy", and if the people there were not of her class—what did it matter? It was the "only place." She "was a gay woman, that was the most important thing—that they were also gay women."

167. Interview, Mary Martinez.
168. Interview, Starling Walter.
169. Interview, Kate Flaherty.
170. Gina Messina Dysert, "Music as a Vehicle of Agency for Marginalized Women," paper presented at the Western Regional Conference of the American Academy of Religion, Phoenix, AR, 2010. I believe music functioned in the gay women's bar cosmology as a vehicle of agency as well.

4. THE 1960s
"IT WAS ... HOLLYWOOD! WE DID A GIRLFRIEND ... DAISY CHAIN!"

Figure 4.1 "It's my party and I'll cry if I want to ... You would cry too, if it happened to you" ("It's My Party", © 1963 [Renewed], Chappell & Co., Inc., used by permission). Photo of Lesley Gore (SMP/Globe Photos Inc. © Imagecollect.com/Globe-Photos). "It's My Party" was recorded by Lesley Gore at the height of her fame in 1963. Gore also sang classics such as "You Don't Own Me," recorded "It's My Party" at 16 and was living a gay life by age 20. In an interview with Shauna Swartz ("Interview with Lesley Gore," June 3, 2005, AfterEllen.com), Gore came out publicly as a lesbian. Note *pinky ring* in photo – a well-known pre-Stonewall gay signifier.

Figure 4.2 The original cover art for the first edition of Ann Bannon's *Beebo Brinker* (1962). *Beebo Brinker* was republished in 1983 and 2001, and each edition had a different cover. Beebo Brinker is remarkable for the 1960s. Readers only once read about her wearing a skirt; she took jobs, and declined a higher education because these vocations would force her to wear feminine clothing (William Dean, "Out of the Shadows: An Interview with Ann Bannon," January 8, 2003, http://www.cleansheets.com/articles/dean_01.08.03.shtml). Bannon describes the image as "god-awful"; the image illustrates how the art was designed for men with no concern for accuracy. Beebo was "a disappointment" in 1962 (Gene Damon, "Book Review," *The Ladder* 7(1), October 1962). In 1969 "a sad failure," Gene Damon, a pseudonym for Barbara Grier, who started Naiad Press—the company that re-released all of Bannon's books in 1983 (Gene Damon, "The Lesbian Paperback," *The Ladder* 13[9–10], 1969). However in *Lesbian Pulp Fiction* (Katherine Forrest, *Lesbian Pulp Fiction* [San Francisco, CA: Cleis Press, 2005]), Beebo was "the most iconic figure in all of lesbian fiction. (Wikipedia, "Anne Bannon, the Beebo Brinker Chronicles," www.wikipedia.com). The above is paraphrased from information originally gathered and provided by Wikipedia. However, all sources used have been sourced back to their original. Permission for use granted by Ann Bannon.

OVERVIEW

It was ... Hollywood! We did a girlfriend ... daisy chain![1]

The Children's Hour, released in 1961, was based on a true case.[2] Shirley MacLaine has said that she and Audrey Hepburn—her partner in the film—never discussed that it was about homosexuality. It was about "a child's accusation".[3] The real-life accusation resulted in women being fired, but not prosecuted, because the court could not believe that such a thing existed. The MacLaine character screams, "I know about it now. It's there ... I resented your plans to marry—maybe because I wanted you ... I couldn't call it by name before, but maybe it's been there since I first knew you."[4] At the end of the film, after the suicide, the remaining character is supposed to marry a young man of the town but walks away without marrying. We do not know where she is headed, but it might be to New York City's fabled homosexual haven, The Village. For, when Hepburn leaves the boarding school, her costume looks remarkably like the character's costume on the cover of the original *Beebo Brinker*, published the very next year, when Beebo arrives in New York City, we presume to the Village.[5]

These images contradict themselves. Beebo actually lives as a gay girl/ butch gay woman, and unlike her cover art, lives in butch or masculine clothing. In fact she will not take higher paying jobs if they demand female attire. Is this where *The Children's Hour*'s fictional character was off to—a gay ghetto such as New York's Village? The film ends with the character realizing that her friend is going to kill herself because of what might be in her; she rushes to save her, busts the door down and is too late. She leaves proud and alone—headed somewhere, but where? The possibility of a gay life *might* not drive her to suicide, but actually to live a somewhat happy life *à la* Beebo Brinker.[6] Today, the story of Beebo Brinker is instructive, whereas in the 1960s it was "disappointing," because of its bar life and butch-femme portrayal.[7]

In 1965 the gay but closeted superstar Lesley Gore recorded "It's My Party" and decided that she could cry if she wanted to.[8] The "party" that

1. Interview, Darlene.
2. Faderman, *Scotch Verdict: Miss Pirie and Miss Woods V. Dame Cumming Gordon*.
3. Rob Epstein & Jeffrey Friedman (dirs), *The Celluloid Closet* (France, UK, Germany, USA: Arte, 1995). The film is based on the 1981 (revised 1987) book of the same name written by Vito Russo.
4. William Wyler (dir.), *The Children's Hour*. The script by Lillian Hellman was based on the stage play of the same name.
5. Anne Bannon, *Beebo Brinker* (New York: Gold Medal Books, 1962).
6. Beebo Brinker was a pseudonym for Ann Weldy.
7. Damon, "The Lesbian Paperback."
8. Shauna Swartz, "Interview with Lesley Gore." AfterEllen, June 3, 2005, http://www.afterellen.com/interview-with-lesley-gore/06/2005.

characterized the 1960s as free love and radical politics did not seriously affect the liberation of gays. Very few informants knew of Stonewall when it happened; the vast majority who came out prior to 1970 found out about Stonewall after lesbian feminism or the advent of second-wave feminism, if they knew of it at all. The summer of love in 1969 was the same summer that Falcon River was being gang-raped in Virginia, and later, in the early 1970s, she was in San Francisco and went to a "drop-in" at which Timothy Leary presided.[9] That year Carolyn Weathers, one of the few women in the Gay Liberation Front, was asked to be the first lesbian on television; in 1970, she would march in the first Gay Pride Parade in Los Angeles, created and attended primarily by gay men.[10] As discussed "the hairpin drop heard round the world" that was Stonewall is still having difficult reception, and the 1960s was not the time of *gay* revolution before Stonewall, for the decade was not radically different from the 1950s. McCarthyism had ended but this did not mean the end of harassment to known or accused homosexuals.[11]

However, surrounding the gay women were the infamous 1960s communities. So Kate could go to a gay bar "for the music," the new rock and roll, and it was everywhere.[12] Sandy told me that she felt the Beatles were speaking liberation for everyone and were cracking open the repression of the 1950s.[13] Darlene said that in Hollywood in the 1960s a bunch of girls would live together in the same apartment complex and a daisy chain was when, "you slept with one girl, and when her girlfriend was returning, you left that bed and entered another bed. Or, when one girl went to work, you could go get in the bed of the girl left behind ... It was the 60s in Hollywood," she smiles, "We were wild."[14]

Gypsy opened the first ever head shop in New York City, a store where you could buy among other things incense, candles, *and* marijuana paraphernalia. However, as counter-cultural as that was, she was not aware of Stonewall. On moving to California and joining a commune, she admitted gay feelings to herself. However, afraid to come out to her "free-love" commune as gay, she secretly went to a small butch-femme bar in Sacramento to test her feelings. There she met her first lover, and later was afraid to tell the commune. "The idea of sixties free love was for men. There really wasn't

9. Interview, Falcon River.
10. Interview, Carolyn Weathers.
11. Interview, John Garcia. Garcia was targeted and believes he was framed for homosexual activity and forced to quit his government job in 1969 at Douglas Aircraft. This happened on the West Coast the same year that the Stonewall Rebellion happened on the East Coast.
12. Interview, Kate Flaherty.
13. Interview, Sandy Clark.
14. Interview, Darlene.

free love for women, and there certainly wasn't any feeling of gay liberation in the hippie movement."[15]

But Carolyn Weathers came into butch-femme culture in Texas in the early 1960s and, later in California, became a hippie. She was able to be open to gender experimentation in the hippie-centered Renaissance Faire, where her gay biological sister, friends, and their lovers felt comfortable being "out."[16] But the gay bar was still where most women needed to go to meet others like themselves, so that even living in a Californian commune one might sneak out to safely meet women.

Hippie culture, aware of gay existence, was more tolerant than the dominant culture if something happened to one of its own—even if what happened was homosexuality. For instance, when Gypsy was in drug culture running her head shop, a good friend was abducted by her Puerto Rican Catholic mother for being gay and forced into a mental institution. She was tied down and force-fed strong drugs "for months."[17] Her treatment may also have included abuse by the institution's guards intended to switch her affiliation from gay to straight, but the woman could never articulate, even after being freed, what happened to her. Even though none of the group was gay, Gypsy and her friends kept the woman's child away from the mother, in safe keeping within the various hippie households. When the woman returned Gypsy said she was "broken" and was never the same.[18] This was true of all informants who had friends incarcerated against their will in mental institutions. This was not true, however, if the women were in actual prisons, or even raped by police or straight men on the street. These women, at least with respect to my informants, were hardened by the abuse but not broken. The ability to withstand the abuse seems to have come from the sense that they were part of a community. When they exited the bar community as part of a police raid, they knew that there *existed* community waiting for them on their return. This was true for Falcon River and her circle, who after having been taken to jail where they were often raped and beaten, would meet at a gay-friendly diner in the early morning consoling each other.[19] But for women in the mental health system, who were placed there overwhelmingly by their parents, their placement occurred often prior to finding the gay bar culture, and so they were unaware of the community it might offer on their release. For instance, Gypsy's friend had not had a chance to come out yet—her mother suspected that she might be gay, but she actually was *not* at the time of her incarceration.[20] This is also true of *The Children's Hour*

15. Interview, Gypsy Powers.
16. Interview, Carolyn Weathers.
17. Interview, Gypsy Powers.
18. *Ibid.*
19. Interview, Falcon River.
20. Interview, Gypsy Powers.

portrayal of gay women and mental illness.[21] Often what made these women insane/suicidal were the accusations and ensuing shame, harassment, and punishment, before they even had a chance to self-identify and create a community that could help them sustain their lives throughout that type of harassment.

One hundred percent of my informants prior to 1973 knew that homosexuals were considered mentally ill. None of them felt that they were in need of mental health assistance for being gay, and none of them believed that they themselves were mentally ill. In fact, several of them had more trouble believing that they were lesbians, because lesbians were *supposed to be* mentally ill and they themselves knew that they were not crazy—so how then could they be lesbian?[22]

As one informant put it,

> I knew I couldn't be a lesbian, because I looked it up in the library—lesbianism—and it said, basically that lesbians were nuts. I knew I wasn't crazy, so I figured, well then, I couldn't be a lesbian. Even though I was sleeping with women and having feelings for them! So, I figured I was something else, but I wasn't sure what that was ...!! It took me a long time to figure out that I could be a *lesbian*, and *not* be crazy![23]

The women's bar of the 1960s was not radically different from that of the 1950s, except that the police raids in northern urban areas were less violent. Police still routinely entered gay bars checking for ID and would continue to do so until the 1980s. However, violence still happened regularly into the 1960s, even in states like California, if outside of the main urban areas such as San Francisco, Los Angeles, Long Beach, or Santa Monica. Falcon remembers being in a bar in Whittier, CA and the police reaching over and grabbing a butch woman's breast and tugging it hard then smashing her head on the counter while they asked her, if she was in fact "a man," why did she have breasts? The butch did not "fight back" and this to Falcon *was* her way of fighting back; she did not respond to the police.[24]

However the 1960s drumbeat of freedom that *surrounded* the gay bar did affect the atmosphere *within* the bar itself. Much depended on where you lived. In Virginia, the 1960s were not summers of love, but a time of extreme repression and overall the "free love" experienced by heterosexuals was not the experience of homosexuals.

Kate's first lover died in a car accident and although she and her girlfriend had apartments in the same building, and so experienced some of the 1960s

21. Wyler, *The Children's Hour*.
22. Interview, Starling Walter.
23. *Ibid*.
24. Interview, Falcon River. Later in Virginia, Falcon would remember much worse.

freedom, when her lover was killed in a car accident there was no one to talk to. She could tell no one even that she had been in a relationship. She pieced together what had happened when the lover did not return and she saw who she deduced was her father cleaning out the apartment.[25]

When I have spoken of this interview I have had friends say, "Oh, I know someone like that. She can't talk to anyone about being a lesbian." And I say—how then do *you* know she is a lesbian—if she can't talk to anyone? It is a slow realization for contemporary queer people to realize that for many pre-Stonewall people being in the closet meant not talking *to anyone* other than the woman or man that they were with. So, if a tragedy happened to that person, there was no one to talk to. The film *If These Walls Could Talk 2* depicts the progression of gay life as experienced within three decades—the 1960s, 70s, and 80s. The first segment depicts two women in 1961 who are closeted. Using foreshadowing, we open with them at the movies—absorbing with grief and awe *The Children's Hour*. When they leave the movie they walk together comforting each other, until we see them realize they are in the open and mutually without words stand apart and continue walking. That night, one of them climbs a ladder to examine a bird feeder, falls and dies. The other has no one to talk to—and no one knows of her relationship. She cannot get into the hospital room—she cannot find out what is happening to "her friend." In fact she eventually loses her house to the lover's relatives, because her name was not on the lease. At the end she simply disappears. She leaves no trace of the relationship and the house is left to her lover's uncaring relatives.[26]

The women's bar did provide a community that could share in the trials and joys of queer life pre-Stonewall. Joan Nestle remembers a butch stumbling into the Sea Colony having been beaten and the community there listening to her story and tending to her.[27] Kate and her lover however had been closeted and so she was truly alone. The only person she shared her story with was her ex-boyfriend fighting in Vietnam, who she could *write* to.[28] The closet also provided a container for Sadie's ten-year relationship. When her lover's husband found out, the lover was forced to choose between Sadie and her children, and had to choose her children. They did not speak after the break-up and Sadie spoke to no one "except for my dogs."[29] The likelihood that a known gay woman's children would be taken away from her was grounded, as homosexuals were considered deviant inverts. As late as 1974

25. Interview, Kate Flaherty.
26. Jane Anderson & Martha Coolidge (dirs), *If These Walls Could Talk 2* (USA: Home Box Office, 2000).
27. Interview, Joan Nestle.
28. Interview, Kate Flaherty. Later he would come out as gay himself; Kate thinks this is why she felt safe sharing with him.
29. Interview, Sadie Smith*.

one informant had her children taken away due to a lesbianism charge and she did not visit them unsupervised until they were adults.[30]

After Sadie's husband died she was placed in hospital-ordered grief sessions and within those she finally grieved—not for her husband but for the death of the relationship with her lover lost over a decade earlier.[31] As I listened to her we both cried and I asked "How did you do it?" It was inconceivable to me that she did not talk to anyone and slept next to her husband for an ensuing decade and she stayed sane.[32] She revealed parts of her story for the first time to me. I was acutely aware, sitting in that woman's kitchen hearing her story that had been silent for so long, how much a gay person's life depends on the decade and place in which they lived.[33] How much do we as queer people owe to women and men who were "in the life" when "the life" was so constricted, given our mostly urban standards today?

"Mostly urban" because neither Sadie's nor Kate's story are confined to the annals of history. While writing this chapter I received an email from a woman transcribing my interviews, a Romanian immigrant currently living in Sweden. "The subject was fascinating. Being originally from Romania, I could say ... we have your 70s—when it comes to gay-lesbian liberation/acceptance and so on. In 2006 I was in a restaurant with a gay friend and when they brought the soup there was spit in it—that's how far acceptance went"[34] While I don't know if this woman is gay or straight, she felt comfortable relating this story to someone she has never met a continent away. I'm not so sure her companion would feel the same, especially if still in Romania.

Also harassment and raids on gay bars in the US have not ceased. In the summer of 2009, there were two widely reported raids on gay bars—one of which took place on the fortieth anniversary of Stonewall at a Ft. Worth, Texas bar, The Rainbow Lounge:

> At least three customers present during the appearance by police officers and Texas liquor commission agents told a CBS-affiliated TV news station that the officers and agents acted in an aggressive and rude manner toward the customers and began singling out people for arrest on public intoxication charges.[35]

On September 12, 2009, there was also a raid in an Atlanta, Georgia gay bar, The Eagle. "Owners of a gay bar in Atlanta claim police unfairly targeted

30. Interview, E.C.
31. Interview, Sadie Smith*.
32. *Ibid.*
33. This woman used a pseudonym in her interview with me, and parts of her story are not shared here.
34. Email correspondence, Armina, June 18, 2008. Obviously she is an ally.
35. Lou Chibbaro-Jr., "Seven Arrested in Texas Gay Bar 'Raid': Men Charged with 'Public Intoxication' on Stonewall's 40th Anniversary," *Washington Blade*, June 29, 2009.

the business and mistreated customers during a late-night raid. Several customers at Atlanta Eagle said they were harassed and witnesses said they were forced to the ground and frisked during the raid Thursday night."[36]

Would I have had the courage to live a homosexual life pre-Stonewall either by going to the period's dangerous yet community-centered gay bars or seeing a woman, but remaining deeply in the closet? In the late 1990s I was dating a woman and we were in a gay restaurant in West Hollywood, and the cooks and waiters kept staring at us. I asked the waiter to bring the cook out of the kitchen and I asked him what he was staring at. He said, "both of you, you are both women." I said, "This is West Hollywood. We're not paying you to stare at us. We're paying you to cook us dinner. Can you do that please?"[37] He laughed and the rest of the night was uneventful. Where did I find the agency to believe that if I was paying for a meal that should include *not* being stared at—simply because I was holding my girl's hand? The deep closet for gays and lesbians in previous decades included the reality that if you had no choice but to act on your homosexuality you would have the decency to keep it to yourself. If you chose to share it—living openly in any way that meant you risked discovery—you were a disgrace, a threat, and finally criminally insane—someone who should be locked up for the protection of others. It was heroic that pre-Stonewall gays breached these attitudes to love "the love that dared not speak its name."

As the 1960s turned to the 1970s and word of Stonewall and other actions around the country[38] spread, the hippie/freedom of expression movement infiltrated butch-femme gay bars and with it came the advent of a new movement—lesbian feminism.

Alice knew she had feelings for women in the 1960s but the definition of "homosexual" was one she could not accept. "It was such a dangerous time," she said. "Being gay was just so awful." She did not identify herself with the group that psychiatrists labeled inverts or deviants. She remembered advertising for a female roommate and a woman calling and identifying herself as a "Greenwich Village lesbian." This identification, and the fact that this woman answered an advert that Alice had made, filled her with so much dread that she became physically ill. Nonetheless she went once to the New York City Public Library and looked up the word "homosexual." She told me that "it was obvious that I was not the only person that had done this—gone through the card catalog over and over again. It was obvious that that entire section of the card catalog was well-used ... others had been there before me searching for information." Did she take out any of the books? "No, I was too afraid. But, at that time in my life, it was very comforting just to know that

36. Associated Press, "8 Arrested in Raid at Atlanta Gay Bar," *Edge*, September 12, 2009.
37. Fran D.* can confirm this story.
38. Belinda Baldwin, "LA, 1/1/67: The Black Cat Riots," *Gay and Lesbian Review Worldwide* 13(2) (Mar/Apr 2006).

there were other people like me out there—somewhere—who had come into that same library and looked at those same cards ... put their hands on the cards ... searching for information."[39]

Alice Myers would not officially come out until the 1970s, when the birth of lesbian feminism provided a different societal definition of being gay that was not accessible in the 1960s. If she had been able to go to the gay bar in the 1960s she might have found other people to help form a different definition other than the one provided by the general culture—but it would have meant identifying with the population *enough* to at least enter bar culture. She could not do that. She could not find a way to be homosexual unless she identified with deviance. She, along with many others, would wait until a space was created that they could identify with—gay pride, lesbian aligned with feminism—and found comfort in the interim perhaps in the library card catalog. However the card catalog did not comfort all who went there. Starling Water lived in the Midwest and, thinking she might be gay, looked up the word "homosexual" and did not relate at all and determined she could not be gay because she was not mentally ill. However, like Alice, she said, "Feminism is what helped me define a new way of being gay."[40] The brewing women's movement created a different window for late 1960s women than for women who came out earlier. If you were confused by the media image early in the decade, you could wait it out, as these two women did (not consciously, but as their lives progressed), and eventually find feminism and a different fit for your sexual identity.

While bar life did not change significantly, the culture around it *did*. The rise of rock n' roll meant it was not crucial to have a partner in order to dance and this helped because in most bars you were not allowed to touch each other and so partner dancing was difficult, to say the least. However, as Helen found out when she tried the "new dance" in her neighborhood gay women's bar in late 1960s Chicago, it got her and her lesbian feminist friends from the Graphics Collective kicked out—especially as they were dressed in overalls and free dancing—as a group, rather than in partners. The bar women made it clear to Helen that "since we were not butch and femme, we had to leave!"[41]

Gay women in the 1970s would for the most part come out as "lesbians" and this was a different definition of self than "gay." Gayle Rubin radically wrote that gay women, especially butch-femme pre-Stonewall, identified with homo*sex*uality and therefore *sex*uality first, where lesbians identified with *feminism* as in lesbian-feminist and therefore *politics* first.[42] These

39. Interview, Alice Meyers.
40. Interview, Starling Walter.
41. Interview, Helen Factor.
42. Gayle Rubin, "Thinking Sex: Notes for a Radical Theory of the Politics of Sexuality." In *Pleasure and Danger: Exploring Female Sexuality*, ed. Carole S. Vance (Boston, MA: Routledge & Kegan Paul, 1984), 267–319.

definitions would prove conflicting by the end of the 1970s and erupt in the lesbian "sex wars."[43] Until the mid 1970s however, in most bar spaces in the US, butch-femme was still, as Sandy Clark said, "the only game in town."[44]

However, since social change was in the air in the latter half of the decade it did infiltrate the lives of the gay women—even if not directly the bars. Gypsy lived in a commune when she moved to California. She is adamant, however, that "the sexual revolution was for men ... It was about *men* getting to sleep with who they wanted to sleep with, not *women*."[45] So although she had to sneak away from her commune in order to find gay identity, she was in counter culture and so felt empowered to search for sexual freedom. This was true not only in hippie culture but also early feminist culture. Tally came out in Iowa in the late 1960s in an old school gay bar because she did not dare tell her feminist collective sisters that she was not *just* feminist—she was also lesbian.[46] Carolyn Weathers and Falcon were also part of hippie culture but also both came out in traditional butch-femme bars—that is, bars where the chief manner in which relationships were organized romantically was butch and femme.[47]

Linda Lack was a UCLA graduate student on a Rockefeller scholarship, but led two lives—one in the bar, and one at school—only staying out late enough in the bars so that she could still get to rehearsal in the morning.[48] G.J. was also a student at this time, and did sex work to pay for her schooling, as her father had cut her off financially. G.J. found her way to this profession because she was in the gay bars and was out to some of her friends. Because she was out, they were able to suggest to her that she might be able to earn some money having "lesbian sex" for voyeuristic men, which she did.[49]

Most of these women lived a double life for most of this decade, either with their families, their jobs or, for some, their husbands. The time was approaching where the bar would no longer be the only place. With it came the option to be out differently to the way that had had been previously available, except perhaps to the wealthy. This time would be ushered in with Stonewall and the gay activism of the late 1960s and 70s and its reverberation throughout the nation. The bar culture would explode with activism in the ensuing decade with cries of "Out of the bars and into the streets."

---

43. Carole S. Vance, *Pleasure and Danger: Exploring Female Sexuality* (Boston, MA: Routledge & Kegan Paul, 1984). This book anthologizes work presented at the 1982 Barnard Conference that resulted in clashes between butch-femme and leather women, and anti-pornography activists during what is commonly called the lesbian sex wars.
44. Interview, Sandy Clark.
45. Interview, Gypsy Powers.
46. Interview, Irene "Tally" Talbert.
47. Interviews, Carolyn Weathers and Falcon River.
48. Interview, Linda Lack.
49. Interview, G.J.

RELIGIOUS AND THEOLOGICAL IMPLICATIONS

Feminist theology[50] would not be a significant part of the feminist movement until the 1970s.[51] Butch-femme bar culture still provided community, even if by the end of the decade women were beginning to ask, "Is this all there is—bars?"

For some, ecstatic and tragic bar experiences gave them information to create a new bar culture in the 1970s. Falcon, a life-long butch, created Mother's Brew in Kentucky, a bar in line with feminist values. However, she says, "The feminists didn't like me because I was butch, even though they called us [the bar women] and I responded, helping to do security at all of their marches and demonstrations."[52]

Gloria Anzaldua writes about being a Chicana lesbian "at the crossroads" in *Borderlands*.[53] Being "at the crossroads" marks the gay women's bars of the 1960s. The bars may have been Hell's Kitchens, but, as the saying goes, "If you can't stand the heat, get out of the kitchen." Most of the informants I interviewed chose to stay.

Because many women lived migratory lives, as did Falcon, they had "big city" experiences even if they were from and would end up in smaller urban areas. The anti-war movement, hippie culture, and nascent women's liberation movement brought about change within the bar and led to actions such as Stonewall, but also prior to Stonewall. Stonewall was the riot that was nationally televised. However, other actions did take place, for instance at the Black Cat bar in Los Angeles, in 1967.[54]

The processes that enabled different ways of being in the gay community resonate with process thought. Marjorie Suchocki writes that process thought is a process *of* thought in which a new creation may be born from the genesis of the old and the new.[55] We are always acting in old ways or birthing new ways—that is our choice.

As noted, Falcon said of watching her drag queen friend walk from the car to the bar, "It was the most courageous thing I have ever seen—before or since."[56] She estimates she was raped once a month for five years. She marched in demonstrations and took, as she says, "hits meant for feminists"

50. Mary Daly, *The Church and the Second Sex* (New York: Harper & Row, 1968). Daly would follow this in the 1970s with several more books. She would re-introduce this book with a lesbian feminist introduction that was truly "beyond god the father," and solidly in the new country of lesbian feminism.
51. Daly, *The Church and the Second Sex*, 2nd edition (New York: Harper & Row, 1975).
52. Interview, Falcon River.
53. Anzaldúa, *Borderlands: The New Mestiza = La Frontera*.
54. Baldwin, "LA, 1/1/67: The Black Cat Riots."
55. Marjorie Suchocki, *God, Christ, Church: A Practical Guide to Process Theology* (New York: Crossroad, 1982).
56. Interview, Falcon River.

when other bar women she had gathered marched between demonstrators against the Equal Rights Amendment and the feminists who were marching for it to the Statehouse in Kentucky. However, she feels that the most courageous thing she has seen is a drag queen walking from her/his car into the bar.

By the beginning of the next decade, lesbian feminism would be identified and a movement would coalesce around that definition. Unfortunately, most of the people who would articulate a movement of fighting back were not the people who had been in working-class, butch-femme bars or who had experienced the police harassment and societal abuse. These women from earlier decades were marginalized and left out of the discussions that formed the working definitions of gay women as they became lesbian feminists in the 1970s. Falcon, a bar butch was asked to leave a NOW meeting she wanted to attend, as were other butch women, among them Jeanne Cordova.[57] The people who articulated feminist resistance were the women identified in women's liberation, although feminism was a movement that affected everyone. So even though Falcon was kicked out of a NOW meeting for being too masculine, in her own Mother's Brew she employed feminist strategies—providing escorts to women's cars, organizing fundraisers for battered women's shelters, and protecting feminists marching in local events.

I believe that the struggle for gay civil rights that exploded at Stonewall had its beginnings in the communities that coalesced inside the previous decades of gay bars, and the feminist theology that would put lesbian separatism at its core[58] had its beginnings in butch-femme bar culture, even though the authors who created these ideologies may not have personally come out of bar culture. The populations who followed these ideologies did owe their existence as communities to women who braved ostracism and worse to create the fledgling political communities in the only spaces available, gay bars that would become the vocal communities outside bars, once those outside spaces were available.[59]

What better way for the newly formed lesbian separatist community to do "away with men"[60] and male culture than the butch-femme bar? This culture eliminated the need for men by having butch women. Of course, there is a logistical hole in this ideology—butches were masculine-identified—but there is also truth in a historical trajectory that posits lesbian feminism following bar culture. Also, there are primary thinkers who articulated lesbian

57. Interviews, Falcon River and Jeanne Cordova.

58. Mary Daly, *Beyond God the Father: Toward a Philosophy of Women's Liberation* (Boston, MA: Beacon Press, 1973).

59. I claim this space/place as political, in line with the work of Kennedy and Davis, claiming more agency for this culture than other writers have, among them Faderman. Faderman has asserted that this culture was not political, but merely proto-political.

60. For example, witticisms such as, "If you can send one man to the moon, why not send them all?"

feminism such as Judy Grahn,[61] and Joan Nestle[62] who came of age in bar culture and credit bar culture with the trajectory of providing space to come to themselves as women and then giving them agency to come into feminism.

The 1970s would see lesbian feminism provide community support, formation, and identification or "theology." However lesbian feminism was able to do this because this support or theology had been *formed* and strengthened in the butch-femme bar.

DEMOGRAPHIC HIGHLIGHTS

I interviewed twenty-nine people who specifically came out in the 1960s—twenty-two women, six men and one transgender person, and heard stories about being out in the 1960s from all of the women I interviewed from previous decades and approximately fifty informal interviews which provided background, quotes, and general information.

In the group of formal interviews there were six butches, eleven femmes, one self-identified "Hollywood lesbian," one lesbian feminist, and five gay men—one gay butch man who participated in the riots at Stonewall and is a bartender there today,[63] one a former gay bar owner who inspired Troy Perry to start the Metropolitan Community Church with his bar activism in terms of support for his arrested clients,[64] one a current bar owner who began his bar career after being accused of homosexuality and having to leave his government job,[65] one who was a drag queen and prostitute in San Francisco and was repeatedly arrested on prostitution charges and who was also a queen in the Imperial Court,[66] and one who was part of the drag queen circle that helped a fallen queen at the 1969 Gay Ball.[67] I also interviewed one person who identifies as "an artist, darling ... one of the transgendered," and still lives 24/7 in that identity. She was infamous in Andy Warhol's circle and participated in his Factory.[68]

One woman worked as a prostitute,[69] and at different times was also a ballerina and a nun. I interviewed a butch who was asked by a group of gay women prostitutes to be their pimp, passing as a man for her own and their protection.[70]

61. Judy Grahn, *Edward the Dyke, and Other Poems* (San Francisco, CA: The Women's Press Collective, 1971).
62. Nestle, *A Restricted Country*.
63. Interview, Tree.
64. Interview, Lee Glaze.
65. Interview, John Garcia.
66. Interview, Miss Rosie*.
67. Interview, Auntie B.*.
68. Interview, Alexis DelLago.
69. Interview, G.J.
70. Interview, Falcon River.

Two women are African American, one part Native American, one married to a Native American and has a daughter half Native, two are Jewish, four are Catholic, and one a former nun,[71] two owned bars, and one of these knew that she was serving drinks to a group in the corner who were closeted nuns. One white woman, a dance student on a Rockefeller scholarship at UCLA, dated a Native American butch woman and felt more comfortable in an inter-racial relationship on the reservation than outside of it, other than in the gay bar which was the most comfortable. All the major events in her relationship "had to happen in the bar—it was the only place."[72] Three Catholic women were arrested and two spent time in jail. One was booked and one was never formally arrested but spent time in jail repeatedly, at least once a month for five years.[73]

The music changed in the mid-1960s with the emergence of the Beatles. As Sandy Clark said, "I felt they were playing for all of us." As a British immigrant she was referring to more than the English connection. "They were singing about revolution. In a very real way, I felt they were setting all of us free."[74]

None were ex-military. Two were employed in bar culture as bar owners, and one performed as a drag king and won awards for it.[75] One woman was arrested and spent the night in jail, as a result of which she lost her children. Her husband used her incarceration as proof of her unsuitability as a mother. Only four women were married, two in lavender marriages.[76] Several women created alternate spaces to go to other than the bar, after seeing the possible gay community *within* the bar. Pat Lamis (Womynz Brunch Bunch), Heather Hamm (Forty Plus) and Bobreta Franklin (United Lesbians of African American Heritage, ULOAH) all created women's social networks in the 1980s, but not before then.[77] Pat and Heather also opened one of the first condom/sex toy stores in response to the AIDS crisis and also eagerly jumped into the lesbian sex wars as entrepreneurs.[78] But in the 1960s the bars were the only spaces they all knew for women to meet. Bar culture would remain through mid-1970 as the primary social community—all women went to bars as their main social outlet.

I met women through Women of Forty Plus, Older Lesbians Organizing for Change, and Coalition of Older Lesbians. One was a feminist publisher and had published my poetry. Two women (both African American) came

71. Interview, G.J.
72. Interview, Linda Lack.
73. Interview, Falcon River.
74. Interview, Sandy Clark.
75. Interview, Falcon River.
76. Interview, E.C. and one other for whom this part of the story was anonymous.
77. Interviews, Pat Lamis, Heather Hamm, and Bobreta Franklin.
78. Interview, Pat Lamis.

through friendship networks of my own. I met two through a former professor and two through women I had dated.

Most women are in their sixties and a few in their seventies. All of them live independently; one in retirement housing. One lives in Gay Elder Housing,[79] and I rode with her and her lover in the gay pride parade in Los Angeles in 2008. All are out to different degrees; three run popular social networks.

I met the men in different ways as well. I met Tree at the Stonewall Inn where he was bartending. I met Miss Rosie in the LA Gay Pride Parade, as she/he is a resident of Triangle Square. Three men I met writing at the gay coffee shop in Long Beach, CA and the manager introduced me—and that one introduction led to the others. I met Alexis at the Gay and Lesbian Film Festival where we complimented each other on our outfits.

VOICES FROM THE 1960s

These informants document the emergent gay female (and male) bar culture community decade leading up to and immediately following Stonewall. Morton encouraged women's theology that is useful, hearing women "into speech."[80] My hope is to create a theology for these women, men, and transgendered people as I heard many of them into speech for the first time.

Hearing women (and others) into speech

Sarge*, 72, butch, Caucasian, Catholic*: Sarge was expelled from high school for kissing a girl. She was a closeted police officer in the 1960s. She worked in a women's jail, had a relationship with an inmate, and later a relationship with another officer. When she went to the police academy there were 100 women to 4,000 men. She never entered a gay bar, nor knew of their existence. She went to "cop bars," bars frequented by cops. She became an alcoholic, keeping all of her secrets, and now is an active member of Alcoholics Anonymous and sponsors gay women. In the 1980s she brought true rape prevention and self-defense to the Los Angeles Police Department. Prior to Sarge, their program was called, "Lady, beware!"[81]

Ellen Ward*, 70, butch, Caucasian, Catholic*: Ellen drove her friend to the Catholic convent she was entering in the 1960s. However, her friend wanted, and had, one last night of gay women's fun by going to all the bars with

79. Interview, Andrea "Andi" Segal.
80. Morton, "Hearing to Speech: A Sermon."
81. Interview, Sarge.

Ellen before she entered the convent the next day! Ellen was jealous that her friend could give up living as a gay woman in a relationship, not necessarily giving up that she was gay-identified, however. Ellen went on to open the lesbian bar, Que Sera. Melissa Etheridge would be discovered there. Ellen was elected the first lesbian mayor of Signal Hill, CA.[82]

***L.N.**, 70, femme, Caucasian, Catholic*: L. had a secret relationship with another wife in 1964. She was still not out to her children, even though she lived with another woman in a long term lesbian relationship. When they were courting, she in her sixties and her partner in her late seventies, they often went out "parking" in her partner's car in the neighborhood park after lesbian events, because L., a traditional femme, would not "have sex right away."[83]

***Ava**, 70s, Caucasian, femme, unknown religious identity*: Ava was a bartender in the Chicago Lost and Found, and conducted marriages there between gay women—some of whom are still married today.[84]

***Alice Meyers**, 69, lesbian, Caucasian, unknown religious identity*: Alice went to the library in New York City and looked up "homosexual" and ran her hands over the cards—many people had obviously come before her.[85]

***Carolyn Weathers**, 67, femme (lesbian feminist), Caucasian, Baptist*: Carolyn self-identified as a Baptist "preacher's daughter" growing up. She did not want to be part of the butch-femme scene in Texas, but "took the role of femme so I could get in. Once I was in, I figured I'd be able to mess around with it a little." One of the only women in the Gay Liberation Front (GLF), Carolyn was also part of the first LA Gay Pride parade in 1970, and the first lesbian on television because, as GLF said, she was "the prettiest."[86]

***Judy Grahn**, 69, butch (lesbian feminist), Caucasian, unknown religious identity*: Judy began with, "When we created Women's Liberation ..." and she is one of the few who can actually say that she was one of the women who created Women's Liberation. She was also dishonorably discharged, classified "undesirable." As they said this to her, she thought, "Well, you just have not talked to the right people."[87]

82. Interview, Ellen Ward.
83. Interview, L.N.
84. Interview, Ava.
85. Interview, Alice Meyers.
86. Interview, Carolyn Weathers.
87. Interview, Judy Grahn.

***E.C.**, 66, femme, Caucasian, Christian*: E.C. lost her children after a Pasadena, CA bar arrest in 1974, which gave her husband ammunition to bring her lesbianism up in court.[88] Her real crime was that she did not respond to an officer who flirted with her, and she believes that's why she was singled out and arrested. She only reconciled with her children when they were adults.[89]

***Sandy Clark**, 65, butch, Caucasian, Christian Protestant*: Sandy wanted to buy a dildo in the 1960s and heard that a woman was selling them in the parking lot of the bar. She went out and bought "a black one" and asked the woman if "she had a bag" for her to put it in. "A bag?! Put it in your pants. That's where it will end up anyway!" Sandy codes everyone on a pink/blue scale based on Kinsey, and gives talks on this at the Women of Forty Plus meetings.[90] She says that, "Prior to Stonewall was a 'terrible time' for homosexuals; The Beatles were singing for all of us to be free."[91]

***Darlene**, 63, femme and gay, Caucasian, Catholic*: Darlene lived in Hollywood in the 1960s and free love was happening with the Hollywood girls she hung out and lived with; she was just "a Hollywood lesbian."[92]

***G.J.**, 63, femme, Caucasian, Catholic*: G.J. was a ballerina with the San Francisco Corps de Ballet, fell in love with another ballerina and had to leave after the woman started seeing a man. She entered the convent and the Mother Superior kicked her out for suspected lesbian tendencies. Her parents cut her off; she became a sex worker and in this way paid for her college education.[93]

***Gypsy Powers**, 63, femme, Caucasian, Jewish (Spiritual)*: Gypsy was part of a group of hippies in New York City in the 1960s. When her best friend was abducted by her Catholic parents and put in Bellevue for suspected gay activity, this group of friends kept the girl's child away from the parents—caring for the child within the hippie group. Before going to the gay bar herself in California and meeting a butch woman, she did not know if, even though she had feelings for women, it "would work [be orgasmic]. Once I found out it worked, I was ready to go for it."[94]

---

88. Faderman & Timmons, *Gay LA: A History of Sexual Outlaws, Power Politics, and Lipstick Lesbians*. E.C.'s story is also documented in this book.
89. Interview, E.C.
90. Sandy and another butch (Carole S. Damoci-Reed) answered questions about sex during this talk.
91. Interview, Sandy Clark.
92. Interview, Darlene.
93. Interview, G.J.
94. Interview, Gypsy Powers.

***Linda Lack**, 63, femme, Caucasian, Spiritual*: Linda called the UCLA information hotline to see if there was a place where women could go to relax and not be "hassled by men," when she was at UCLA on a Rockefeller scholarship. A woman on the hotline gave her information on how to get to such a place—without telling her that it was gay. She credits the ability to have a sexual life to that woman who told her how to get to her first bar.[95]

***Andrea "Andi" Segal**, 62, Caucasian, femme, Jewish/Christian*: Andrea, or "Andi," was in the first march for gay rights with Reverend Troy Perry (founder of Metropolitan Community Church). She hung out at Anna's Coffee Shop in Silver Lake because she and her friends were underage, and was later "recruited" by Rev. Troy right out of the bar Joani Presents where she and her long term lover went after softball games. "He did most of his recruiting in the bars." They were the first lesbian couple Rev. Troy married and the reception was at Joani Presents. She lives in Triangle Square, LA's first gay elder housing complex.[96]

***Bobreta Franklin**, 61, femme, African American, Catholic (Science of Mind)*: Bobreta co-founded ULOAH, United Lesbians of African American Heritage, in 1990 with, among others, informant Sandra Tignor. It was founded as an alternative to the bars for African American women and the organization then also coordinated Sista Fest, a Black lesbians retreat. "Femme and butch never went out of fashion for the Black lesbian community; I always felt comfortable dressing up femme, and still do."[97]

***Cynthia Robinson**, 60, African American, femme, Christian*: Cynthia was living in Chicago when her friend, a prostitute, was picked up by the police "and ... probably raped. I know it was true ... because the cops ... picked us up once, me and a friend, and they tried to scare us, by telling us that they were going to kill us and get rid of the bodies—I figured they could get away with it if they wanted to." Cynthia danced professionally in Vegas as an out lesbian.[98]

***H.C.**, 60, butch, Caucasian, no specific religion*: H.C. dressed as a butch, and snuck into bars underage. Once, when she was out walking, she was detained by the police because of how she was dressed. She was terrified they would tell her parents. Once she escaped from a gay bar raid, aided by older patrons in the bar, by hiding on the roof and thus avoided arrest. She

95. Interview, Linda Lack.
96. Interview, Andrea "Andi" Segal.
97. Interview, Bobreta Franklin.
98. Interview, Cynthia Robinson.

felt that many of the older patrons would help a younger person avoid arrest if at all possible.[99]

***Pat Lamis**, 60, butch, Caucasian, Catholic (Goddess)*: Pat at first was femme but, "I couldn't get the butches to leave me alone with my long blonde hair." So she cut her hair and became butch. Pat and her long term lover Heather both founded groups in the late 1980s for women to socialize outside bars. However, for both, the bars were necessary—the bars were "the only place" for both of them in the 1960s, and decades later, they organized outside the bars. The Womynz Brunch Bunch, a social community Pat organized, has over 5,000 subscribers.[100]

***R.C.**, 60s, butch, Caucasian, Catholic*: R.C. worked for a famous Hollywood personality and had access to a crowd and parties outside bars attended by Hollywood's working class, as well as middle and upper classes. This was somewhat unique to the LA area as the classes working within "the industry" mingled together outside of bars, and this class mingling tended to not happen elsewhere.[101]

***Delia Silva**, 56, butch (femme), Chicano, Catholic*: Delia entered the bars underage with a fake ID in the late 1960s and loved the East LA bars specifically for Mexicans; her first night was "ecstatic". Her favorite was the Plush Pony, and butch-femme was "the only way" to go. The style was more formal and the dancing strictly Latin at the all-Spanish butch-femme Redz—a bar taken over from heterosexuals by gay women (including informant Nancy Valverde).[102]

***Falcon River**, 55, butch, Caucasian/Native American, Protestant (Wicca-Dianic)*: The KKK burned a cross on Falcon's lawn in Virginia in the 1970s for dating a black woman. She was crowned Mr Roanoke, a drag king, and had "the time of my life in the bars" even though repeatedly raped by police. "It was the first time I ever felt home—the bars. Nothing was keeping me from that, from the women. The cops couldn't stop me." In 1972, she and others were arrested, locked in a paddy wagon and forced to watch a drag queen being raped on the floor in front of them by the cops. A gay dentist helped people after beatings, for "we were afraid we might get hurt worse" by homophobic staff if they went to the hospital.[103]

99. Interview, H.C.
100. Interview, Pat Lamis.
101. Interview, R.C.
102. Interview, Delia Silva.
103. Interview, Falcon River.

***Vanessa Romain**, 51, butch, African American, Catholic*: Vanessa came out at 13 and was used to police brutality because the LA police were brutal to her and her brothers on the streets of South Central. She hitch-hiked to Long Beach's women's bars to get to a different environment than downtown LA. Her favorite bar was Que Sera, operated by informant Ellen Ward. Arrested many times in the bars, Vanessa today sits on the Long Beach Gay and Lesbian Pride board.[104]

Men

***Miss Rosie**, 70s, cross-dresser/prostitute/drag queen, Caucasian, unknown religious identity (Unity Fellowship Deacon)*: Miss Rosie was arrested repeatedly for prostitution in San Francisco and put in the Queen's tank—a jail for drag queen prostitutes. She[105] was also a Royal Queen of the Imperial Court (a formal Court of drag queens, butches, and cross-dressers across the US, started in San Francisco, 1965).[106]

***Tree**, 69, gay male, Caucasian, unknown religious identity*: Tree still bartends at Stonewall Inn and was involved in the Stonewall Rebellion the night it happened. He says, "Definitely women were there—Stormé Delarverie" was there. Stormé was a well known female impersonator and butch woman, believed by many to be the first person to throw a punch at Stonewall.[107]

***John Garcia**, 65, gay male, Mexican American, unknown religious identify*: John was accused of homosexuality while at Douglas Aircraft and asked to leave. Approached by a man at work, they went to a hotel and had sex. Later his supervisors showed him photos of that encounter—he assumes he was set up because he was up for a security clearance. He never saw the man again. He tried to deny the charge, saying he only had one encounter. But work was intolerable after the charge. He left and went to his first gay bar and felt "at home" for the first time. John opened one of the now oldest and most successful bars in Southern California—Ripples.[108]

***Auntie B.**, 60, former drag queen, Caucasian, unknown religious identity*: Aunti B. was at the 1969 Gay Ball in LA and witnessed cops, who ringed the ballroom, say that that if anyone touched anyone else—because they were

104. Interview, Vanessa Romain.
105. This informant is biologically male, and wears male clothing unless specifically "in drag." I use the pronoun (in this case "she") that the informant used during the interview.
106. Interview, Miss Rosie*.
107. Interview, Tree.
108. Interview, John Garcia.

all known to be homosexual—they would be arrested. Auntie B. remembers a drag queen falling on the runway and breaking or twisting her ankle; she began to crawl to the door. No one was helping her at first. Finally drag queens and queers helped, "if you're going to arrest us, then arrest all of us." There were too many that night to arrest, according to Auntie B. But he also remembers when Lee Glaze and others created the Rose Brigade.[109]

Lee Glaze, *late 60s, gay male/"The Blonde Darling," Caucasian, unknown religious identity*: Lee ran The Patch, an infamous club where Troy Perry witnessed his first gay activist action. Lee Glaze said if anyone was arrested at his club, he would bail them out, which he did—with a dozen roses: eleven for the drag queen arrested and one for the arresting officer, creating "The Rose Brigade." This was the force behind Troy Perry starting in 1968 with twelve members[110] the now world-wide Metropolitan Community Church, a gay-friendly Church, now with over 43,000 members.[111]

Father Joe**, 57, male ally, Caucasian, Catholic*: Father Joe was in a seminary close to the Stonewall Riots as a teenager when he saw the televized riots on TV. He couldn't afford to go to Selma and march for black civil rights but felt he could go to Stonewall and went the second day, participating as a witness. Observing how gays were treated, he found his ministry.[112]

Transgender

Alexis Del Lago*, 70s, artist/transgender/drag queen, Puerto Rican, Catholic*: Alexis was part of the Warhol Factory and made films with Andy Warhol. Alexis also knew Valerie Solanis, the lesbian who "shot Andy Warhol."[113]

109. Interview, Auntie B.*.
110. Rev. Elder Troy Perry, "How Did MCC Begin?," http://www.mccchurch.org (accessed April 16, 2010).
111. Interview, Lee Glaze.
112. Interview, Father Joe*.
113. Interview, Alexis Del Lago.

5. THE 1970s "WE WERE . . . WOMEN IN OVERALLS DANCING WITH WOMEN IN OVERALLS. THEY KICKED US OUT."

Figure 5.1 Chicago Women's Graphic Collective (group photo), 1972. (Photo from the CWLU Herstory Project. Photo donated to the Collective by Estelle Carol.) Photo used with permission, CWLU Herstory Project.

(a) (b)

(c)

Figure 5.2 Posters by the Chicago Women's Graphic Collective, 1970–83. Using silkscreen to create prints in large quantities on a low budget, and later offset, the Graphics Collective wanted feminist art to be a collective process to set it apart from male-dominated Western art: each poster created by committee of two to four women, and led by the designer. Thousands were sold all over the world until the group dissolved in 1983 (Chicago Women's Graphics Collective 2009). (a) "Midwest Lesbian Conference" (CWLU Herstory Project); (b) "Sisterhood is Blooming" (CWLU Herstory Project); (c) "Isis" (CWLU Herstory Project). "Isis" text: "Woman Spirit/I am the center./I am the point from which all directions start./I am the past and present united in eternal flight." Images used with permission, CWLU Herstory Project.

OVERVIEW

> A bunch of us went to the lesbian bar in our overalls. We were lesbian feminists. The bar was still butch-femme. We were dancing with each other—women in overalls dancing with women in overalls. They kicked us out.[1]

Chicago Women's Liberation Union housed the Chicago Liberation Graphics Collective. Helen Factor was a member. The 1970s were when lesbian feminists became "the point from which all directions start," to quote the infamous "Isis" poster. This generation created lesbian feminism which I came out into in 1979. My first lover and I had "Isis" above our bed in New Hampshire as did other lesbians we knew in Boston.[2] The poster "Midwest Lesbian Conference" was hanging in the lesbian household I moved into, in Colorado, 1983. These anonymously created posters were *everywhere* within the lesbian nation—sold at women's bookstores, where you could also buy women's or womyn's[3] music[4] and find consciousness-raising groups and services like women's health clinics, rape hotlines, and battered women's shelters. The lesbian separatist world sought to be separate from the patriarchal or male-centered world. Within a surprising amount of time, approximately a decade, this lesbian world would flower in every urban area from Los Angeles to Des Moines to New York. Lesbians were no longer mentally ill (since 1973) and this gave them the ability to open services such as health centers as openly lesbian health centers. Prior to 1973 a self-identified lesbian considered mentally unstable by the establishment running a mental health clinic would be a misnomer. During the 1970s, however, feminist therapy would develop as a *bona fide* field. Women-only spaces opened and lesbians exploded from the feminist movement to populate them.

Nature abhors a vacuum. Gay women exploded from within the Second World War. The contested story is that General Eisenhower, aware of the extent of gay women in the force, decided he wanted to purge them out of the military. The woman taking the directive, Johnnie Phelps, said that roughly 95 percent of the military women were gay and asked to have her name put first, and then another woman asked for her name second.

1. Interview, Helen Factor.
2. That I would meet one of the Collective members and "anonymous" creators of that famous poster during this research has been one of the myriad joys of the project.
3. "Womyn" became so much a part of the feminist lexicon that it is now an entry in the *Oxford English Dictionary* and is defined as referring to womyn's space, such as a "womyn's music festival." Lesbian feminists of the 1970s created the word to remove "men" from "women"—thus "womyn," plural, "wimmin."
4. Michigan Womyn's Music Festival, www.michfest.org (accessed July 20, 2013). "Michfest" or "Michigan Womyn's Music Festival" has been in continuous operation since 1975.

Eisenhower took back the initiative.[5] The war meant that people could do a daring thing such as stand up as a gay woman, and one might expect someone to stand with you. After the war, the bars provided places for connection during the decades that had the least public places available; and gave women of these decades physical spaces to develop a sense of community, and to take pride in belonging.

However, by the mid-1970s lesbian feminism afforded different physical places—such as women's bookstores which, although almost a thing of the past today, were common meeting places in any major city during this period. "Women's bookstores constituted political and educational organizations ... from the 1970s to 1990."[6] When I first moved to Los Angeles with my then lover in 1987, one of our first stops was Sisterhood Bookstore, where we checked the bulletin board for apartments. We were staying with a woman we had not met before we left Colorado, but had contacted from the "Contact Dykes" list in *Lesbian Connection*.[7] We moved in with this woman—two women, two cars, our stuff, and three cats for three weeks, and we remained friends. Lesbian nation was thriving.

Queers in Space: Communities, Public Places, Sites of Resistance documents queer space as necessary for community in order for place to become a "site of resistance."[8] Nestle also documented the restricted and important nature queer space had for the 1950s woman,[9] particularly the butch-femme bar. Why do certain spaces fill a community's need for place in such a way that the space then defines the community in the way that women's bookstores, and festivals of the 1970s, and the women's bars pre-Stonewall, helped to define the communites that they served? Martin Meeker writes that homosexual community was founded by its participants through a complex web of communication;[10] homosexuals had to "coalesce around an identity ... into communities and specific places."[11] Communication systems served as pathways for homosexuals to find their way towards meeting places. For working-class gay people gay bars were "the only place," so com-

5. Schiller & Rosenberg (dirs), *Before Stonewall*. This story has been criticized as being false (various websites). However it has also been reprinted in several authoratative texts, as well as included in documentaries such as this one. What seems certain is that whether or not Johnnie Phelps heard or responded to this order, the facts—that there were that many qualified gay women in the military and removing them would be a great loss to the military—was true enough for the story, if it is that, to remain in circulation.
6. Junko Onosaka, *Feminist Revolution in Literacy: Women's Bookstores in the United States* (New York: Routledge, 2006), 1.
7. *Lesbian Connection* was founded in 1974 and is still going (as of this writing, 2013).
8. Gordon Brent Ingram, Anne-Marie Bouthillette, & Yolanda Retter, *Queers in Space: Communities, Public Places, Sites of Resistance* (Seattle, WA: Bay Press, 1997).
9. Nestle, *A Restricted Country*.
10. Meeker, *Contacts Desired: Gay and Lesbian Communications and Community, 1940s–1970s*, 1.
11. *Ibid*.

munication systems would lead them to the gay bar. Del Martin and Phyllis Lyon founded the gay women's rights organization Daughters of Bilitis (DOB) in 1955 as an *alternative* to the bars, and created the *Bay Area: North Beach Bars Guide*, a map of gay bars, for the attendees at their first conference in 1960 in San Francisco.[12] Without the bar where *would* the communication system lead? We can't know because for gay people the place to which they were led was the gay bar—"the only place." Some pre-Stonewall gay women did go to discreet house parties or a DOB meeting and did not use the bar as their primary space. However in the ninety-two interviews conducted for this study there was only one woman who had *never* gone to a gay bar; she was married and "out" as she said, between "eight to three when the kids were in school."[13]

Communication systems lead to physical spaces to create community that establishes lived identity and claims place; today we also add virtual space. When that community establishes itself it may not need that system, as it has reached enough members. It may no longer even need the physical space, for example the forbidden bar. Even organizations that are alternatives to a place become obsolete, as people no longer need the alternative—as with the dissolution of DOB in the 1970s. Lesbian feminists had created public spaces and the removal of official status as deviant made it possible for lesbian feminists to align themselves with the group known as *feminists*.

Lesbian feminism was more identified with political practice than sexuality; and gay women's bar culture was more identified with sexuality, that is, butch-femme.[14] Bar culture butches and femmes tagged with the cultural mores of the 1950s masculine and feminine codes were not the androgynous gender identities that flourished with the hippie movement. Gender *costuming*, such as long hair for men, made androgyny more possible for everyone. This look was not available pre-1960s: women looked like *women*, and men like *men*. Butch women looked masculine, not androgynous, and this difference between bar dykes and lesbian feminists was pronounced. Lesbian feminists dressed androgynously and older generations had strong gender divisions in costume.

However, although written histories deem them less visible, and less present, this does not mean that butches and femmes were not present in 1970s lesbian feminism or that lesbian feminists did not sneak off to older butch-femme bars, or that many women who came out in the 1970s in fact

12. Gallo, *Different Daughters: A History of the Daughters of Bilitis and the Rise of the Lesbian Rights Movement*, Map reprinted in photo insert section (between pp. 116–17). This map of gay bars, 1960, includes comments regarding the bars such as "reserved gay" of the Paper Doll or "mostly tourist trade" of Finnocchio's.
13. Interview, Sadie Smith*.
14. Elise Chenier, "Lesbian Feminism." In *An Encyclopedia of Gay, Lesbian, Bisexual and Queer Culture*, ed. Claude J. Summers (Chicago, IL: glbtq, 2004).

never embraced lesbian feminism but embraced bar culture—as legions of women had done for decades—despite the new alternatives to bars.[15] For in the early 1970s butch and femme coupling was *still* the primary *organizing principle.*[16]

However the quote, "The past and present united in eternal flight" from the "Isis" poster celebrated not the lesbian feminist's *actual* recent past, which would have been the gay bar, but rather a *created* "herstory," often depicted as mythical (perhaps real, perhaps legendary) goddess history, or the *belle époque* history of France populated by among others Collette,[17] or perhaps the early feminist suffrage struggles. While these women could populate herstory, the butch woman, even the butch war veteran, and certainly the inveterate pool player, the drag king (or queen), and those who might authenticate them as valued precedents for "herstory" such as the femme in her poodle skirt and bouffant hairdo, were not seen as creating "her" story, but as writing gay history that looked like "his"story due to the masculine persona of its actors. Women's liberation, which had trouble accepting lesbians or "the lavender menace" coined by Betty Friedan,[18] could not accept butch-femme, with what *looked* like women being subservient to men, or femininity subservient to masculinity. Since lesbians were trying to gain purchase within feminism, they created a *her*story that began with lesbians, as in the 1970 manifesto, "The Woman Identified Woman," that stated a lesbian was "the rage of all women condensed to an explosion."[19] It was not "the persistent desire of butch-femme"[20] and its dangerous bar culture, even though for many gay women the initial meeting ground for feminist activity was the bar culture. However the masculinity valorized in butch-femme was not welcome in emerging lesbian feminist circles outside of bars, and not at all in standard feminist circles, such as the National Organization for Women.

15. Amber Hollibaugh & Cherrie Moraga, "What We're Rollin' around in Bed With," *Heresies* 3(4) (issue 12, "The Sex Issue") (1981): 58–63. This is the original publication of this oft-anthologized article. Hollibaugh and Moraga articulate the necessity of lesbian feminism recognizing that butch-femme was what many (as they identify themselves here) feminists were actually "Rollin' Around in Bed With."
16. Kennedy & Davis, *Boots of Leather, Slippers of Gold: The History of a Lesbian Community*. Kennedy and Davis were the first to put forth academically that butch and femme were an "organzinig principle" for gay women's community prior to Stonewall. This was very much supported by my informant interviews, as when an informant said that there were two ways to find a gay bar, one of them being to "follow a butch woman."
17. This was true even though Collette had a very butch cross-dressing lover, Willy.
18. Susan Brownmiller, *In Our Time: Memoir of a Revolution* (New York: Random House, 2000), 71. Friedan used "lavender menace" referring to lesbians within women's liberation, 1969. Brownmiller's work also documents the use of the word as it was taken up by the activist lesbian feminist movement who in defiance began naming themselves as The Lavender Menace.
19. Radicalesbians, "The Woman Identified Woman," Pittsburgh, PA: Know, Inc., http://scriptorium.lib.duke.edu/wlm/ (accesssed December 17, 2009)
20. Nestle, *The Persistent Desire: A Femme-Butch Reader*.

Tally wanted to come out to her straight women's liberation collective in Des Moines, Iowa but was afraid to talk to the collective about her feelings.[21] Tally's story, anthologized in *More Strong-Minded Women: Iowa Feminists Tell Their Stories, is* the story of a strong-minded woman.[22] The group to which she belonged created the first battered women's shelter, rape hotline, woman's health collective, and other radical feminist interventions in Des Moines such as the first women's bookstore. However, she was afraid to come out because the collective was straight-identified. Later in the decade many collectives would promote "feminism is the principle, lesbianism is the practice," but earlier feminism was considered heterosexual. Early 1970s feminists talked about revolution that would upset patriarchy but did not articulate a need for a female partner. For Tally, the advent of lesbian feminism mid-decade "allowed all of the parts of me to come together—the feminism part and the lesbian part. I didn't have to be in a straight women's collective and going to a bar on the side, or vice versa."[23]

Lesbian feminism took root around academic institutions and the establishment of women's studies courses, as well as in institutional buildings. The working-class gay women's or lesbian community that gained access to the public place of the bar did coalesce around *working-class* institutions and *the bar* was where their community congregated. Holding and occupying this place—the bar—was not seen as political for lesbian feminists. A 1950s butch like "Matty" in *Boots of Leather* felt strongly that by going to the bar and defending a public place she was political:

> I'm not the type that will put a sign around my neck as I said earlier and parade around and say, "Hey, my name's Matty and I'm gay." But I won't deny it, and if I have to proclaim it in some way to make it easier for the gay people who are going to come along I'll gladly do it ... In years to come I believe that we're going to be talked about and we're going to be legends, just like Columbus is. I'm serious.[24]

While lesbian feminists did not necessarily see keeping a bar space open as a revolutionary act, because they were building alternate spaces *to* the bar, at the same time many of them continued *to go* to the bar.

However holding the bar space was still fraught with danger and there continued to be police harassment. A chance encounter with a police officer in a 1974 Pasadena bar meant that E.C., as the most feminine woman in the

21. Interview, Irene "Tally" Talbert.
22. Louise R. Noun, "Irene Talbert." In *More Strong-Minded Women: Iowa Feminists Tell Their Stories* (Ames, IA: Iowa State University Press, 1992), 17–30.
23. Interview, Irene "Tally" Talbert.
24. Kennedy & Davis, *Boots of Leather, Slippers of Gold: The History of a Lesbian Community,* 184.

bar that night and one who refused police sexual advances when they asked for ID, led her to spend a night in jail for "resisting an officer." As a result, her husband brought lesbianism up in their divorce courtroom and she lost custody of her elementary school children.[25]

Laura, remembers police coming in and asking for ID at the Happy Hour,[26] in Garden Grove. In the butch-femme bars of Orange Country, California such as the Lioness, and the Huntress, others remember a continual police presence that involved harassing ID checks that could result in arrest if there was any resistance.[27]

This harassment could escalate quickly. Jewel started the first US black disco, The Catch One, in South Central Los Angeles in 1970 and remembers the harassment as a severe threat to shut her down. She believes the only reason the harassment stopped in the 1980s was that the Los Angeles Police Department (LAPD) was afraid to enter a gay establishment due to the AIDS epidemic.[28] Vanessa, also African American, remembers the early 1970s in South Central Los Angeles as a time of rabid police violence, especially against black youth, and felt targeted as a recognizably butch woman, along with her brothers on the streets of South Central. She hitch hiked or bussed to Long Beach to attend gay bars, particularly Que Sera, her "gay home." This was true despite her numerous arrests inside and outside the bar for "being butch and being mouthy," that is, "speaking up if the police harassed someone else," or "her woman."[29]

Jeanne Cordova, founder of the first *Gay and Lesbian Yellow Pages* and former president of DOB, LA, came out in the burgeoning, mostly lesbian, softball leagues of Los Angeles. However, the existence of butch-femme awakened her sexual preference. She was dating another androgynous woman in the league but at the lesbian bar after one of the games when she was accepted by the lesbian members and invited along, she noticed something that made her heart

> skip a beat ... butch-femme. I was looking at these women and I realized ... that my girlfriend ... was more butch than me, and that made me almost the femme ... I didn't want to be the femme; I wanted to be *with* the femme. Seeing a butch-femme couple at the bar made me realize all of this in flash. And I proceeded quickly to break up with the girl I was seeing and date a femme![30]

25. Interview, E.C.
26. Interview, Laura Hill.
27. Interview, Mary. Mary was one among several who remembered this.
28. Interview, Jewel Thais-Williams. They failed to close the bar down and The Catch One still operates.
29. Interview, Vanessa Romain.
30. Interview, Jeanne Cordova.

Jean came into butch-femme in the early 1970s, after leaving the convent because she realized there that she was a lesbian, and discovered the butch-femme bars of East Los Angeles, specifically Redz and The Plush Pony. Redz was the bar taken over by Nancy Valverde and her pals of the early 1950s,[31] and it was also here that the underage Delia marveled at the older Latina butch-femme couples who "knew how to dance."[32] Jean, Nancy, and Delia were part of the East Los Angeles butch-femme scene. Nancy dated outside of East Los Angeles in the 1950s at the primarily white Pink Cadillac, and had a girlfriend there (as well as at other bars) but felt most comfortable in East LA, the barrio in which she grew up and where most Mexican Americans lived.[33]

Jean, however, was integrally also part of the emerging lesbian feminist LA scene, being a core member of the women's coffeehouse.[34] The lesbian feminist *place* was often not a bar, but might be a coffeehouse, or a performance place, such as the Women's Building, or a women's center where feminism and politics ruled rather than the raw sexuality of the butch-femme bar. This is why Delia, a working-class 1970s gay woman, only went to Redz and the Plush Pony, having no interest in traversing lesbian feminist places as she was not part of that community but very much part of the East LA gay bar scene.[35]

However Rita, a professional woman who moved from Mexico in 1979, only went to a mixed gay and lesbian, but primarily Mexican, East Los Angeles bar once, with her cousin whom she stayed with when she first moved to the US. A dentist, she had been out as gay in Mexico. But she had never had a long-term girlfriend or gone to an all women's bar before she moved to the States. In Acapulco she lived a closeted gay life for ten years before emigrating; all of her girlfriends wore heels and make-up. It wasn't until she came to the United States that she saw the "tough Mexican girls—the cholas ... and I totally didn't relate to that." As a professional she moved to Westwood and created community with primarily white women:

> Maybe I am racist. But I couldn't afford to be around someone who told me they couldn't have this and that because they were Mexican ... I moved in with white women who spoke English. I was so ambitious ... I just couldn't see how hanging out with those women would help me. I was always only attracted to white women. Look at my cousin ... that I moved here with and stayed with at first? He is still selling furniture as a salesman. And he is still dating the East LA guys that

31. Interview, Nancy Valverde.
32. Interview, Delia Silva.
33. Interview, Nancy Valverde.
34. Interview, Jeanne Cordova.
35. Interview, Delia Silva.

> are box cutters downtown! Still! Over twenty years later ... how would that kind of mentality help me? He still can't even speak English! No, I wanted something different. I was determined to make it here.[36]

Still, that didn't mean she didn't participate in bar culture. Although the bars of East LA did not appeal to her, she "lived at Peanuts and The Palms," two prominent 1970s West Hollywood bars. While Peanuts appealed to a middle-class and more white crowd and The Palms was more working-class, both were located in the gay environs of West Hollywood, CA. Rita never felt the need to enter total Chicana space, after her early ventures there; in fact, she felt the need to distance herself from it.[37]

Not all Chicana lesbians entered the butch-femme bars of East LA, but many did, and some managed to bridge the gap between professional lives lived out in lesbian feminist activism, and a dating life in the working-class butch-femme bars, and dated women in both.[38] However butch-femme did cede its primary place in the late 1970s, even if it continued in bars populated by older or working-class lesbians and lesbians of color.

As young lesbians were attracted to lesbian feminism, butch-femme began to be considered passé. Jeanne Cordova said, "I hate when people call butch-femme role-playing; I never felt like I was role playing; it always felt natural to me. Anything else *would* have felt like a role."[39] Falcon River said the same thing, as did most self-defined butch women of this and other periods,[40] and this was also true for working-class and women of color femmes. Bobreta Franklin, a black lesbian femme, said butch-femme never went out of fashion no matter "what the rest of lesbians were doing or what they considered butch-femme to be. I enjoyed dressing up as a femme and I kept doing it. I liked it; that's why I did it and I will always do it."[41] Since both cultures were operating, a young middle-class butch like Jeanne Cordova could still work in feminist activism and yet find herself as a Chicano butch within the bars of East LA.

It appears that no other Los Angeles area group had the continuity with the gay women's bar culture as did and do Chicana women. For example, the 1950s bar Redz is still a gay bar and a primary place for Chicana women to gather.[42]

36. Interview, Rita*.
37. *Ibid.*
38. Jeanne Cordova, "When We Were Outlaws." In *Sundays at the Mazer (Lecture Series)* (West Hollywood, CA: June Mazer Lesbian Archives, 2008). Jean said she "was very busy in the 70s," and showed pictures of herself. Complimented on the picture, she chuckled, "That's why I was so busy."
39. Interview, Jeanne Cordova.
40. Interview, Falcon River.
41. Interview, Bobreta Franklin.
42. On a visit with Nancy Valverde in 2009 to Redz, we met a young Guatemalan woman who runs a taco stand in downtown Los Angeles. She told us that she saves her money

Black women often went to Cookies, The Star Room, and others and felt integrated in these bars, but according to Jewel Thais-Williams, black women's bars were scenes of fights that ended up closing them down. Jewel, who frequented these bars herself, made her bar, The Catch, a gay *male* black disco. "Black girl bars fall apart. I would never open a woman of color bar—the fights ... the drama. They never work."[43]

There wasn't a specific black gay women's bar, such as Redz for Chicanas, until the 1970s when The Catch opened. Although a black male disco, it was quickly discovered by the black gay women's community as well. However, Redz and the Plush Pony did not continue because of a *lack* of fights, for within Chicana East LA lesbian life, there were many fights and most Chicana informants engaged in at least one fight, mostly jealous fights over women. "And the femmes were the worst," says Delia, noting that it was not only butch women who fought.[44] Nancy always carried a knife as well as other weapons and used them.[45] While true of other informants, particularly Falcon, it was very true of informants from East LA. However such violence did not deter Chicana lesbians from embracing butch-femme dating, and going to the site where that was possible. Even Jeanne Cordova, a self-defined "gentleman butch" as opposed to "chola," engaged in at least one fist fight.[46]

While all races encountered violence in the gay bars, the black community in particular encountered obvious prejudice. Sandra Tignor was asked to leave The Canyon Club located in bohemian Topanga, CA because she was black;[47] this happened in 1969, a year after the fabled 1968 summer of love.

Although 1970s middle-class urban bars were less violent and experienced less police harassment, anywhere in the South and also rural working-class areas, experienced sometimes more violence than inner city bars of any race. Falcon in West Virginia felt it necessary to teach her girlfriends to fight. She taught her black lover to use a gun, and Falcon held off the KKK because she was dating this black woman.[48]

The mid-1970s, however, could be different for a woman with a college degree, especially an acknowledged professional. Lawyer Roberta Bennett[49] had a very different experience with the police than any other informant.

---

to go to Redz once month. We happened to meet her during her once a month trip—for which she saves her money. Clearly Redz, this Spanish East Los Angeles, primarily butch-femme bar is, for this young Latina, still "the only place."

43. Interview, Jewel Thais-Williams.
44. Interview, Delia Silva.
45. Interview, Nancy Valverde.
46. Interview, Jeanne Cordova.
47. Interview, Sandra Tignor.
48. Interview, Falcon River.
49. Roberta Bennett was the real life lawyer on whom the lesbian lawyer character of "Joyce" in the popular *L-Word* television series was based.

When confronted by police conducting an ID check in order to intimidate patrons and owners, Roberta approached them. She told them she was an attorney and asked their business. She then asked if they were looking for someone particular and what the reason was. The police gave up their ID check and left.[50] Whether due to Roberta's credentials, race, class, or all of these factors is open to speculation. But the fact that as a gay woman she used her agency to confront the police shows how much changed in urban Los Angles for a segment of the population. Within this class would have been Lillian Faderman a decade and a half earlier. However, Lillian was afraid to take a gay women's academically themed book[51] out of the library.[52] But by 1975, Roberta felt free enough to confront the LAPD's routine discrimination. That the 1974 *Diagnostic and Statistical Manual of Mental Disorders* (DSM) in its seventh printing no longer listed homosexuality as a category of disorder meant that if there was ever a good time to confront the police, it was after the official decision that you were not mentally ill.

As meaningful as this historical event was, it did not change the fact for many people that they were still considered mentally ill by authorities. E.C.'s story that her children were taken from her because a lesbianism charge deemed her unstable happened in 1974, a year after this ruling, in urban Pasadena. Minnie Bruce Pratt also lost her children due to being lesbian,[53] and wrote about it in *Crime against Nature.*[54]

Lesbians continued to lose their children, deemed unstable or unfit mothers, throughout the century. Although there have been significant advances in equality, as of this writing gay marriage is still not legal throughout the US.[55] Well into the 1980s it was so well known in California that you could lose your children if you were gay, that Jayne, who was helping male friends with a Gay Pride Parade float, was thrown to the ground by them when cameras passed by, because they knew she was in a custody suit with her homophobic ex-husband and were afraid what could happen if a picture was

50. Interview, Roberta Bennett.
51. Foster, *Sex Variant Women in Literature; a Historical and Quantitative Survey*.
52. Passet, *Sex Variant Woman: The Life of Jeannette Howard Foster*. Lillian documents this story in the "Introduction" to this biography, about the life of Jeannette Foster who wrote the book that Lillian would read between the stacks, not daring to check it out.
53. Interview, Minnie Bruce Pratt.
54. Minnie Bruce Pratt, *Crime against Nature* (Ithaca, NY: Firebrand Books, 1990).
55. Lawrence Hurley, "Gay Marriage Gets Big Boost in Two Supreme Court Rulings," Reuters.com, June 26, 2013, http://www.reuters.com/article/2013/06/26/us-usa-court-gaymarriage-idUSBRE95P06W20130626 (accessed July 13, 2013). While gay marriage may be legalized by the court in states like California, there has been a trend to put that right as an amendment on the public ballot which resulted for instance in the Proposition 8 battle. Gay marriage which was ruled as legal in 2008 then became illegal the same year with the passage of Proposition 8. As of June 29, 2013, gay marriage has once again been ruled as legal in California—this time by the US Supreme Court who struck down Proposition 8.

taken of her around gay people. To this day, she will not use her real name in print regarding these issues, fearing for her child custody.[56]

What did the gay bars provide for people who had their children taken away? You cannot have a religion without a community; you can have a mystical experience but not a religion. In fact, for a mystical experience to be recognized, it needs a believing community. The individual person with such a phenomenological experience cannot speak of it without it losing the quality that makes it sacred,[57] for speaking of it makes it profane. For the experience to have the deep meaning accorded to mystical experience, and for the person to be deemed a mystic, the narrative must be told and held by a believing community, whose members believe in the existence of such experiences.

E.C. knew that the bar she went to would give her community,[58] a slice of humanity that did not feel the way the judge did, the way her ex-husband did, the way his divorce lawyer did, or the way the arresting officers or even perhaps her own lawyer did. As a closeted hairdresser who would she be able to talk to about her children being taken away because she was a lesbian? Who would understand what this story meant for her? For these stories did not have the same type of meaning to those who imposed their narratives on those deemed inverts, deviants, felons, dangerous and/or mentally ill as they did to the homosexuals who were at the *receiving* end of such impositions.

Instances of such community understandings are, among others, Falcon's story that she "owes her face" to a dentist who was part of the crowd. "He wasn't a medical doctor, he was a dentist—but he was 'our' doctor,"[59] and Joan's story about the bloodied butch staggering into the bar, having been beaten up blocks away. "The fact that she had someplace to go ... where someone would understand was so radically important. There was so much caretaking that went on in those bars."[60]

By the 1970s the need for all-women spaces where "someone would understand" became even more pronounced. Many lesbians embraced lesbian separatism and so rejected men. Safe space was women-only space; woman and women were "wimmin" or "womyn" to get the men/man out.[61] The spaces that women's collectives created, such as those that Helen and Tally were part of, were the first of their kind. *Womyn* would call and demand

56. Interview, Jayne Doolittle*.
57. Rudolf Otto, *The Idea of the Holy: An Inquiry into the Non-Rational Factor in the Idea of the Divine and Its Relation to the Rational*, 2nd edn (New York: Oxford University Press, 1950).
58. Interview, E.C.
59. Interview, Falcon River.
60. Interview, Joan Nestle.
61. Laurie J. Kendall, *The Michigan Womyn's Music Festival: An Amazon Matrix of Meaning* (Laurie J. Kendall, 2008). Michigan Womyn's Music Festival is still so labeled to designate it "womyn's only" space

to speak to a woman insurance agent, police officer, dentist, or doctor and doing this resulted in services designated for this new community—from women's health clinics and battered women's shelters to domestic violence training for police officers.

Butch women however were often asked to leave feminist meetings, including Jean, Falcon, and Robin Tyler. Falcon was pointedly asked to leave, and her girlfriend went with her,[62] for what was unwanted was not necessarily the butch look, for many women looked butch in the 1970s, but the persona that *found a femme* woman attractive.

So while lesbian feminists created coffee houses, music festivals, and an underground of *womyn* spaces, gay women who still identified as butch-femme still relied on the bars as "the only place." The gay women/butch-femme community often felt these new places were not open to them. And for the pre-Stonewall butch-femme/bar dyke/"role-playing" lesbian to give up bars meant giving up not only identity but community, for the bars were still "the only place" to freely exhibit the contested identity of butch-femme.

In 1987 when I first visited the butch-femme bar The Happy Hour in Garden Grove, California, I was horrified that the bouncer passed her hand through my and my hippie girlfriend's bodies to make sure we were "not touching" and told us it "was not allowed."[63] Coming from a 1980s hippie Colorado culture I could not understand how lesbianism was not allowed in a gay bar. I had never experienced this. The bar was not raided that night and most informants indicated bar raids were not in effect past the early 1980s, although ID checks were still conducted. There was no ID check that night but clearly bar personnel were prepared if cops entered with that intention. The bouncer held onto the rules of conduct, for if raids were stopped by this time, they ceased less than five years earlier, and in effect held onto the space. The Happy Hour in the late 1980s was also a butch-femme bar—another first for me, where only one person was allowed in the bathroom at a time, and if the flashlight beam played across the dance floor it had to pass *between* dancers.

Nonetheless many gay women entering lesbian feminism from bar culture missed butch-femme and yet felt there was no going back. Some of them bridged the divide as did Jean, active in DOB and later in the National Organization of Women, which earlier asked her to leave a meeting, as well as being an out butch in East LA. Falcon opened Mother's Brew in Kentucky infused with lesbian feminism after she left drug dealing in Virginia. Mother's Brew sponsored feminist institutions such as battered women's shelters

62. Interview, Falcon River.

63. Although the Colorado *gay bar* may have seemed at the time more permissive, this did not translate to the *general* culture. For example, when I called a battered women's shelter in 1984 to escape an abusive girlfriend, the shelter informed me that they could not take me—because I was a lesbian.

and marches in support of NOW even though its owner, Falcon, had been kicked out of a NOW meeting.[64]

Most middle-class white lesbians were now *lesbians*—not *gay women*, or *butch or femme* or *he/she* or *invert* or *homosexual* or even *gay*—but definitely *lesbian*, and this marked a population not just lesbian but also *feminist*. No informants used lesbian to describe themselves before the 1970s. Many would never use that word or claim feminist politics, unless they *did* come out in the 1970s and many butch women were not allowed to claim it. Nestle wrote of her difficulties articulating that the butch-femme culture in privileging femme desire *was* feminist, and so articulated pre-feminist politics within bar culture.[65] The fact that I found bar culture worthwhile surprised even many of my own informants.

However, it is my contention that the years and the women who were publicly out in bar culture from 1945–75 were the actual mothers of contemporary lesbian feminism. This period, lesbian feminism, is often defined by its reference to a mythical goddess figure in the past—for instance, the Isis of the Chicago Graphics poster.

I believe however that the missing historical link between that past and the 1970s is the butch-femme couple, the true "point of connection" between the two.[66] The butch-femme years were more than a pre-political or even political ground for the breeding of the lesbian feminist movement to come, or the gay rights movement and its Stonewall uprising. I propose that there was something sacred, something religious, in the community building and protection that took place within the bar culture, and this culture, that deserves re-framing—*baby, you are my religion.* This phrase, said to me by an ex-lover, was incorporated into my 1997 one-woman show *Ballistic Femme.*[67] I came to see this as having meaning both in butch-femme history and my own life as well.

Religion and belief systems differ. The bars gave butch-femme culture a physical space *for* community, and the articulation of rituals that enabled these separate and isolated individuals to *form* community. Was it a believing community? Yes. It believed in the unfairness of what was happening to its members, when almost no one outside of the four walls of the bar shared that vision. The community's theology, or word of God (*theo*—God, *logos*—Word) approached that of a lived liberation theology.

The 1970s saw the birth of the second wave of feminism (the first wave being suffrage), lesbian feminism, and lesbian separatism. "Feminism is the

64. Interview, Falcon River.
65. Nestle, *A Restricted Country*.
66. Chicago Women's Graphic Collective, "Isis: Poster" (Chicago, IL: CWLU Herstory Website Gallery One, 1970–83). I am referencing here the quote on the Isis poster, "I am the point from which all directions start."
67. Cartier, *Ballistic Femme*.

theory; lesbianism is the practice," so *lesbian feminism* was theoretically feminism and practiced as lesbian.[68] Ti-Grace Atkinson wrote that maxim and also:

> The price of clinging to the enemy [a man] is your life. To enter into a relationship with a man who has divested himself as completely ... from the male role as much as possible would still be a risk. But to relate to a man who has done any less is suicide ... I will not appear with any man publicly, where it could possibly be interpreted that we were friends.[69]

The idea of being *in love* with another woman and having sex with her *supposedly* was second to the idea that you were giving your energy to women, rather than to men.

"Women are the only oppressed group in our society that lives in intimate association with their oppressor," said Evelyn Cunningham.[70] Since most women were with men romantically, how could there ever be a definition of that oppressor that would allow women to fight back? As the decade wore on Rita Mae Brown wrote, "An army of lovers shall not fail,"[71] referring to the army of lesbian lovers in the women's movement as it became *de rigueur* to experiment with lesbian sex. However, such practice was not universal and depended on where participants lived. It was not true that belonging to a feminist community (Tally's story[72]) or a hippie community (Gypsy's story[73]) would also create the window for lesbian expression.

While butch-femme bars still flourished and were a major venue for people to come out, they were no longer the only way. Women in universities, or those who had access to feminist discourse communities—women's rap groups, or the new consciousness-raising groups—might never need to set foot in a bar to meet an actual lesbian. While bar culture had been essential for earlier gay women to *knowingly meet* other gay women (unless you had access to the limited windows where you might meet gay women such as

68. Ti-Grace Atkinson, *Lesbianism and Feminism*, Chicago Women's Liberation Union, 1971. This early pamphlet is reprinted in the anthology *Feminism and Sexuality: A Reader*, ed. Stevi Jackson & Sue Scott (New York: Columbia University Press, 1996), 282.
69. Ti-Grace Atkinson, *Amazon Odyssey* (Links Books, 1974), 90–91.
70. Evelyn Cunningham in *A Few Good Women Oral History Collection*, 1938–2000, bulk 1969–2000, creator: Barbara Hackman Repository: Special Collections Library, Pennsylvania State University. Cunningham transcripts of interviews are in series 4, Oral History Tapes, boxes 9 and 11. Evelyn Cunningham was an African-American civil rights era journalist.
71. Rita Mae Brown, "Sappho's Reply," in *Poems from the Women's Movement*, ed. Honor Moore, American Poets Project (New York: Library of America, 2009), 41. Used with permission of author.
72. Interview, Irene "Tally" Talbert.
73. Interview, Gypsy Powers.

college or the military), 1970s lesbian feminism was the first political movement outside of bar culture that was publicly accessible to *most* women.

However, the early movement was not accepting of lesbians. The president of the National Organization of Women (NOW), and a founder of the second wave of feminism, Betty Friedan,[74] called lesbians in 1969 "the lavender menace," and omitted the DOB from the list of sponsors of the First Congress to Unite Women in 1969.[75] In 1966 Friedan told a college audience not to become part of the "anti-man, politics of orgasm" school. Nonetheless, she seconded a resolution protecting lesbians at the NOW Conference in 1977, where lesbians staged a protest and encircled the membership wearing "Lavender Menace" T-shirts and demanded to be heard.[76]

Falcon reports being called at Mother's Brew often to provide security for "the feminists," which she often did, most notably for the rally that resulted in the passage of the Equal Rights Amendment Bill in Kentucky.[77] Both self-identified butches Jeanne Cordova and Robin Tyler ended up working together as feminist activists, often with other butches, among them Ivy Bottini.

Cordova believes that she was "too butch" for a national audience,[78] so when her work, as well as the noted activism of butch Ivy Bottini, received national attention, they were contacted by NOW Headquarters and asked to step down,[79] and were replaced by a more traditionally feminine face.[80] Friedan's thesis in 1963, which was considered reactionary at the time, was that many, if not most, women were not satisfied by motherhood and housework, and that the assertion that they should be was why women were depressed and anxious.[81] As feminism gained a foothold in the US and became less suspect, so did the leadership of women—who went beyond Friedan's assertions. Friedan never meant to let go of heterosexual family as a primary activity. The fact that women, some lesbian, saw feminism as an outlet for their rage at the entire paradigm of heterosexual relations was not her intention. However, by the end of the 1970s, even Friedan was willing to vote that yes, lesbians needed to be *and were* part of the feminist movement and deserved protected status within the NOW umbrella.

The Radicalesbians asked in 1970, "What is a lesbian?" And they answered, "A lesbian is the rage of all women condensed to the point of explosion."[82]

---

74. Friedan, *The Feminine Mystique.*
75. Kathy Belge, "What Is the Lavender Menace?," lesbianlife.about.com.
76. Associated Press, "Feminist Author, Icon Betty Friedan Dies at 85," *USA Today*, February 4, 2006.
77. Interview, Falcon River.
78. Interview, Jeanne Cordova.
79. Ivy Bottini, "Everything You Wanted to Ask This Old Dyke—Answered." In *One Culture Series* (Los Angeles, CA: One Gay and Lesbian Archives, University of Southern California, 2008).
80. *Ibid.*
81. Friedan, *The Feminine Mystique.*
82. Radicalesbians, "The Woman Identified Woman."

This rage of "all women" meant that lesbian separatists, who only wanted to deal with women and have as little contact with men as possible, devised a new definition of lesbian. The political lesbian was still having sex with women, but she was a political animal—she was the "rage of all women," not the bar dyke who wanted the freedom of sexual expression.

While women were enraged and women's liberation demanded anger, many women *who were having sex with other women* did not identify as lesbians. For these women "gay" still fit best because lesbian was inextricably linked with lesbian feminism. These women did not fit into the political model, for example, bar dykes like Falcon, were often not welcome at feminist events. Lesbians were afraid to identify as gay women for fear they would be ostracized in feminist political circles as Falcon was, so the manner in which Falcon was treated served as a deterrent.[83] That a lesbian, or woman-loving woman, was political and not *just* sexual, led ultimately to confusion.

In 1980 the feminist poet Adrienne Rich wrote her "compulsory heterosexuality" treatise, in which she proposed that not only lesbians as self-defined sexual beings were entrapped by conventional heterosexuality, but heterosexuals as well. Because heterosexuality was compulsory, in order to prove that one was "straight" one would go to extraordinary measures to escape the gender police who would enforce heterosexuality/make it compulsory. Rich wrote that *lesbian* might mean a woman who avoided conventional married life and resisted male domination, not just a sexual woman loving another sexual woman. This meant that "lesbian relationships" were possible between any two women.[84] Such a stance was provocative because the identification "lesbian" to many gay women meant that they did not just *love women*; they were *making love to women*. This point, and what constituted acceptable sexual behavior, would undergird the sex wars that erupted between lesbians and feminists in the 1980s.

Bar life reflected these dynamics. There were bars that became more androgynous and lesbian feminist planning spaces. There were bars that used butch-femme as the primary structure. Many lesbians switched back and forth between these communities, enacting different parts of their social life in these different spaces. Among them would be Jeanne Cordova,[85] but in the early part of the decade feminists could be asked to leave because they didn't conform to bar standards, as was Helen Factor and her friends because they didn't partner dance and were dressed without butch or femme distinction.[86]

83. Anderson and Coolidge (dirs), *If These Walls Could Talk 2*. The second segment portrayed 1970s feminism perceiving *obvious* lesbians, i.e., butch lesbians, and the ostracizing that resulted, even from other lesbians, i.e. lesbian feminists.
84. Rich, "Compulsory Heterosexuality and Lesbian Existence."
85. Cordova, "When We Were Outlaws."
86. Interview, Helen Factor.

But by the end of the decade, a *butch-femme couple* could be asked to leave even the bar. In 1979, an obvious butch-femme couple were surrounded by a group of mostly androgynous lesbians (myself included) and made to feel so uncomfortable that they left the Boston bar, named Somewhere. Because we were lesbian separatists we felt the couple was "male-identified," the femme woman in heels and a dress and the butch in masculine clothes, and felt agency in putting pressure on them to leave "our bar,"[87] much as the butch and femme women made Helen and her Collective Graphic sisters leave their bar.[88]

Prior to this period, everyone interviewed identified as "gay," "gay woman," "gay girl," or "a woman who loved another woman." A majority of these would use "lesbian" in the 1970s if they entered a feminist community. Otherwise, they continued to use "gay." Lesbians in the 1970s, whether gay or lesbian, had the option to identify *politically*. Previous to this decade it was very difficult to identify as political *and* gay.

Gays and lesbians lived *lives* in bars prior to the event Stonewall and so created the beginning of gay and lesbian civil rights because they claimed public space by occupying urban bars and walking the streets, many times as open homosexuals. Most of these women, especially if they cross-dressed/dressed opposite their biology, did not identify themselves as part of a political movement. A few did feel, as the narrator Matty did from *Boots of Leather*, that they were "like Columbus" and were keeping the bar space open for the young gay people "coming up."[89] In contrast, however, most lesbian feminists as part of a political movement easily verbalized holding both political and sexual identities by identifying as not just gay or lesbian but as lesbian feminists.

For many butches and femmes, the lesbian feminists were not primarily sexual and lost the sexuality behind the word gay. This was not the reality for lesbian feminists who were actually very sexual; although certain customs that prior to the 1970s had been *de rigueur*, such as penetrative sex with dildos, were now considered *passé* and male-identified. Lesbian feminists should be able to orgasm through the clitoris alone; the newly discovered feminist erogenous zone named after *The Hite Report* was published in 1976.[90]

The lesbian feminists, as part of the sexual revolution, paid lip service (literally) to non-monogamy, and experimented with vibrators and other toys,

87. Today, of course, I feel awful about this act and can still hear the femme's heels clicking as she walked out of the door, opened for her by her butch.
88. Interview, Helen Factor.
89. Kennedy and Davis, *Boots of Leather, Slippers of Gold: The History of a Lesbian Community*.
90. Shere Hite, *The Hite Report: A Nationwide Study on Female Sexuality* (New York: Macmillan, 1976).

supposedly with the exception of dildos. Feminist health groups sprung up where these empowered lesbians found their cervix with plastic speculums and a flashlight. The idea that this was *your body as a woman* quickly found a large audience, as illustrated by the history of the still updated and re-issued *Our Bodies, Ourselves*. This Boston Women's Health Collective *Women and Their Bodies* came out in 1970, published by the collective;[91] the next year it was published as *Our Bodies, Our Selves* by the collective and a radical New England Free Press;[92] by 1973 it found a home with a major press, and was given the slightly less radical title *Our Bodies, Ourselves* ("Ourselves" as all one word, rather than the authoritative "Our Selves"), and continues so in print to this day.[93] Women longed to have information about their bodies passed from women and to women, and lesbian feminists were at the forefront of this major movement. At the center of the 1970s movement was the ownership of the body—from battered women's shelters, rape hotlines, abortion clinics, and freedom of choice debates—to feminist health centers and finding your own cervix. There was no doubt that so much of the movement involved protecting basic rights to "*our bodies*" and helping other women to do the same. The personal became political, and topics such as how you made love, and with whom, how you lived, and what you ate (I was at a potluck where a lesbian who brought barbequed ribs was severely criticized by the vegetarians in the room) were *all* open for discussion.

This was in marked contrast to the world of the "stone" butch, or silent butch and femme, who wanted to win her heart. The 1970s still provided the option that you could go to either a political feminist hangout or a more butch-femme bar, or to both. It was however true in this decade that the feminist hangouts were not being raided—whereas the butch-femme bars were still being policed and would continue to be into the 1980s.

While true that most women lived in one camp or another, women also traversed the territory if they found it expedient. Rory talks about being primarily "a bar dyke" but also of hanging out on the back porch of the "women's collective" house, getting high and waiting for her girlfriend to be done with her meetings to go out on a date.[94] This is similar to the relationship between the 1970s feminist and 1970s bar lesbian in *If These Walls Could Talk 2*,[95] but in Rory's real life, this was not as conflicted as has been portrayed.

91. Boston Women's Health Collective, *Women and Their Bodies: A Course* (Boston, MA: The Collective, 1970).
92. Boston Women's Health Course Collective, *Our Bodies, Our Selves: A Course by and for Women* (Boston, MA: Boston Women's Health Course Collective and New England Free Press, 1971).
93. Boston Women's Health Book Collective, *Our Bodies, Ourselves* (New York: Simon & Schuster, 1973).
94. Interview, Rory Devine*.
95. Anderson & Coolidge, *If These Walls Could Talk 2*.

Kim Palmore related troubles gaining entrance to the popular Long Beach bar, Ripples, and being told that lesbians must wear closed-toe shoes, so popular-among-lesbians Birkenstocks were not allowed, and feeling that butches were discriminated against by the manager who wanted men in the bar.[96] Laura reports that at Newport Station women were not able to enter wearing Levis, but men could go in without shirts.[97]

Prior to the 1970s, many bars asked black lesbians for two or three pieces of ID, as opposed to white lesbians who were asked for only one piece of ID. Jewel Thais-Williams, who experienced this, cites this reason as the main reason that she opened Catch One in Los Angeles.[98] However one mixed-race African American lesbian said she never felt comfortable at The Catch as she was not "dark enough;" however, she also felt that she did not fit into the more lesbian feminist bars either.[99] Prior to this time, because being gay was closeted, gay people were lucky to find each other at all. While it is true that some bars were segregated, depending on geography, the lines were not as clearly drawn as they would become in the 1970s, when "lesbian" and "women of color" became commonplace terms and marked territory that could not be crossed by someone not clearly marked with that identity.

Since lesbians were no longer considered to be mentally ill, they could create alliances with communities—the same communities with whom feminists aligned themselves. This meant that the prostitution and drug-running connections of the past decades were no longer wanted community partners as the bar was no longer the only place. A whole range of different options had opened.

Butch and femme were deviant, linked with bars, and political lesbians wanted to distance themselves. In response Nestle founded the Lesbian Herstory Archives,[100] wrote A *Restricted Country*, and gave a home to the bar women who first gave her "a home."[101] Enterprising butch lesbians like Falcon did create spaces with feminist trappings such as Mother's Brew which offered escorts to and from your car, and gave donations to feminist services such as battered women's shelters. However, Falcon was interested in bar culture prior to this, and although interested in feminism, it was not that interested in her. However Falcon says, "They [feminists] needed their own space. Butches were just not welcome. I understand it. Everyone needed feminism; we [butches] did, too."[102]

96. Interview, Kim Palmore.
97. Interview, Laura Hill.
98. Interview, Jewel Thais-Williams.
99. This comment was made by an informant who wished to remain anonymous.
100. Warshow, *Hand on the Pulse.*
101. Nestle, *A Restricted Country.*
102. Interview, Falcon River.

RELIGIOUS AND THEOLOGICAL IMPLICATIONS

Father Joe (not his real name), a Catholic priest for the past forty years was seventeen years old and in seminary when Stonewall proved to be "one of the most liberating things that ever happened to me."[103] Father Joe, then an acolyte, saw the first night of the rebellion on television. He had wanted to be a priest since age five and entered seminary at age thirteen. He was particularly moved by images of civil rights actions where he saw "nuns and priests with their collars marching with the blacks in the South. I wanted to march with them, but couldn't afford to go there. When I saw the images from Stonewall I knew I could get to the Village, whereas I couldn't get to the South."[104]

He relates that what he saw at Stonewall touched him in

> a core way. I wanted to go up to the snickering cops and reprimand them. I saw things I had never seen before—men dressed as women, men holding hands, masculine men—it was all so new to me. And these people were being brutalized by the cops. I had already seen the police batons used on people the night before on television. I decided then, I think, that this would be my ministry. I wanted to stand with these people, the way the nuns and priests had stood in Selma with the civil rights activists.[105]

Father Joe would see this come full circle in 2007, when a butch-femme couple stood up in his congregation in response to a challenge he issued asking his parish to speak of what they were afraid of. The butch stood up and said she was afraid if people knew she was "a lesbian that I will get kicked out of the Church." Father Joe put his arm around her saying, "Not as long as I am in the parish. As long as I am here, there is a space for you at the table." He had tears in his eyes as he related this and he is part of the country-wide movement in urban Catholic parishes that have a designated ministry to "welcome home" gay and lesbian Catholics.[106]

Father Joe grew up in Hell's Kitchen in New York and came from a family of alcoholics. He was raised in part in bars and, although his parents were both alcoholics, he found that people in the bar "took care of us." As his choice of ministry literally poured out of the bar Stonewall, Father Joe also does ministry with alcoholics. "People often go to bars looking for 'Spirits with a big S' but find 'spirits with a small s' … it is not an accident that priests

103. Interview, Father Joe*.
104. *Ibid.*
105. *Ibid.*
106. *Ibid.*

drink wine at the Mass, rather than tea or coffee," he says. Alcohol does pave the way for social interaction, if used responsibly, and is a "spirit."[107]

Reverend Troy Perry, founder of the gay Metropolitan Community Church, conducted the first Gay Pride March in West Hollywood in 1970. Andi was part of that march and is proud of having taken part, and for being recognized as a spiritual being. "I loved the bars and my girlfriend played softball so we were always in them. And I loved them; we had a great time, and a lot of friends. But, we were ... not considered real people, somehow. Reverend Troy Perry changed that. He made us more legitimate. It was like we were no longer dirty, or something." Andi points out that Reverend Perry organized for his March within the bars. "It was the only place," she says. "We all came out of there."[108]

However, since butch-femme and bar culture remained isolated from feminist community the larger feminist uprising of women's spirituality would not largely affect butch-femme communities until almost the millennium. Z. Budapest, recognized as starting the women's spirituality movement, founded the Susan B. Anthony Coven Number l, the first feminist witches' coven. She published *The Feminist Book of Lights and Shadows* in 1976,[109] later re-titled *The Holy Book of Women's Mysteries* and published in Oakland[110] and in Los Angeles[111] by small presses. This book has a similar trajectory to the publication of *Our Bodies, Ourselves.* Z. Budapest was seen as *the* witch for the lesbian feminist movement, just as the Boston Health Collective was seen as the health collective. By 1989, Z.'s book would be published[112] and is still in print today, recently published in a highly-illustrated text,[113] as part of a series. Part of Z's success was her and others' insistence on owning their lives. The book documents her struggle as she was thrust into the spotlight when she was tried as a "witch" in 1975—she was found guilty after being arrested on Venice Beach for reading tarot cards. She fought the charges for nine years and won the right for every tarot reader to do so legally. As with *Our Bodies, Ourselves,* such was the need for feminist material, and her book became the spiritual classic for a new population, lesbian feminists.

107. *Ibid.*
108. Interview, Andrea "Andi" Segal.
109. Zsuzsanna Emese Budapest, *The Feminist Book of Light and Shadows* (Los Angeles, CA: Feminist Wicca, 1976).
110. Zsuzsanna Emese Budapest, Helen Beardwoman, & Sue Whitson, *The Holy Book of Women's Mysteries,* 2 vols. (Oakland, CA: Z.E. Budapest, 1979).
111. Zsuzsanna Emese Budapest, *The Holy Book of Women's Mysteries* (Los Angeles, CA: Susan B. Anthony Coven No. 1, 1979).
112. Zsuzsanna Emese Budapest, *The Holy Book of Women's Mysteries* (Berkeley, CA: Wingbow Press/Bookpeople, 1989).
113. Z. Budapest, *The Holy Book of Women's Mysteries* (Newburyport, MA: Weiser Books, 2007).

As a lesbian feminist, however, Z. Budapest did not allow men into her circles. This model of feminist witchcraft, the oldest religion, was widely adopted throughout the country. Women wore buttons that read, "WITCH—Woman In Total Control of Herself," and T-shirts that celebrated women's "blood mysteries" by proclaiming, "Woman—I can bleed for days and not die," and asserted that you could say "I Am A Witch" three times and "be a witch."[114]

"WITCH—Women's International Terrorist Conspiracy from Hell" was a radical women's group composed of members who would later split into two groups—Redstockings and New York Radical Women—and who dressed as traditional black-garbed witches and hexed the Wall Street Stock Exchange on Halloween, 1968. The Stock Market fell the next day and again the next.[115]

This women's spirituality movement was not receptive to butch women or to femme women who loved butches. Falcon would join women's spirituality circles after experiencing the Michigan Womyn's Music Festival in 1975. But she felt out of place until she created a path that she felt was an open path for butch as well as other women, called The Guardian Path, founded in the very late 1990s.[116]

Father Joe pointed out that Church, as originally defined by the early Christians, was to gather and tell stories and break bread: where "two or three are gathered in my name" then there is "Church." Were the butches and femmes of previous decades gathered in "His Name?" Father Joe believes so, as they were gathered in the name of each other, community support and telling stories, and to him that is in the "name of Christ." "People forget 'Matthew 25' all the time," he says. "'Whatever you do to the least of me, you do unto me.' So 'the least of me' in the 1960s might certainly have been gays and lesbians. To create spaces for these people was to do it, in some sense also, for the Christ in them."[117]

For women, denied entrance to many religious institutions, Catholic convents were still a viable option for women's community. However, as Bronco,[118] Jeanne Cordova,[119] Melanie DeMore[120] and others found, lesbian identity was a reason to be removed from the convent or rather for them to be removed from the women's community that they knew and loved. And this was painful especially for Bronco whose dismissal was "one of the

114. I experienced all of these—I own the button and T-shirt. I was told by a woman who lived on womyn's land in Oregon that I could be a witch if I said "I am a witch," three times. She said this is how lesbian feminists became witches—we were to take charge of it ourselves and proclaim it ourselves.
115. Freeman, "WITCH—Women's International Terrorist Conspiracy from Hell."
116. Interview, Falcon River.
117. Interview, Father Joe*.
118. Interview, Bronco Alda Moonwater.
119. Interview, Jeanne Cordova.
120. Interview, Melanie DeMore.

most painful experiences of my life." It was her women's community from age fourteen into her twenties (as the seminary was for Father Joe during this same period). Until she found the Michigan Womyn's Music Festival and lesbian feminism, Bronco was adrift. "Even with how bad it ended, I wouldn't want to have not had that time in the convent. I would still do it, knowing how it ended," she says. "It was incredible for me to be part of a women's community."[121]

Rory also found women's community after she went AWOL because of sexual harassment in the military. She did not find women's community stationed on a tugboat as one of the only women on that boat. During her AWOL year she lived on the edge as a prostitute, finding solace in the lesbian bar, just as she did on her weekend leaves when stationed in the military. However, upon returning to the military and facing trial, she was cordoned into a unit with other lesbians also awaiting trial. "That's when it became great—I was with other lesbians!"[122]

For many women in the 1970s the reality of finding women's community was not as easy as entering a women's liberation circle. While this became an option for many women, especially academic and/or political women, and some urban women who were interested in feminism, it was not the option that was available or of interest to many other women. The lesbian bar was still the place of community and breaking bread.

Father Joe talks about going to Dignity meetings founded by Catholic gays and lesbians in the 1970s. He went to his first one in 1977 and following the meeting everyone agreed to go to a bar. He didn't realize until they got there that it was "a gay bar." "Of course it makes sense it would be a gay bar. But I was shocked when so many people in the bar knew the priest I was with—they were coming up to him saying 'Father John,' and telling him stories. It was Church right there."[123] With the formation of LGBT religious groups, liberation theology was implicit—gays and lesbians were denied civil rights such as marriage, so gay *liberation* was *why* these congregations gathered.

DEMOGRAPHIC HIGHLIGHTS

I interviewed twenty-two people specifically who came out in the 1970s and also heard stories about "being out" in the 1970s from all women I interviewed from earlier decades, particularly those from the 1960s. I also conducted numerous informal interviews with people from this period which provided background and general information.

121. Interview, Bronco Alda Moonwater.
122. Interview, Rory Devine*. She won this case and was able to leave the military without a dishonorable discharge because one of the men on the tugboat stood up for her.
123. Interview, Father Joe*.

The formal interviewees were nine self-identified butches, two femmes, one gay woman, and eleven lesbian feminists who came out in lesbian feminist communities; of the lesbian feminists three now identify also as femme; the gay woman now identifies as metrosexual and/or butch; and at least one of the lesbian feminists now identifies also as butch. One of these women worked as a prostitute and dealt drugs. Three were arrested, but none of those arrests happened specifically because of being lesbian.

Two women are African American, two Chicano-identified and two Filipino; and three are former nuns. One performed as a folk singer in a lesbian bar,[124] one helped to open a lesbian feminist café and was also prominent in the butch-femme Chicana bars in East Los Angeles.[125] Women who came out in the 1970s came out on the brink of, or in the midst of, a lesbian feminist explosion dependent on where they lived geographically. Many of them bridged the divide between lesbian feminism and butch-femme bar culture by participating in both cultures and having the cultures compartmentalized. N. Amazon was a bar regular, with Vanessa Romain (who came out in the 1960s), at the Que Sera in Long Beach, California, but was also a member of the lesbian feminist collective Califia.[126] Irene "Tally" Talbert came out in a butch-femme bar because it was the only place she knew to meet lesbians, but she was also part of a feminist collective where she was afraid to talk about being lesbian.[127]

Of the women I interviewed who came out in the 1970s, one was ex-military; she went AWOL because of sexual harassment after being assigned as one of the first women on a Navy tugboat. She spent the year AWOL—before she returned to the military thinking she was facing court martial. By the time she returned, however, other women had come forward to make a charge against her commanding captain, and a man from the tugboat stood by the women's stories. This helped make the charge against the captain stick. Rory was discharged, but not dishonorably, and did not face court martial.[128]

Five of the women I interviewed were married to men prior to coming out, four of those had children, and three were able to keep their children; one from the South lost her children in the divorce because of being a lesbian. This woman, Minnie Bruce Pratt, has written about that loss[129] and also about coming into lesbianism as a feminist and then discovering butch-femme with her current partner[130] Leslie Feinberg, author of *Stone Butch*

124. Interview, Melanie DeMore.
125. Interview, Jeanne Cordova.
126. Interview, N. Amazon*.
127. Interview, Irene "Tally" Talbert.
128. Interview, Rory Devine*.
129. Minnie Bruce Pratt, *Crime against Nature*.
130. Minnie Bruce Pratt, *S/He* (Ithaca, NY: Firebrand Books, 1995).

Blues.[131] Another woman got pregnant and had to give up her child for adoption but luckily they were re-united when the child turned of age and sought her out.

Most of these women created or helped create alternate spaces for lesbians. Linda Garnets created the first-ever lesbian psychology course at UCLA, and perhaps anywhere;[132] Roberta Bennett created the first interface organization fundraising for politicians who agreed to support gay issues;[133] Jeanne Cordova the first gay and lesbian yellow pages;[134] Tally a battered women's shelter, bookstore and rape hotline in Des Moines, Iowa;[135] and Vivian Escalante the first Dykes on Bikes, the lesbians riding motorcycles contingent that is a tradition in front of most US Gay Pride Parades.[136]

Bar culture also served as a pipeline of communication to the opening of well paying jobs, and was the precursor to a more formal affirmative action policy that would be enforced in the ensuing decade. Laura, who came out in the 1970s, was an office worker and movie usher/janitor prior to becoming one of a handful of women working in the power plants. She had an ex-girlfriend who was one of the first three women in the power plants in the 1970s. Edison had eleven power plants and these three women were the first to go into three different plants and then work their way up. White men held all the jobs in the power plants in the 1970s until a class action suit forced them to hire people of color and women. Laura was a plant equipment operator, which she says was "absolutely a man's job" prior to this time. As Laura puts it, in all of southern California:

> There were only a dozen women hired and only two of them were straight girls. Although none of us talked about our sexuality—it was still pretty closeted. But, I remember being at the Que and seeing a woman I worked with dancing with her Edison hard hat on. She had run out and got her hard hat and came back into the club to dance. So we did run into each other in the bars.[137]

As she says:

> That fact that women had been in plants and could do that job—à la Rosie the Riveter—showed that it had already been proven—women could do those jobs—so it made it much harder for the plants to say no. It's closer for me, however, than Rosie because my ex broke the barrier

131. Feinberg, *Stone Butch Blues: A Novel.*
132. Interview, Linda Garnets.
133. Interview, Roberta Bennett.
134. Interview, Jeanne Cordova.
135. Interview, Irene "Tally" Talbert.
136. Interview, Vivian Escalante.
137. Interview, Laura Hill.

> in the southern California plants. I learned about the job because of word of mouth from another lesbian—"Hey, if you want a good paying job and are willing to get dirty ... you might want to go down to the plant." That is why most of us doing it were lesbians—straight women just didn't find out about it. A lot of this information came through the bars from one lesbian to another.

For those early women working in the plants Laura says "the hazing was incredible." She remembers that her ex was told to run different errands until she was sweaty and then to go to a lower floor and there they dumped "tons of bird shirt on her—and of course it stuck, because she was sweaty. But she took as much as they dished out and eventually she was respected more than some men." Laura also remembers that few women were working as longshoremen and in the refineries. Laura pioneered a program that trained high school youth to learn different Edison jobs and targeted both girls and boys. "There was this one girl, little high-school girl, who loved to weld. She learned that she loved to weld which she never would have. She just wouldn't have been exposed to it."[138]

So the feminist movement that targeted job equality was in many instances *powered by 1970s lesbians* and often *through bar connections* by transgressive women such as butches. Laura says, "Most of the women were butches or more androgynous ... and all tough. You just wouldn't survive otherwise."[139] The masculine factory-working woman, the Rosie image, was resurrected by the lesbian community and some of its bar culture attendees did find their way into jobs through the underground system that relied on common meeting places, such as bars, for the passing of information.[140]

Butch-femme bar culture was central to some and adjacent to other women's lives, playing its part in addition to what else they were doing. However, for Delia, a young Chicano who came out in the 1960s, butch-femme bars were central for community as they had been for women in previous generations.[141] For Kim, Vanessa, and Tinker,[142] the gay bar was the primary place, although they operated in limited ways outside the bars. Tinker ran a successful hair shop, with its advertisement of, "have you been tinkered with lately?" as an out lesbian, and did hair shows and events and/or benefits within the community.[143] Vanessa did work with local charities and became part of the early organizing for the Long Beach Pride Committee,

138. *Ibid.*
139. *Ibid.*
140. Meeker, *Contacts Desired: Gay and Lesbian Communications and Community, 1940s–1970s.*
141. Interview, Delia Silva.
142. Interviews, Kim Palmore, Vanessa Romain, and Tinker Donnelly.
143. Interview, Tinker Donnelly.

the second largest Pride organization in the country.[144] Kim trained in karate and other martial arts as an out lesbian and was active also in leather culture and events and today is a college professor.[145] But for many, butch-femme became a historical reality, even as it remained current. N. Amazon talked about emulating an "old school" butch who was the bouncer at Que Sera because she wanted butch-femme culture and didn't know how to get it. She was also in a feminist collective where butch-femme was contentious.[146] In fact, Pat Gozemba would write one of the only academic studies of the butch-femme community, *Women of the Lighthouse*, about a bar in Lowell, MA; because she felt the bar women of the previous decades were being left behind.[147] While she went to the bar, she also operated in a wider lesbian feminist circle, while the "Women of the Lighthouse," as they were older and not in feminist circles, operated only within the bar circle. She felt that since they gave her so much community as she was coming out, she "didn't want to leave them behind."[148] This is the same sentiment that drove Nestle to write about butch-femme culture and found the Lesbian Herstory Archives.[149]

Fourteen women I met within my friendship circles, two specifically at the Michigan Womyn's Music Festival. Several were lovers. Several others came through Forty Plus contacts and another was a former professor.

Most of these women are in their fifties and early sixties. All live independently; one lives with her mother and helps run that household. All of them are out and for all but one lesbian identity is important to her professional life. For instance, N. Amazon is an out lesbian within the social work system, and is often assigned cases involving gay clients and or issues.[150] For Dr. Tanya Gilbert, the fact that she is lesbian is important in her work as a psychotherapist.[151] And for Pat[152] and Kim,[153] who both do research involving lesbians, their sexuality is a plus rather than a hindrance to their work.

144. Interview, Vanessa Romain.
145. Interview, Kim Palmore.
146. Interview, N. Amazon*.
147. Interview, Pat Gozemba.
148. Janet Kahn & Patricia Gozemba, "In and Around the Lighthouse: Working-Class Lesbian Bar Culture in the 1950s and 1960s." In *Gendered Domains: Rethinking Public and Private in Women's History, Essays from the Seventh Berkshire Conference on the History of Women*, ed. Dorothy O. Helly & Susan M. Reverby (Ithaca, NY: Cornell University Press, 1992), 90–106. The article by Gozemba is as far as I know one of the very few ethnographic studies of this population besides the study of Buffalo, NY done by Kennedy and Davis, *Boots of Leather, Slippers of Gold*.
149. Interview, Joan Nestle. See also Nestle's *A Restricted Country* and *The Persistent Desire: A Femme-Butch Reader*.
150. Interview, N. Amazon*.
151. Interview, Tanya Gilbert.
152. Interview, Pat Gozemba.
153. Interview, Kim Palmore.

VOICES FROM THE 1970s

As with the other chapters, it is essential that the women be "heard into speech."[154]

Hearing women into speech

These informants are from the 1970s, and document the continued gay female bar culture community in the US, as well as emergent lesbian feminism.

In this section, many women still felt they must use pseudonyms. Also women used many identifiers for gender as well as religious identity, and even when describing their racial identity as different now than earlier in their lives.Many of these women would have identified as "feminist," but the question put to them was gender identity as butch, femme, gay, lesbian, and so on. I have indicated those that answered with feminist or lesbian feminist as a primary identity; however many of these women might have used feminist as an additional identifier—if that question had been posed.

Doreen Brand*, 80, feminist (also now femme), Caucasian, unknown religious identity*: Doreen came out later in life in the 1970s as a lesbian feminist running a bookstore she named The Well of Happiness which was in Florida—a humorous take-off on the famous book by Radclyffe Hall, *The Well of Loneliness*.[155]

Ivy Bottini*, 71, lesbian feminist/butch, Caucasian, unknown religious identity*: Ivy was president of the New York Chapter of the National Organization of Women in the late 1960s, when she penned an essay to the NOW membership entitled, "Is Lesbianism Dangerous to the Women's Movement?" She believes she was not re-elected to the presidency because of that and because she "outed" herself as a lesbian. She moved to California where she became a leader in the lesbian feminist movement.[156]

Marilyn Taylor*, 68, femme. Caucasian, Jewish*: Marilyn paid for her butch lover's sex change operation, one of the first in the country in the 1970s. Marilyn owned seventeen wigs, long "wigs like Cher," and loved to go dancing at Joani Presents in Los Angeles where she wore go-go boots and minidresses. She was always looking for "the hard to find in the 70s" butch woman when she went to the bar.[157]

154. Morton, "Hearing to Speech: A Sermon." Intentional repetition of quote.
155. Interview, Doreen Brand.
156. Bottini, "Everything You Wanted to Ask This Old Dyke—Answered."
157. Interview, Marilyn Taylor.

***Roberta Bennett**, 65, lesbian (also now butch), Caucasian, Jewish*: Roberta came out right after homosexuals were declared mentally fit. And this is how she felt able, as a degreed lawyer, to question an armed policeman when he was questioning the bar habitués where she was having a drink. She identified herself as a lawyer, questioned his tactics and questioned him strongly enough that he left.[158]

***Irene "Tally" Talbert**, 62, lesbian feminist, Caucasian, atheist*: Tally was afraid to tell her feminist collective in Des Moines, Iowa that she might be a lesbian and then that she was a lesbian, and so she lived a double life—one hidden from the collective where she found herself as a feminist, and one where she found herself as a lesbian—in a butch-femme bar.[159]

***Bronco Alda Moonwater**,[160] 61, feminist (also now butch), Caucasian, Catholic*: Bronco experienced her first realization of love for women in the convent at age fourteen.She was kicked out of the convent by the Mother Superior for having lesbian tendencies. This was one of the most painful periods of her life, but she says she would not trade it—it was in the convent where she first experienced women's community. She went on to play semi-pro football; "Bronco" was the team's nickname for her, and it stuck.[161]

***Helen Factor**, 60, lesbian feminist, Caucasian, Jewish*: Helen came out in 1973 as a member of the Chicago Women's Graphics Collective. Collective members went into the bar the Lost and Found, and danced together, rather than partner dancing. This resulted in the group being kicked out by the management who saw the new lesbian feminism as bad for business.[162]

***Deborah Edel**, 60s, butch, Caucasian, unknown religious identity*: Deborah founded the Lesbian Herstory Archives with her then lover Joan Nestle, because she believed the bar culture women's stories were being forgotten.[163]

***Pat Gozemba**, 60s, gay, Caucasian, Catholic*: Pat felt indebted to the women in the butch-femme bar where she came out, The Lighthouse, named after the Virginia Woolf novel, *To the Lighthouse*.[164] Even though she "moved on" into lesbian feminism, she could not move on from these women and so, with Janet Kahn wrote the groundbreaking, "In and around the Lighthouse:

158. Interview, Roberta Bennett.
159. Interview, Irene "Tally" Talbert.
160. Although "Bronco Moonwater" is not the name Bronco went by when she first experienced loving women, it is her actual name today, and not a pseudonym.
161. Interview, Bronco Alda Moonwater.
162. Interview, Helen Factor.
163. Interview, Deborah Edel.
164. Virginia Woolf, *To the Lighthouse* (New York: Harcourt, Brace & World, 1955).

Working Class Lesbian Bar Culture in the 1950s and 1960s," about the women at that bar.[165]

***Minnie Bruce Pratt**, 60s, lesbian feminist (also now femme), Caucasian, Presbyterian*: In 1975, Minnie Bruce lost custody of her sons when she came out as a lesbian in Fayetteville, North Carolina. Later she wrote a book of poems *Crime Against Nature* about that and her successful struggle to stay connected as mother to her children. The sodomy statute, the "crime against nature" law, which the state and her husband used to take her children, was repealed at the national level in 2003. She is partnered with Leslie Fienberg, the groundbreaking author of *Stone Butch Blues*.[166]

***Jeanne Cordova**, 59, butch (now also radical feminist), Mexican American, Catholic*: Jean left the convent because she wanted to be a lesbian; she identified gay feelings in the convent with another nun who wanted her to stay and be in the closet. Jean felt that she now knew who she was and did not want to be in the closet.[167] She hung out at The Plush Pony, an East Los Angeles bar, and also organized the first National Lesbian Conference in 1973 and founded and published *The Lesbian Tide* from 1971 to 1980.[168]

***Yolanda Retter**, 59, lesbian feminist/butch, Chicana, Catholic*: As a member of Califia, the Southern California women's collective, Yolanda challenged white women on internalized racism, demanding that women of color be heard and incorporated into discussions. She earned her doctorate from UCLA, and went on to write academically about "queers in space,"[169] and to be the first librarian at UCLA for the Chicano Studies Library; she compiled the first Lesbian Legacy Collection at the One Archive at USC (now named the Cordova-Retter collection).[170]

***Rosie Roeper**, 58, butch lesbian, Filipino, Catholic*: Rosie got involved in lesbian bar culture, after she joined a softball team—that's where the team went after games, and Rosie eventually went with them. She had been married, and has children. Her husband was abusive and she left him. She went on to be the first woman certified to do the kind of mechanical work that she does and felt that the bars gave her a place to find herself—they "were home every weekend."[171]

---

165. Interview, Pat Gozemba.
166. Interview, Minnie Bruce Pratt.
167. Jeanne Cordova, *Kicking the Habit: An Autobiographical Novel: A Lesbian Nun Story* (Los Angeles, CA: Multiple Dimensions, 1990).
168. Interview, Jeanne Cordova. See also Jeanne Cordova, "When We Were Outlaws."
169. Ingram *et al.*, *Queers in Space: Communities, Public Places, Sites of Resistance.*
170. Interview, Yolanda Retter.
171. Interview, Rosie Roeper.

Laura Hill*, 55, gay/lesbian, Caucasian, Protestant*: Laura went to the first Disneyland "Gay Days," organized by the LA Tavern Owners Association. When Disneyland found out the "LA Tavern Owners" was a gay organization, they tried to take back all the tickets. They were unsuccessful and "Gay Days" was born. Today this is an international event drawing thousands of people. One of the first women to work in an Edison Power Plant, Laura found out about the job opportunity through a conversation at the bar.[172]

Rebecca H. Rhoades*, 53, gay/butch,*[173] *Caucasian, Methodist ("no longer identifies with religion")*: Rebecca had never felt that anyone was attracted to her—although she was certainly attracted to others, most often women. It was after going to her first gay bar in Denver, CO, that she realized people would also be attracted to her. It was a shock and a gift to realize she could participate in dating, love, and sex. She was a cowgirl and later went on to be a veterinarian, and the executive director of a Humane Society.[174]

Melanie DeMore*, 53, butch, African American, Catholic*: Melanie joined the convent, and was with the Sisters of Charity for five years in the 1970s, even though she knew she was a lesbian. She left the convent because she knew she could not hold to the order of celibacy. She still however belongs to the order. She was once pulled over by police and a gun put to her head, because "they were looking for a black man" in Texas. Her first job was playing music in a women's bar.[175]

B.R.*, 53, feminist (now also femme), Caucasian, Dianic/Jewish*: B.R. is the high priestess of a well-known Dianic coven. She believes that she had a kundalini, Tantric-type of sexual self-awakening with her first butch lover. She then moved from a feminist identity to that of a femme feminist.[176]

Tanya Gilbert*, 53, femme, African American, Catholic*: Tanya ran a bar in Chicago geared towards serving African American lesbians. She often had to go down to the jail and bail out butch lovers and "get their stuff,"

172. Interview, Laura Hill.
173. Rebecca's story exemplifies the amorphous gender labeling of this period. She specified that she knew she was butch in some way when she entered bar culture in the 1980s in her early twenties, but she identified primarily as gay. It was when she went to the bar, however, that she first realized women could be attracted to her, as well as her being attracted to them—she had never felt attraction coming back to her before she entered bar culture—it was a revelation. She came into butch identity in the bar at that time, but did not use the word "butch"—however, she did feel the identity of being butch. She now uses both words, butch as well as gay, as identifiers.
174. Interview, Rebecca H. Rhoades.
175. Interview, Melanie DeMore.
176. Interview, B.R.

i.e. their dildos, before the women were taken into jail. Tanya also worked to integrate white and black women's bars, one time staging an action at a predominantly white women's bar, until they allowed equal access to the bar for women of color.[177]

***Vivian Escalante**, 53, butch, Spanish, Catholic*: Vivian realized she was getting in one fist fight at The Plush Pony because her and another butch felt they were "supposed to" fight and remembered how they rolled down the hill fighting and then decided they had "done what they needed to do" and decided to stop. She started the well-known tradition of having a contingent of Dykes on Bikes ride at the front of Los Angeles's Gay Pride Parade, a tradition now in many other cities as well.[178]

***Kim Palmore**, 52, butch, Caucasian, atheist*: Kim came into queer theory as a millennium scholar, and an old school butch, and is currently a professor. She remembers being denied admittance to Ripples, the bar in Long Beach, CA because she felt the manager did not want women there—especially butch women. She remembers being in the bars during a raid, being physically abused by police and also physically abused by straight men on the street.[179]

N. Amazon*, 50, butch, Caucasian, Jewish*: N. was mentored by an old school butch, just by watching to see what she did that was so successful. N. wanted to date the kind of women that this butch, the bouncer at the gay bar she went to, the Que Sera in Long Beach, California, dated. These women she wanted to date were femmes. So she watched the bouncer and imitated what she did—and began to be successful as well. N. coupled this bar culture with also attending the lesbian feminist Califia meetings.[180]

***Tinker Donnelly**, 50, butch, Caucasian, Christian (Spiritual)*: Tinker felt she was "raised by gay men" and made Ripples, the mostly male gay club, her "home." She came out at sixteen and was almost sent to a sexual re-orientation camp by her step-mother. She went on to become a licensed hairdresser, well known not only for her haircuts ("Have you been tinkered with lately?") but also for the myriad of benefits she performed for the gay community. She identified then and now as a butch, and went to the bar at least five times a week during the 1970s.[181]

177. Interview, Tanya Gilbert.
178. Interview, Vivian Escalante.
179. Interview, Kim Palmore.
180. Interview, N. Amazon*.
181. Interview, Tinker Donnelly.

***Linda Garnets**, 50s, lesbian, Caucasian, Spiritual*: Linda identifies as a "red diaper baby," and strongly socialist. However, her first therapist and psychology professor in graduate school was an old school butch with a femme girlfriend. She had a profound influence on Linda, reducing her homophobia, even though Linda did not, and does not, identify as butch or femme, but lesbian. Linda taught the first psychology class on lesbians at UCLA in the 1980s,[182] a class she still teaches.[183]

Rory Devine, 48, gay/bar dyke/butch, Asian (now as Hapa-Filipino American), no specific religion (Spiritual)*: The first night in a gay bar for Rory was exciting. She remembers Donna Summer playing and she felt "energized, thrilled and enthralled. I would get to be a better man than my father." She joined the Navy in the late 1970s, but had to go AWOL because of severe sexual harassment, eventually going back, and with others putting the captain who harassed her on trial. However, during the time she was AWOL, she had no other options for employment other than prostitution. During her stint in the Navy she remembers saving her checks and using all of her money to get to the gay bar twice a month, "As long as I had cab fare and enough to buy one drink, I would go. It was home."[184]

182. Linda Garnets & Douglas Kimmel (eds), *Psychological Perspectives on Lesbians, Gay, and Bisexual Experiences* (New York: Columbia University Press, 2003).
183. Interview, Linda Garnets.
184. Interview, Rory Devine*.

6. THE 1980s
"I REALLY DID THINK I WAS JESS FROM *STONE BUTCH BLUES* REINCARNATED."

Figure 6.1 Andrea Dworkin (foreground) at an anti-porn demonstration in New Orleans (New York News and Features; photo: John Goetz). Her husband John Stoltenberg, with moustache, is on the right (John Stoltenberg, *Refusing to Be a Man: Essays on Sex and Justice* [New York: Penguin, 1990]). The Association of Community Organizations for Reform Now (ACORN) sponsored the march through the French Quarter. Organized in Dworkin's Fairmount Hotel suite in conjunction with a NOW conference, the huge divide happened between anti- and pro-pornography advocates from the American Civil Liberties Union. NOW was against the march taking place. After her death, Dworkin's picture illustrated an article subheaded, "A victim of child abuse as a child, briefly a prostitute as a young woman, Andrea Dworkin married a gay man and spent three decades fighting hyper sexualized America. She lost." (Ariel Levy, "The Prisoner of Sex." *New York Magazine*, May 29, 2005).

Figure 6.2 Front cover image for the first edition of Andrea Dworkin's *Pornography: Men Possessing Women* (Illustrator: Terrence M. Fehr). The publication of this book in 1989 was a signature event for the anti-pornography movement as they structured discourse defining pornography as men possessing women. Used with permission.

Figure 6.3 Lesbian Sex Mafia logo (used with permission of one of the founders, Dorothy Allison). Founded in 1981, the Lesbian Sex Mafia (LSM) is one of the oldest women's BDSM support and education groups in the country: "membership primarily in the tri state area of New York, New Jersey and Connecticut. ... also have members along the East Coast, across the country and even in Europe!" (Lesbian Sex Mafia. "Welcome to the Lesbian Sex Mafia." www.lesbiansexmafia.org). The group was first established in 1981.

Figure 6.4 "We believe that S/M can and should be consistent with the principles of feminism." "As feminists, we oppose all forms of social hierarchy based on gender. As radical perverts, we oppose all social hierarchies based on sexual preference." (Gayle Rubin, "Samois," *Leather Times: News from the Leather Archives and Museum*, Spring 2004). The image shows the logo of Samois, the lesbian leather organization. (Reproduction of this photo is with the permission of copyright holder Gayle Rubin.)

I Want a Twenty-Four-Hour Truce During Which There Is No Rape[1]

OVERVIEW

I came out in a consciousness raising group in the 80s, a feminist consciousness raising group, ALICE— Alliance for Lesbians Interested in Consciousness Expansion. They did not understand

1. Andrea Dworkin, "Talking to Men About Rape (Original); I Want a Twenty-Four Hour Truce During Which There Is No Rape (Revised)," *Out!* 2(6) (1984). From the speech given at the Midwest Regional Conference of the National Organization for Changing Men, fall 1983, St Paul, Minnesota. Published in Andrea Dworkin, *Letters from a War Zone* (Brooklyn, NY: Lawrence Hill Books, 1993), 162.

> butch-femme. I knew I was butch, but I tried to be androgynous. Then I read Joan Nestle. I wished so often that I had been born in the 50s so that I could be part of that time and fit in.[2]

> After I read *Stone Butch Blues*, I related so much to Leslie Feinberg's character that I seriously thought maybe I was Jess [the main character] reincarnated. I actually sort of believed that for a while.[3]

The 1980s were when butch-femme came back into fashion. The Barnard Conference in 1982 officially started what became known as the "lesbian sex wars."[4] The Conference was to take place in 1981 and word of invited speakers became known to some members of Women Against Pornography (WAP). This group was strongly associated with feminist writer and anti-porn advocate, Andrea Dworkin, who was one of the founding members of the New York group, along with Adrienne Rich, Grace Paley, Gloria Steinem, Shere Hite, Robin Morgan, and others. Included in the speaker list for the conference was Gayle Rubin, founder of Samois, the first lesbian feminist sadomasochist group.[5] Also included in the list of speakers were Joan Nestle and Dorothy Allison. Nestle had written of being femme in the 1950s, of her sexual awakening with butch women, and of butch-femme community in *A Restricted Country*, and Allison had written of being attracted to butch women as well as to leather sexuality in *Trash*. Members of WAP protested the event and demanded that at a feminist conference there be no speakers promoting violence against women and this included leather sex practitioners, as well as those speakers promoting butch-femme. The conference decided not to proceed with its scheduled speakers, but an alternate conference was organized at which the protested speakers did speak. Carol Vance, the conference organizer, published the original Barnard speaker line-up in the anthology *Pleasure and Danger.*[6]

How did butch and femme become so inextricably linked with leather sex? There were sex radicals coming of age in the lesbian feminist 1970s that had ties to older butch-femme community and to lesbian feminism, as well as some who had ties to leather sex, as did Allison. This group also included Joan Nestle and others and they espoused the writing of white, working-class femme Amber Hollibaugh and Chicana butch Cherrie Moraga in

2. Interview, Angela Brinskele.
3. Interview, Robin Finkelstein.
4. Vance, *Pleasure and Danger: Exploring Female Sexuality*.
5. Gayle Rubin, "Samois." *Leather Times: News from the Leather Archives and Museum*, Spring 2004.
6. Vance, *Pleasure and Danger: Exploring Female Sexuality*. This is now used in Women's Studies classes.

"What We're Rollin' Around in Bed With," first published in 1981,[7] that highlighted how many avowed lesbian feminists, especially working-class women and women of color *were* involved in butch-femme—despite it being politically incorrect during lesbian feminism. Because lesbian feminists distanced themselves from butch-femme and accused them of role-playing, when leather sexuality played itself across the lesbian landscape of the 1980s there was no place for the displaced butch- and femme-identified women to go except with the new sex outlaws—the leather sex community.

In and of itself, it should be said that leather sex and butch-femme are no more synonymous than lesbianism and heterosexuality are. However, because they were both outlawed sexualities—for example denial of butch and femme at feminist meetings and denial of leather sex reality within lesbian feminism—the two factions banded together.

Prior to lesbian feminism, being gay was about who you had sex with and your gender identification was most often butch, femme, or kiki. After lesbian feminism, one did not necessarily identify as gay *first* but as lesbian. Lesbian was your political identification as in *feminist* lesbian or lesbian feminist (usually the latter). "The personal is political," was coined as a feminist maxim,[8] and although many feminist second wave women were heterosexual, this phrase became the coinage with which many lesbians felt free to comment on another's personal life—that is, sex life.

Several 1980s informants longed for a time that none of the informants from that actual period wish still existed;[9] this is emblematic of how much butch and femme people of the 1980s wished that butch and femme was still the *de rigueur* expression of lesbianism instead of lesbian feminist androgyny. Nonetheless, they admitted they did not want police harassment, or arrests for masquerading, as Nancy Valverde experienced in the 1950s,[10] or to have the only place where they could congregate be a bar. None of these were the things they wanted. What they wanted was for the sexualized lesbian community, butch-femme and leather, to be embraced. Joan Nestle herself warned me "to not romanticize" this 1950s culture.[11] This is interesting because Joan's sexually-charged writings on the era are what caused many 1980s informants, among them Angela Brinskele, *to* romanticize the

7. Hollibaugh & Moraga, "What We're Rollin' Around in Bed With," 62–84.
8. Carol Hanisch, "The Personal Is Political (March 1969)," in *Feminist Revolution*, ed. Redstockings (New York: Random House, 1979), 204–5. Hanisch states "One of the first things we discover in these groups is that personal problems are political problems. There are no personal solutions at this time." By "groups" she meant the burgeoning consciousness-raising groups that women created in order to incorporate feminism into their lives.
9. Interview, Angela Brinskele.
10. Interview, Nancy Valverde.
11. Interview, Joan Nestle.

era.[12] In the end, however, it may all be valid: the romance and the tragedy. For instance, I wrote two short stories about two different women, one of whom walked into the mid-twentieth-century gay women's bar and saw the opportunity for self expression and embraced it with excitement—the smoke, the secretiveness, the hidden world, the sexuality. And the second story was about a woman who walked into a gay women's bar, and saw to her horror that "the only place" to exist as a female homosexual was within four dirty Mafia-owned or police-paid-off walls, playing a role which included alcohol, cigarettes, pool playing and, especially for the butch-femme bar attendee, traveling to dangerous parts of the city. For this second woman, as for my 1960s informant Marj, the butch-femme bar did not provide entrée to "the life" but was a doorway through which she walked and just as quickly walked back through.[13]

For Ginny from the 1940s, the roles of butch and femme were so off-putting that she never went back to the bar.[14] A few informants, for example, were followed into the restroom by a butch woman who then approached them and tried to have sex with them there, among them both Ginny and Marj. However, going to a restroom alone *was* a signal to butch women at the time that they were to follow the woman and approach her. Ginny and Marj did not know that bar code, although it was well known to most bar attendees. Joan Nestle wrote about The Sea Colony's "bathroom line" and how the bouncer monitored the bathroom door, giving each woman a requisite number of toilet paper squares, ensuring only one woman at a time would go in.[15] But for the novice bar goers, such behavior was terrifying and they never went back, preferring instead a closeted life, revealing themselves as gay to a few friends and/or to their lover only. Marj's case, from the 1960s, reveals someone who went to a gay bar once, saw the "tough butches ... femmes" and "was scared." "I couldn't relate—I didn't go back."[16] Being closeted to a certain extent[17] was preferable to finding out how the bar culture system worked and learning how to operate within it.

For butch women like Carole, who also went to The Sea Colony in the 1950s,[18] the fact that butches followed them and tried to have sex with them was an experience, scary and a bit exciting and not something they would re-do, but as a result of which they figured out that if this could happen,

12. Interview, Angela Brinskele.
13. Interview, Marj Johnson.
14. Interview, Virgina "Ginny" Borders.
15. Nestle, *A Restricted Country*, 92–102.
16. Interview, Marj Johnson.
17. I say "to a certain extent" here because the idea of being "out" is a post-Stonewall one. For decades prior to Stonewall coming into a gay consciousness *in whatever way* someone was able to create that was what we today would call "being out"—even though today that has a different meaning.
18. Interview, Carole S. Damoci-Reed.

other things could happen too. They could figure out how to have sex with women by figuring out the codes of sexual conduct within the bar. Even Carolyn, who had to choose butch or femme on her entrée to a 1950s San Antonio bar, said, "If I had to be a femme to get in, so be it; I don't think I was femme, but ... I was more that than the other, so I chose it, and I'm so glad I did, otherwise I couldn't have gotten *into* the life of the bar, and that was worth almost *anything* I had to do."[19]

Within feminist circles and the organizing groups of lesbian feminism the sex wars raged. However, outside of feminist circles, butch-femme relationships did continue within the bar culture that existed in working-class and women of color communities. However, since some educated and articulate women came to consciousness as lesbians within lesbian feminism *and* were also invested in butch-femme, arguments for sexual expression within these contested communities were presented that lesbian feminist did engage. Women like Dorothy Allison[20] and Joan Nestle[21] expressed allegiance to both butch-femme and lesbian feminism and they created books that helped form these new alliances between butch and femme, feminism and leathersex culture. These women, who had originally connected to butch-femme, found strong allies within both camps. So a woman like Joan Nestle could belong to both the Lesbian Sex Mafia and also found the Lesbian Herstory Archives.[22] As the decade wore on, a woman like Dorothy Allison could write the acclaimed *Bastard Out of Carolina*,[23] a semi-autobiographical novel about incest survival that became a staple within feminist discourse that analyzed domestic violence, and also write *Two or Three Things I Know for Sure*[24] about how difficult it was for her to "wear the coat woven" for her by those who identified her as the incest survivor they imagined her to be, rather than the queer femme–lesbian feminist–leathersex woman she actually *was*.

Because of their shared outlaw history, butch-femme and leathersex became synonymous to lesbian feminist coalitions such as Women Against Pornography (WAP) and those WAP members actually organizing the Barnard Conference.

However, for the average butch or femme woman in the working-class gay women's bar, butch-femme and leathersex were not synonymous with their expression, and many were totally unaware of these factional fights. They followed a tradition established as gay from the 1950s. This tradition

19. Interview, Carolyn Weathers.
20. Allison, *The Women Who Hate Me: Poetry, 1980–1990*.
21. Nestle, *The Persistent Desire: A Femme-Butch Reader*.
22. Warshow, *Hand on the Pulse*.
23. Dorothy Allison, *Bastard out of Carolina* (New York: Dutton, 1992). This was a finalist for the National Book Award.
24. Dorothy Allison, *Two or Three Things I Know for Sure* (New York: Dutton, 1995).

was established when the outlaw status of being gay itself *was* the outlaw status, and the gay bar was "the only place" to establish community. Because middle-class and upper-class lesbians did not have a majority public presence, their public outlaw status within the gay community was muted. Some lesbians did go to upper-class bars in urban areas such as Los Angeles' The Laurel Club populated by movie stars, and later Joani Presents in the Valley, and this attendance had a certain status. But for butch-femme working-class women, status might come from spending the night in jail, or participating in the ritual of dressing butch-femme and dating within the culture. Lillian Faderman remembers being in The Laurel Club in the 1960s and seeing two rich women who had given each other full length fur coats for Christmas. "I felt like—I wanted that," she said, "that kind of power. I couldn't believe it. That was very sexy. And it was amazing to me—that lesbians could have that."[25]

This admiration of "power" would change within the power exchange (also the name of a leather bar in San Francisco) discussions that emerged within leathersex discourse. While Lillian's youthful admiration of gay women enjoying power did prefigure the leathersex discussions of the 1980s, in the 80s leathersex lesbians engaged in debates, and sometimes protests, against lesbian feminists asserting opposition to the values of collective consciousness, androgyny and prioritizing politics. These leathersex lesbians frankly enjoyed power—playing with power, power over, topping and bottoming. New terms such as *femme top* and *butch bottom* helped explain these relations to the rest of lesbian culture and this did explain leathersex to some but further confounded others. In many ways then, the leathersex communities of the late 1980s and the sex wars can be seen to have *queered* butch-femme.

Further confounding the traditional butch-femme community was the embracing of the sex worker community by young queer and leathersex lesbians, where the previous decade's younger community had denounced it. While COYOTE's (Call Off Your Old Tired Ethics) founder, Margo Saint James, had been embraced by feminists asserting that women's work, even sex work, should be paid and unionized, the idea that sex work was a valid form of work *for lesbians* was not popular. Feminism has had a history of having to embrace, however reluctantly, sex radicals if they are heterosexual, such as Victoria Woodhull the free love activist and suffragette, who ran an infamous Presidential platform.[26] But lesbians within lesbian feminism wanted to assert their independence completely from men and this included sex with men in all forms, and this did distance working-class sex worker

25. Interview, Lillian Faderman.
26. Amanda Frisken, *Victoria Woodhull's Sexual Revolution: Political Theater and the Popular Press in Nineteenth-Century America* (Philadelphia, PA: University of Pennsylvania Press, 2004).

women from lesbian feminism. The arguments Andrea Dworkin (herself a former prostitute) made with Catherine A. MacKinnon—that women could sue the makers of pornography for harm done to them in the name of pornography or because of its effects—endeared many prostitutes to them and testimonies from prostitutes played a major part in their argument against pornography.[27] However, the underlying assumption that no woman would choose prostitution if given the chance and the skills to choose other professions, was not necessarily true.

Leathersex and radical sex communities celebrated sex work as valid and sometimes chosen work for queer culture and empowered leathersex lesbians. However this population often conflated sex work arguments to mean all sex work, legal and illegal, such as the legal work of exotic dancing, work within strip clubs, and illegal work such as prostitution. This often obscured the real dangers faced by illegal work and concentrated research in empowered urban communities such as San Francisco. This is true of the groundbreaking work *Sex Work*, which included feminist analyses of how empowering sex work was, at the same time concentrating research in urban spaces where a queer discourse was present.[28] This newly sex positive, *as sex work positive,* discourse created distance between lesbian feminists and prostitutes. Prostitutes themselves often viewed sex work as a necessary profession, and a wise choice given their options. This created another outlaw community from lesbian feminism—prostitutes. These women then bonded with the welcoming communities of leathersex and outlawed butch-femme lesbians (which historically had never broken rank with prostitutes[29]). These distinctions further cemented the bond between the outlaw communities of leathersex and butch-femme. Of course, such distinctions were often restricted to intellectuals, as working-class bar lesbians (and working-class prostitutes of any gender identification) were often not asked to engage in the discussion.

Prostitution was one of the few ways that the butch and femme community made a living throughout its history. Many informants asserted that the position of the displaced communities of prostitution and lesbian bars created coalitions just by geographical positioning, and there are crucial works that substantiate this relating to the heyday of women's bars in the 1950s

27. Catherine A. MacKinnon & Andrea Dworkin, *In Harm's Way: The Pornography Civil Rights Hearings* (Cambridge, MA: Harvard University Press, 1997).
28. Priscilla Alexander Frederique Delacoste (ed.), *Sex Work: Writings by Women in the Sex Industry*, 2nd edn (San Francisco, CA: Cleis Press, [1987] 1998).
29. Donna Penn, "The Sexualized Woman: The Lesbian, the Prostitute, and the Containment of Female Sexuality in Post-War America." In *Not June Cleaver: Women and Gender in Post-War America, 1945–1960*, Critical Perspectives on the Past, ed. Joanne J. Meyerowitz (Philadelphia, PA: Temple University Press, 1994), 358–81.

and 1960s.[30] This placement created a historical link between prostitutes and gay women of the period that flowered into liaisons between the patrons of prostitutes and the women's bars, with the creation of butch pimps and femme (and butch) prostitutes. Many informants did engage in prostitution and or sex work-related activities, such as actual sex work, pin up work, lesbian sex play for heterosexual voyeurs, and pimp work for gay women/lesbian prostitutes. In the 1950s this was being "on the game" and most informants related that many of the feminine, femme women (and a large number of butch women as well) in any gay bar in America might be "on the game" in some way.

The coalescing in the late 1980s of these three communities—leathersex, historical, and 1980s butch-femme, and sex work contributed to the formation of an allied force that overshadowed the dominant expression of 1970s lesbian feminism. By the mid 1990s, then, *lesbian feminism* as an organizing principle began to seem *passé*.

So, with the rise of queer theory and queer culture in the late 1990s, there would be *another* generation of distance added to the distance from historical butch and femme than the one originally installed by 1970s lesbian feminism. As many young newly-identified *queer* people embraced transgender identity, traditional butch or femme was left behind with the rise of queer culture which would result in Queer Studies programs in universities across America. The cry that many lesbian feminists yelled at femmes in the 1970s that still loved butches was, "If you want a man, why don't you just go get a real one?" And at butches the claim they leveled was that lesbian feminists were womyn, with a "y", and they loved other womyn with a "y." A butch who looked like a man/masculine was not so dangerous, for many 1970s women looked butch. But that he/she wanted to date a feminine woman, a woman a man might date, and not a lesbian "womyn," was dangerous.

However, as the 1980s progressed what might be leveled at young and old butch women was "If you want to be a man, why don't you just be one?"[31] And this discourse increased as the ability to "become a man" became reality with the advent of transgender operability and the sex war became a war (as of this writing not officially declared as such) on what determined "biological" sex.[32]

---

30. Nestle, *A Restricted Country*; Penn, "The Sexualized Woman: The Lesbian, the Prostitute, and the Containment of Female Sexuality in Post-War America." These and other works discuss the intersections between prostitutes and working class gay bar women. Also several informants noted this (see 50s and 60s chapters); among them Falcon River, who witnessed pay-offs to the police in the form of "free" prostitute "servicing."
31. Interview, N. Amazon*.
32. Anne Fausto-Sterling, *Sexing the Body: Gender Politics and the Construction of Sexuality* (New York: Basic Books, 2000). While the queering of masculinity as it took shape pre- and post-millennium is outside the time frame of this study, it is discussed in many works, including *Sexing the Body*.

Bar culture changed in the 1980s because of the possibility afforded to lesbian students by women's liberation to organize outside of bar culture. This began to change in the 1970s, and by the 1980s the *pre-Stonewall* gay bar experience became historical and one that could not be re-created outside of its historical context. For the sex wars that facilitated an alliance between the newly out leathersex women and butch-femme referred to butches and femmes who straddled the divide from butch-femme to lesbian feminism. Such an alliance did not, by and large, include the actual historical bar denizens who never came to lesbian feminism—the gay women who came out in the 1940s–60s and did not have access to feminist discourse *per se.* The women who came to leathersex through butch-femme and feminism demanded acknowledgement from both camps, such as the lesbian S/M camp Samois, that made the double circle of the lesbian women's symbol a pair of handcuffs. Their numbers, as they were younger, began to overshadow the numbers of lesbian feminists, as the once younger lesbian feminists had overshadowed the older butch-femme bar culture, and thus eventually this community became a somewhat more dominant lesbian expression. Lesbian sex and sexuality became the catch phrase. *On Our Backs*[33] officially replaced the lesbian feminist newspaper *Off Our Backs*[34] as *the* magazine that young lesbians read—a leathersex triumph of newer values of sexuality over older values of pure politics.

By the time older butches and femmes caught on to the fact that butch and femme were cool again, with the advent of leather sex, the times would change again. The new queer culture celebrated the queering of masculinity and femininity in butch-femme as radical gender expression, but at the same time did expect allegiance from its members towards transgender expression. Many butch and femme members of the pre-Stonewall period were simply left out of the loop for many reasons, chief of which might have been that much organizing of queer culture happened/happens on the internet. Most informants pre-Stonewall simply do not use this system of communication at all, or very rarely. Also many, but not all,[35] pre-Stonewall butch and

33. *On Our Backs*, the first erotic magazine run by women was published in San Francisco from 1984 to 2006 (with no issues produced from 1994–98). Their website's home page reads, "Welcome to On Our Backs: the Best of Lesbian Sex." This magazine was considered to represent the voice of the newly identified sex positive lesbian.

34. *Off Our Backs: The Feminist News Journal* was published from 1970–2008, in Washington, DC, and was considered the official news journal of the women's liberation movement. I remember sitting on the couch in the Colorado collective house I lived in, in the mid-1980s, and reading it for the first time—and to use Muriel Rukeyser's phrase "the world split open." It contained the truest statements I had ever read about women's lives. I immediately subscribed. I ended up publishing articles for "*oob*" as well as consulting it for conferences, events, and journal deadlines—as it was the organ of information for women's liberation's various tribes.

35. Leslie Feinberg, *Trans Liberation: Beyond Pink or Blue* (Boston, MA: Beacon Press, 1998), among others.

femme women did not support transgender as they felt it left biologically born female butches out of the category they once occupied and had defined.

Former drag king Falcon laments, "What took real courage was being a different kind of *woman*, not a man. Why would I be a man? What I fought for is for a woman to be like me, not for me to become a man."[36]

The urban flourishing of butch-femme as culture and community in and of itself was *prior* to Stonewall, the actual event, and Stonewall *as a time period, à la* pre-Stonewall. But even though major urban areas such as Los Angeles had a gay pride parade immediately following the Stonewall uprising in New York City in 1969, as late as 1980 the butch-femme bar The Huntress forty-five minutes south of Los Angeles in Orange County, "behind the Orange Curtain," would experience police harassment[37] and would remain primarily working-class butch-femme until it closed in the 1990s.

In the mid-1990s when I first entered a lesbian-operated sex store, I felt like I had been living under a rock for most of the decade. This store was, and is, called Good Vibrations with its moniker being, "the clean well-lighted sex toy store" and its original location opened in 1977, (with other branches opening soon after in other cities), was San Francisco, CA.[38] For women who came out in the 1980s these were the established spaces they entered into. For those of us coming out in the 70s, we entered lesbian feminist political spaces. This was a major issue which surfaced in the 80s—the difference between older *identified* more political lesbians and younger *identified* more sexual lesbians. However as discussed, this difference was also prevalent in the reverse in the 70s—where older gay bar culture primarily butch-femme women saw lesbians as political and not concerned with sex/social life, and young lesbian feminists saw themselves as part of the political women's liberation movement.

For butch-femme, the major identity shift of the 1980s was that butch-femme, rather than being a contested identity, was by the end of the decade and into the 1990s a more fashionable identity than lesbian feminism—in no small part because it was seen as more sexual, and as the winner in the sex wars. The lesbian leather community claimed a younger constituency than what was now seen as the old guard—lesbian feminism which in the 1970s was the younger force when butch-femme was the old guard. The difference was that *this* butch-femme was as Lillian Faderman describes it, a "neo" or new butch-femme, a butch-femme identity that came out as sexual and *not* proto-political, as she defines the butch-femme cultures pre-Stonewall.[39]

36. Interview, Falcon River.
37. Interview, Mary. Former Huntress DJ.
38. Good Vibrations, "Good Vibrations: Making the World a More Pleasurable Place," http://www.goodvibes.com/content.jhtml?id=1786 (accessed July 15, 2013).
39. Faderman, *Odd Girls and Twilight Lovers: A History of Lesbian Life in Twentieth-Century America*, 268.

The new butch-femme of the 1990s was sexual and publishing magazines like *On Our Backs*, whereas throughout the 1980s lesbian feminism was still the organizing principle. However pre-1970, historical butch-femme was the organizing principle.

Another queer historical movement that occurred in the 1980s was that the AIDS epidemic ran unchecked throughout the US.[40] This forced a decision by lesbian feminists and new gay youth who came of age during this period. Sayings of lesbian feminism like, "If you can put one man on the moon, why not put them all?" took on an entirely different meaning when so many men that you knew were dying and literally "going to the moon." The lesbian response to the AIDS epidemic was overwhelmingly positive and has been written about extensively—particularly in the history of ACT UP (the AIDS Coalition To Unleash Power).[41] The settlement of the sex wars in favor of sexual experimentation like leather sex, and the AIDS epidemic which made many lesbians question lesbian feminism, especially its separatist element, created a space for butch-femme as a *gender* identity to re-emerge. However this was a gender expression within the emerging sex positive culture, not an embracing of older butch-femme community members, many of whom were still closeted in old school bars.[42]

These old school butch-femme bars existed, as The Huntress did in Orange County, California, and they were still patrolled by police. Several informants said that because The Huntress was known as a butch-femme bar where gender expression had deviant/masculine and feminine women together, it was still patrolled by police. Police regularly entered the bar for ID checks, whereas that did not happen in the more lesbian feminist bars of the decade.[43]

In the late 1980s and into the 1990s, because affiliations grew between the newly out lesbian communities of leather and culturally outlawed under lesbian feminism butch-femme community, what resulted was sex clubs that featured leather play parties for lesbians, but also celebrated the new butch-femme identity.[44] These new clubs were not necessarily populated by old school butch-femme couples, who for one thing were older and not going as much to bars as previously.[45] The Forty Plus group began in the late 1980s

40. Randy Shilts, *And the Band Played On: Politics, People, and the Aids Epidemic*, revised edn (New York: Penguin Books, 1988).
41. ACT UP/New York Women and AIDS Book Group & Marion Banzhaf, *Women, Aids, and Activism* (Boston, MA: South End Press, 1990).
42. This is why Faderman asserts that historical butch-femme is different from "neo" butch-femme, or butch-femme post-Stonewall.
43. Interview, Laura Hill.
44. Interview, Vivian Escalante. Vivian founded one such club in Los Angeles, The Cunt Club.
45. But, these were populated by women who bridged the divided community consciously, such as Joan Nestle, Dorothy Allison, and Madeline Davis—all members of the Sex Mafia.

as an alternative to bars,[46] however it was as much that as it was to provide a space where older women would feel comfortable who felt they no longer fit into the younger crowd that would go to any bar, of any persuasion. The affiliations that were woven tended to be between leather lesbians and the new butch-femme, *as well as* lesbian feminists—all negotiating identity among and between these contested identities. Most lesbians also supported gay men in their private lives,[47] and many became involved in public arenas, such as ACT UP.[48]

If someone was not party to lesbian feminism and did not cross the divide between butch and femme and lesbian feminism as did writers like Joan Nestle, Dorothy Allison, and Judy Grahn, then it did not necessarily follow that they developed these new connections. Butch-femme women who came out prior to Stonewall and the new neo-butch-femme of the 1980s and 90s could remain much separated. Pat Gozemba explores this writing about her feelings of not wanting to leave the women of The Lighthouse bar of Lowell, Massachusetts behind as she moved into another more feminist community.[49] This was also Joan Nestle's reasoning.[50]

The old school butch and femme were left in bars because they came of age in and as a community that stayed in bars despite changes. For many of these women the bars remained "the only place." The new butch-femme was about a gender expression that was foreign to them, as the older butch-femme was not necessarily a leather community. The new affiliations between the leather communities were not necessarily with these older butch-femme women who continued to connect in bars that remained for them "the only place."[51]

46. Interview, Heather Hamm. Heather was the founder of the group Forty Plus. She died in 2010. I led the memorial service for her, with her partner of twenty-one years, Pat Lamis, founder of the Womynz Brunch Bunch. There were at least 75 people who attended—with three days' notice of the event, most of them members of the Women of Forty Plus group that Heather had started in the late 1980s.
47. Interview, G.J. This is supported by an informant story that involved taking care of a significant gay man in a lesbian life during the AIDS crisis. There were many more of these informant stories, as well as my own story, which involved personal caretaking and/or being involved in the more public activist struggle.
48. ACT UP/New York Women and AIDS Book Group & Marion Banzhaf, *Women, Aids, and Activism*.
49. Kahn and Gozemba, "In and around the Lighthouse: Working-Class Lesbian Bar Culture in the 1950s and 1960s."
50. Nestle, *A Restricted Country*.
51. Different bars were popular during the different decades. For example, consider The Muff Diver in San Francisco, a popular 90s lesbian bar, or the Clit Club, a Los Angeles lesbian sex club, as opposed to popular bar names of previous decades—The Lost and Found (Chicago), The Huntress (Boston), or The Saints (southern California).

RELIGIOUS AND THEOLOGICAL IMPLICATIONS

The Metropolitan Community Church (MCC) had been established for over a decade, having its first march in West Hollywood in 1970.[52] Pride Festivals were actually incorporated as nonprofit public benefit corporations. Long Beach Lesbian and Gay Pride became incorporated in 1983, and had its first festival in 1984. As Ken Davis, former Pride Board member, said:

> We had to get incorporated first, and get the money up front or we wouldn't have been able to get the permits. Fred Kovell, owner of the lesbian bar, The Executive Suite, was a straight man who owned a lesbian bar, and he lent Pride the money to get the permits to have its first Festival. There was not a march separate from the Festival. There was always a Gay Pride march and festival. It was not a small thing—it was huge, that he was able to lend the money—I've heard stories that money came in a suitcase, in pennies and small bills. There are a lot of tales around that, but that the money for our first Festival *was lesbian bar money*[53] is undisputed.[54]

This illustrates how the emerging, and newly titled alphabet soup, LGBT, community was now also a business. The gay pride march and action that began at Stonewall as a riot, was now incorporated as a not for profit business. "Today the Long Beach Pride, Inc. has a budget of 1.6 million," added Davis.[55]

The original Stonewall resisting community perhaps imagined this kind of explosion and perhaps did not—many were just struggling to have a better life, or even struggling to have that bar, the Stonewall Inn, stay open that one night.[56] In any case, the out-ness of all aspects of gay and lesbian life changed radically in the 1980s. Religion was available to gay people with churches like MCC and other congregations that allowed gay and lesbian members such as Unitarian Universalist meetings and even the gay Catholic Dignity meetings.[57] There were lesbian rabbis at Kohl Ami, the Los Angeles reformed Jewish congregation where I went to a lesbian wedding in the late 1980s, and there were also the new spiritual identities such as Wicca and other New Age groups where many lesbian feminists chose to receive spir-

52. Perry and Lucas, *The Lord Is My Shepherd and He Knows I'm Gay; the Autobiography of the Rev. Troy D. Perry, as Told to Charles L. Lucas.*
53. This may be why Long Beach insists proudly that they be called Long Beach Lesbian and Gay Pride, as opposed to putting "gay" first.
54. Interview, Ken Davis.
55. *Ibid.*
56. Carter, *Stonewall: The Riots That Sparked the Gay Revolution.*
57. Interview, Father Joe*.

itual sustenance.[58] This meant that bars did not have to be *the only place* if one chose to look elsewhere.

LIBERATION THEOLOGY CONNECTIONS

The connections between newly emerging theologies as well as theologies in established religions that occurred during this decade opened new spaces for gay and lesbian theology. This began with the codification of liberation theology over a decade earlier. The very term "liberation" made liberation theology a template for other groups to use in forming liberation theologies of their own—among them feminist and gay/lesbian/queer.

Liberation theology emerged in the 1970s, and was established by the 1980s. First used in 1973 by Gustavo Gutierrez, a Catholic Peruvian priest,[59] it was a theology used among Latin American Catholics in which the Gospel of Christ was interpreted to demand that the church liberate its people from poverty. It gained currency because the believing people were fighting revolutions, such as in Nicaragua, and were often controlled by dictators. While liberation theology as a social movement was inspired by the Second Vatican Council and in particular the 1967 papal encyclical, its foothold as a movement began in the 1970s with Leonardo Boff of Brazil as a primary articulator who espoused that Jesus came not only to bring peace, but "to bring the sword" to injustice and it was incumbent on oppressed people to liberate themselves from oppression.[60] Liberation theology declares that the Church should support these insurgent people's movements, as exemplified by the subtitle of a seminal text which reads, *Democracy or Revolution?*[61] Latin American bishops adopted a resolution in support of liberation theology in 1968 at a Colombian conference; however the Roman Catholic Church hierarchy did not support the use of Marxism that liberation theologians utilized to make their arguments. The Church hierarchy also did not support the critiques leveled at the Church itself that castigated how the Church had dealt with social revolutions in its past, nor did the hierarchy support the revolutionary movements that liberation theologians supported and joined. For example, members of the Sandinista leadership in Nicaragua were Roman Catholic clergy, a Maryknoll and a Jesuit.[62]

58. B.R. is a lesbian priestess of a large goddess circle.
59. Leonardo Boff & Clodovis Boff, *Introducing Liberation Theology* (Maryknoll, NY: Orbis Books, 1987).
60. *Ibid.*
61. Paul E. Sigmund, *Liberation Theology at the Crossroads: Democracy or Revolution?* (New York: Oxford University Press, 1990).
62. *Ibid.* In 1985 the Vatican censured Leonardo Boff but in 1986 amended that censure to support a more moderate form of liberation theology.

At a time when social movements were changing, and had changed the face of America, liberation theology threatened the canons of the Church. In the late 1980s Father Joe walked into a Dignity meeting of exiled Catholics, after which the members adjoined to a gay bar where the inhabitants all knew the fellow priest that Father Joe had attended the meeting with and he was moved to think, "church was *happening*—we were in community."[63] Liberation theology as a methodology for gay and lesbian religious texts was a natural fit. Liberation theologians espoused support of the oppressed and that idea fit into the post-Stonewall fabric of revolutionary community. By the 1980s and thereafter gay life would have published theological articulators—chief among them Troy Perry[64] and Nancy Wilson[65] of the MCC.[66] As the decade progressed more texts were published which supported gay life, for example James Nelson's *Body Theology*, which while not an explicitly gay text, was an embodied theology revelatory in that it centered on the sacrality of the body and created a theology for liberating the body,[67] and begged the question, which body needed more liberation than the gay body?

When these more traditional religious physical spaces opened up, for example MCC had actual church spaces as early as the 1970s, the bar simply was not the only space. Andi, who marched in the first LA gay pride parade with Troy Perry, and was part of the first lesbian couple to be married by him, said that while Perry declared gay people fit subjects for a "church" community in 1970 it is also important to remember that "the MCC Church came out of the bars—most definitely."[68]

Liberation theology then had its genesis for gay and lesbian people in the gay civil rights movement, and in the lived communities that claimed space for community—the bars. These were contested dangerous spaces throughout the twentieth century, but particularly in mid-century when bars were regularly raided. Liberation theologians espouse that Jesus states that the Church must support the freedom of the oppressed to truly support the people it parishes. The Biblical parable of the loaves and fishes reveals that if the people are hungry they cannot hear the word of God.[69] They must be fed. Gays and lesbians found a way to live in spaces fraught with danger, much like the early Christians in the Catacombs,[70] keeping a population and

63. Interview, Father Joe*.
64. Perry and Lucas, *The Lord Is My Shepherd and He Knows I'm Gay; the Autobiography of the Rev. Troy D. Perry, as Told to Charles L. Lucas.*
65. Nancy L. Wilson, *Our Tribe: Queer Folks, God, Jesus, and the Bible* (San Francisco, CA: HarperSanFrancisco, 1995).
66. Interview, Troy Perry.
67. James B. Nelson, *Body Theology* (Louisville, KY: Westminster/John Knox, 1992).
68. Interview, Andrea "Andi" Segal.
69. Matthew 14:13-21.
70. Benko and O'Rourke, *The Catacombs and the Colosseum: The Roman Empire as the Setting of Primitive Christianity.*

its practices alive, feeding them as it were, until such time as it would be possible to "let freedom ring."[71]

DEMOGRAPHIC HIGHLIGHTS

I formally interviewed thirteen people who came out in the late 1970s and early 1980s.[72] I also heard stories about being out in the 1980s from all women I interviewed from previous decades, as well as corroborating those stories as I myself came out in 1979,[73] and I conducted several informal interviews which contributed to the background information for this decade.

I interviewed four self-identified butches and four femmes. One femme always identified as a femme while another became more femme after originally coming out as gay. Two women came out as femme after starting to date butches and leaving heterosexual life. Two women self-identified as lesbian feminists and now identify primarily as gay, and two women self-identified as androgynous. I also interviewed one gay man with the self-identification of "bear."

One woman is African American, one mixed Asian, two Jewish, one a current Protestant minister, five Catholic, and one a former nun and current Catholic Charity worker. One performed as a deejay in a lesbian bar and one was a bartender in a lesbian bar and lesbian strip club. One started a butch-femme social network and also was a safety monitor at lesbian leather events in San Francisco. Several were very active in lesbian feminism and two founded networks for lesbian feminists.

Women who came out in the 1980s came out into established lesbian feminist community replete with bookstores, concerts, *womyn*'s only spaces such as the Michigan Womyn's Music Festival, and other events. In the mid 1980s this culture would crash headlong into the lesbian sex wars and many of these women would take differing paths in these sex war arenas. This is also true for the women from past decades as they took different arenas that were offered in their time periods of coming into gay culture, as gay culture

---

71. Samuel F. Smith, "America (My Country 'Tis of Thee), Song Lyrics," http://www.hymnsite.com/lyrics/umh697.sht (accessed April 16, 2010).
72. For consistency, I have material in this chapter as relating to the 1980s, even though I have included informants whose stories begin in the mid-1970s, and continue into the 1980s.
73. As I noted in the chapter on the 1970s, "being out," "coming out," or how "out" one is, are all post-Stonewall conversations. It is true that after Stonewall people did ask each other, "When did you come out?" This would not have been the case for pre-Stonewall women; for these women the conversation would more have been along the lines of, "Do you like women? When did you first know?" and I have included these indicators of when a person's story starts in previous chapters.

opened into gay liberation and lesbian feminism. However, the divide in the 1980s was not so much between lesbian feminism and butch-femme *bar culture* as it was between lesbian feminists and activists who wanted to *resurrect* butch-femme. This is demonstrated in the essay by Hollibaugh and Moraga,[74] where Moraga wrote that whatever white working-class and women of color were doing in feminist *meetings*, what they were "rollin' around in bed with" was often "butch-femme" identified.

I interviewed women who were ex-military and five who were married to men prior to coming out, and four of those women had children. All of them were able to keep their children. One became a lesbian after her husband died in her late seventies, and one is still not out to her children, although she is separated from her husband.

Many women created or helped create spaces for lesbians, among them Robin, Fran D., and Maria. Some spaces were decidedly feminist, for example an all-women's karate dojo, and some were bar culture spaces, created to serve the sex war combatants who were now seen as the sexual outlaws. However many of these women would straddle both worlds—lesbian feminism and the new leather lesbian culture. For instance, Fran D. and Vivian Escalante[75] created the first Dykes on Bikes contingent riding in the front of Gay Pride Parades, and Fran was instrumental in creating Los Angeles Radical and Wild Women, LA's longest running lesbian leather group. However, she also pioneered women teaching women motorcycle safety.[76] Feminism and *lesbian as sexual* would became less problematic at the end of the decade, but in the beginning the disjunction between leather lesbian and/or butch-femme was seen as antithetical to lesbian feminism.

Most women went to bars; three did not. One went to more feminist events such as collective meetings, and social functions deemed lesbian feminist rather than bars, and two came out later in life and went to older lesbian social clubs meant to replace bars. As with the 1970s women, butch-femme was central to some and for others was in addition to their lesbian lives. However if they were involved in the new leather community, as Fran D. and others were, then bar culture played a big part—as their identity as "leather dykes" was as ostracized an identity as butch-femme had been in the 1970s.

Eight women I met within my friendship circles. One I met through Women of Forty Plus and two I met through Catholic organizations that *welcome home* gay and lesbian Catholics, one of these being the National Conference of Gay and Lesbian Catholic Ministries, where I heard Bishop Vera speak on gays and lesbians as a disenfranchised population who helped

74. Hollibaugh & Moraga, "What We're Rollin' Around in Bed With."
75. Interview, Vivian Escalante.
76. Interview, Fran D.*.

him see Christ more clearly.[77] One I met volunteering in the Catholic booth at Gay Pride in Long Beach, California, Comunidad, an organization at my home parish of St Matthews where I serve on the board.[78]

All women interviewed for this decade lived independently. Five were in their forties, one in her eighties, one in her sixties, and the rest in their fifties at the time of the interviews. All but one self-defined as "out." For six of them lesbian identity was an important part of their professional lives; for three it was not important to professional life but they were not closeted in their work lives either. Two women were closeted outside close friendship circles.

VOICES FROM THE 1980S

As with the other chapters, it is essential that women and men who informed my work be "heard into speech."[79] It is my hope to create a theology useful to these women and men themselves, having heard many of them into speech ... for the first time.

Hearing women and others into speech

These informants continued gay female bar culture community in the US as well as continuing lesbian feminism, and contributing to the emergence of queer culture, and queer theory and politics.

The women

***Evelyn Basa**, in 70s, femme, Caucasian, unknown religious identity*: Evelyn found her current partner online and left Texas when she was over seventy-five—in order to move in with Sunne, her first lesbian lover. She waited until her abusive husband died, and then when her boys started "to boss me around, I said, 'Oh your Daddy's dead, and that's the only man that is going to boss me around. I'm leaving.'"[80]

***Anna Totta**, 60s, androgynous, Caucasian, Catholic*: Anna was a nun for thirty-three years. She loved the intensity she felt in women's community

77. Raul Vera Lopez, Bishop of the Diocese of Saltillo, Mexico, "Closing Plenary Speaker" (paper presented at the National Association of Catholic Diocesan Lesbian and Gay Ministries (NACDLGM) Conference, Long Beach, California, September 21 2008).
78. Interview, Anna Totta. Also, as I do here, I refer in this decade to myself and my own story.
79. Morton, "Hearing to Speech: A Sermon." There is an intentional repetition of introductory language here.
80. Interview, Evelyn Basa.

but it went further for her—she was actually a lesbian. She came out in the 1980s and worked until her retirement for a Catholic Charity organization, as an out lesbian.[81]

Fran D.**, *50, butch, Caucasian, Jewish*: Fran is a sign-language interpreter and motorcycle safety instructor; and also a former bartender in gay bars. She considers herself a "lipstick butch," and found herself in leather culture, and not in lesbian feminism.[82]

D.A.M., *50s, femme, Caucasian, Catholic*: Father Joe welcomed her and her partner as a lesbian couple in his parish. Her partner had been kicked out of her former Catholic parish because she was a lesbian. D.A.M. had never been with a woman and was straight before meeting her partner.[83]

Karen Kahn, *50s, gay, Caucasian/Asian, unknown religious identity*: Pat Gozemba's partner, Karen did not relate to the butch-femme bar culture, but does strongly relate to the bar as an important space for community and identification.[84]

Maria Doest, *50s, gay, mixed Asian, unknown religious identity*: Maria was in the military and then married an abusive man. She started competing in karate, earning her black belt. She went on to be a stunt woman, and to be inducted to the Martial Arts Hall of Fame. The bars, especially for her in Texas, helped her trust gay community before she came out.[85] A fifth degree black belt, Maria founded three karate schools, among them KarateWomen in Venice, CA.

RevSisRaedorah*, *50s, femme, African American, Presbyterian*: RevSisRaedorah is an ordained minister. When coming of age in Texas she was a law enforcement officer, and also entered and won many beauty pageants. She remembers how she loved hanging out with her gay male friends. She also remembers having butch women fall for her—but she was always monogamous so was not available that often![86]

Angela Brinskele, *45, butch, Caucasian, Catholic*: Angela read Joan Nestle's *A Restricted Country* and longed to have been born where butch was celebrated. She came out into radical feminism in 1981 at age nineteen in

81. Interview, Anna Totta.
82. Interview, Fran D.*.
83. Interview, D.A.M.
84. Interview, Karen Kahn.
85. Interview, Maria Doest.
86. Interview, RevSisRaedorah*.

the Southern California consciousness-raising group, Alliance for Lesbians Interested in Consciousness Expansion, ALICE, and worked at being "androgynous" even though she was "really butch." Angela sent a check to Joan Nestle, after reading *Restricted Country*—saying that if she could she would take her to dinner, lacking that she wanted to pay for her dinner.[87]

Jayne Doolittle*, *40s, femme, Caucasian, unknown religious identity*: In 1987 Jayne helped gay male friends decorate a Gay Pride float and they threw her to the ground when press came by because they knew she was in a child custody case. They were afraid even in the late 1980s that her children might get taken from her. Later this was reinforced for her when she went to the lesbian bar The Happy Hour and was introduced to women who had lost their children because their lesbianism had come out in court during their divorce process.[88]

Mary, *40s, androgynous, Caucasian, Catholic*: Mary was a deejay in a butch-femme bar in the 1980s and did not realize that culture "really existed" until she deejayed within that Southern California, Orange County bar, The Huntress. She remembers cops parked across the street, and still remains closeted because her ex-lover was in law enforcement.[89]

Lisa Samson, *age 39, butch, Caucasian, Catholic*: The first time Lisa was in a gay bar she felt she was "living on the edge ... it felt scary to be enjoying myself so much." She recently wore a tie for the first time, and identified as butch after having been "out" for a decade.[90]

Robin Finkelstein, *39, butch, Caucasian, Jewish*: When she first came out Robin felt that she was a reincarnated Jess, of *Stone Butch Blues*. She feels that butch is not role-playing but natural—she is butch as a natural gender identity. She is also strongly feminist and goes every year to the Michigan Womyn's Michigan Festival. She started the now annual Butch Strut, a parade of butches at "Michfest," now still going strong after many years.[91]

Men

Ken Davis, *40s, gay male/bear, Caucasian, unknown religious identity*: Ken identifies as a "bear;" bears are "big, burly, gay guys" who love other bears. There is even a special night at the Long Beach, CA gay bar, Ripples, dedicated as Bear Club night.[92]

87. Interview, Angela Brinskele.
88. Interview, Jayne Doolittle*.
89. Interview, Mary.
90. Interview, Lisa Samson.
91. Interview, Robin Finkelstein.
92. Interview, Ken Davis.

7. HISTORICAL ANTECEDENTS

QUAKERS AND FRIENDS

The language of "thee" has strong roots in various religious traditions, and I drew on these roots especially as they related to the Quakers and to Martin Buber's concepts of *thee*.

"Thee" is the objective case of thou, and is rarely used today except in contemporary wedding rituals, as in, "*With this ring, I thee wed.*" However, thee is today in general usage by the Quaker Society of Friends. Quakers emerged as a Christian denomination in England during a period of religious turmoil in mid-1600, and Quakerism is practiced today in a variety of forms around the world. Friends (or Quakers) are involved in movements for pacifism, social equality, and simplicity, and, like many indigenous religions, Friends include care of the planet as their mission.[1]

Quakers do not have an official creed, nor do they believe access to God must be mediated by a hierarchal figure. Quakers have "meetings" and there is no officiating central figure. When an individual Friend feels moved to witness—share the word of God speaking through him or her—they stand and do so. The Quaker definition of "Friend" is the other person in religious community, with whom one is in community. In Quaker praxis there is no official intermediary that hears the word of God and passes it back to the congregation. Each Friend can hear the word of God, can "witness" that word of God and inform other Friends in the meeting what she/he has heard and then speak what they witnessed. In listening other Friends declare it valid through the act of witnessing. While Friends do not commonly use "thee" today, it is historically used in their discourse to denote a non-hierarchal relationship between Friends.

1. Chel Avery, "What Do Quakers Believe?" www.quakerinfo.org, http://www.quakerinfo.org/quakerism/beliefs (accessed July 28, 2013).

SALLIE McFAGUE: A MODEL OF GOD AS FRIEND

Why is it valuable to see God as a friend?

Sallie McFague proposes a useful model. She creates parallels between human friendship and the divine human relationship. She exposes the creative and useful possibilities a God/divine human relationship has as a beneficial model for a relationship we might have with God/the divine. A friend is accessible. A friend often loves us unconditionally. A friend is someone we feel close to and confide in and are in community with. She asks—can God be divine and also have those qualities that a friend has?[2] The Merriam Webster Online Dictionary describes "friend" as one attached to another by affection or esteem or one that is not hostile. A friend is also a favored companion.[3]

One, however, assumes that if one were to attempt to have a friendship with God then one would have had other friends before one attempted to have *God* as a friend.

God as friend would have been very useful for the bar culture population. Unfortunately this was not a possible religious relation available to them. For homosexual women in the mid-twentieth century to have a friend at all, or to have friends and to feel accepted in community was a salvific act in and of itself—that *was* their baptism into an identity seen as a redeemable and necessary part of culture. For most bar women, the bar was the only place where community and recognition of friendship that created self-identity (baptism) was possible. So, although there are models (Quakers and McFague's model) of *God* as friend, for bar culture mid-century gay women, *God as friend* was unlikely. By naming the relationship they had with each other as religious community, I am naming what happened for *many* of these women in terms of their relationships *with each other*. The bar culture provided not only what might have been provided by a house of worship, if they had been accepted at such a place, but also a space where a community was formed that allowed bar women to be *baptized* into an identity as gay *and* in relation to others.

Don Norman, one of the narrators in the documentary *On These Shoulders We Stand,* speaks to this. He says that the first time he went to the bars of the 1950s in Los Angeles he felt like he had "gone to heaven." Obviously he had never before experienced anything like it.[4]

God as friend is useful as a way to view this culture religiously because *prior to* God being friend, or hearing the word of God through a Friend (or

2. Sallie McFague, *Metaphorical Theology: Models of God in Religious Language* (Philadelphia, PA: Fortress Press, 1982), 177–92.
3. Merriam Webster Online Dictionary, "Friend", http://www.merriam-webster.com/dictionary/friend (accessed July 15, 2013).
4. McElhinney, *On These Shoulders We Stand.*

friend), one must first be, and have, a friend. It makes sense that having God as a father is not as useful for daily living in Christian community as having God as a friend. McFague argues that comparing God to father is idolatrous. For what does one owe an idol other than worship? With a friend one often owes a much more heartfelt commitment. However in order to be and have a friend, I must have access to the conditions where I can know *myself* as someone who could *be* a friend—where I can practice friendship *knowing myself as a possible friend* to someone, even a mythic someone at first and then friendship with another actual person. For most mid-century gay women the only place where they could experience these conditions was in the gay women's bar.

MARTIN BUBER: I/THOU

> Then shall he answer them, saying, Verily I say unto you,
> Inasmuch as ye did it not to one of the least of these,
> ye did it not to me.[5]

There were few populations that lived a public or semi-public life during the period 1945–75 that could be considered as "least of" as was the homosexual of the period—who was not only considered, but officially deemed, mentally ill, a sinner, a national security risk, and a pervert so dangerous that he or she could destroy anything from her own family, husband, children, neighbors, to someone else's reputation, her own or someone else's livelihood, and on up to the ability to destroy their entire country.[6]

> *So faith, hope, love, abide,*
> but the greatest of these is love.[7]

In *I and Thou* Martin Buber writes that life is about the encounter with the other, the *I* and the *Thou*,[8] and argues that a person is at all times engaged in relations. We need each other to have authentic existence and this is not merely philosophical, but actualized in encounter after encounter between the other and ourselves. While we cannot prove that this *happens*,

5. Matthew 25:45.
6. Johnson, *The Lavender Scare: The Cold War Persecution of Gays and Lesbians in the Federal Government*. This book documents how the Cold War's witch hunts had more to do with routing out the national security risk that homosexuals posed than the risk that Communists posed.
7. 1 Corinthians 13:13. The actual Biblical passage that Ava, a Chicago gay bartender, used to "marry" gay female couples in her 1960s bar, The Lost and Found. Some of those couples are still married today.
8. Martin Buber, *I and Thou* (Edinburgh: T. & T. Clark, 1953).

nonetheless we know it does, and it happens not only between two people but between people and nature, or animals. Buber also argues that a relationship with God is only possible through an *I–Thou* relationship with God as *the other*. Buber contrasts the *I–Thou* relationship with what he calls the *I–It* relationship where we confront the other not as *Thou* but as *It*. We connect with the other as *It* not to connect with an *other* like us, but to clarify our ideas. Therefore we create a monologue and not a dialogue, and we turn the other into an object and not a living thing. These two relationships are opposites of each other. The other in the *I–It* relationship serves to help the *I* advance his or her position, not to create a communal exchange. In the face of modernism, Buber cautioned that the *I–It* relationship was on the rise while the *I–Thou* was rarely found.[9]

The secrecy of the pre-Stonewall period excluded queer people from the dominant culture—there was practically no way to meet a queer person in the dominant culture and know that that person was queer—unless one met that person in a gay bar. Queer people often had to use false names in the gay bar to protect themselves and each other; this means that in the world outside the gay bar, the ability to meet in a Buber-istic *I–Thou* relation was almost impossible for queer people. Queer people were invisible. They lived in "the twilight" as it was known, and were often called "twilight lovers"—reflected in the title of Faderman's *Odd Girls and Twilight Lovers*.[10] While for Buber a relationship between God and *I* is the highest form of relation, queer people pre-Stonewall did not have the ability to avail themselves of it. And also they were often left out of human relations that would connect them on an *I–Thou* continuum because of the need for secrecy.[11]

THEOLOGY—THE WORD OF GOD

> i found god in my self and i loved her—i loved her fiercely.[12]

ntozake shange[13] wrote this piece after working with women, among them Judy Grahn, in performative events in San Francisco.[14] Judy Grahn, an out

9. Martin Buber, *Between Man and Man* (London: Kegan Paul, 1947).
10. Faderman, *Odd Girls and Twilight Lovers: A History of Lesbian Life in Twentieth-Century America*.
11. It is true that it is difficult for anyone to have an *I–Thou* relationship, or friendship—embedded soliders in combat are a contemporary example. This example is also what many pre-Stonewall people felt like in their relations with each other.
12. ntozake shange, *For Colored Girls Who Have Considered Suicide, When the Rainbow Is Enuf: A Choreopoem* (New York: Macmillan, 1977), 63. Used with permission.
13. ntozake shange traditionally uses lower case initial letters in her name in her publications—in honoring that choice I am using that here as well.
14. shange, *For Colored Girls Who Have Considered Suicide, When the Rainbow Is Enuf: A Choreopoem*.

butch lesbian who was dishonorably discharged from the military for being a lesbian in the 1960s,[15] said that the gay bar was her first place of knowing and, as noted, said that when a woman entered a gay bar she opened to the *possibility* of herself as a sexual self often for the first time.[16] It was only *in* the women's bar that a gay woman might be seen without first being seen through the filter of sinner. The experience of being in that bar *space/place* allowed a woman to create *place* in her body without sin and therefore create a place where she acknowledged her sexual self freely and could find an unspoken god. For there was little sense of a God with a capital "G" in the bar community, and there was no language yet available for discourse on a small "g" god. This would have to wait until the New Age provided that language with which one could articulate the version of god in the self.

THEALOGY—THE WORD OF THE GODDESS

Thealogy is another variant of *theo*logy. Carol P. Christ, Goddess scholar and feminist theologian, writes, "The word thealogy comes from the Greek word Thea or Goddess and logos or meaning. It describes the activity of reflection on the meaning of Goddess in contrast to theology, from theos and logos which is reflection and meaning of God."[17] In her works, particularly *Rebirth of the Goddess,* Christ speaks of how her version of thealogy, as opposed to theology, is rooted in experience. She believes the earth is holy and our true home. She also believes that women's experience (like all human experience) is a source of insight about the divine.[18] Patricia Monagham noted that in Christ's rendition, we find that feminist theology arises "from experience, rather than moving from theory to practice." Of course more orthodox theology, she argues, does originate from theory as opposed to originating from practice.[19]

Black lesbian/essayist Audre Lorde wrote of something similar when she argued in *Sister Outsider* that "the master's tools" would never "dismantle the master's house":

> Those of us who stand outside the circle of this society's definition of acceptable women; those of us who have been forged in the crucibles

15. Grahn, *Edward the Dyke, and Other Poems.*
16. Judy Grahn, *Another Mother Tongue: Gay Words, Gay Worlds* (Boston, MA: Beacon Press, 1984).
17. Carol P. Christ, "Feminist Thealogy as Post-Traditional Theology." In *The Cambridge Companion to Feminist Theology,* ed. Susan Frank Parsons (Boston, MA: Cambridge University Press, 2002), 79–98.
18. Carol P. Christ, *Rebirth of the Goddess: Finding Meaning in Feminist Spirituality* (Reading, MA: Addison-Wesley, 1997).
19. Patricia Monagham, "Book Review: *Rebirth of the Goddess,*" *Booklist* 93(19–20), 1624.

> of difference—those of us who are poor, who are lesbians, who are Black, who are older—know that survival is not an academic skill. It is learning how to stand alone, unpopular and sometimes reviled, and how to make common cause with those others identified as outside ... For the master's tools will never dismantle the master's house. They may allow us temporarily to beat him at his own game, but they will never enable us to bring about genuine change.[20]

It is this feeling that propelled Christ to extricate herself from the master's house of theology as it is not possible to house "thealogy" or language of the goddess within the master's house. It is this same impetus that propelled me from theology or from situating the system I created within the house of theology—even with a defining adjective such as queer or feminist or even liberation in front of the noun theology. While all of these ways of talking about the sacred inform the sacred *today*, for the *historical period 1945–75 in queer people's lives* these terms do not fit. These women (and men) were cast out of the house of God and had no agency/theology to speak of Him (as it was decidedly "Him"). The master's tools of discourse regarding the sacred at that time could never construct a house of discourse to describe their experience as anything other than sinful.

20. Audre Lorde, "The Master's Tools Will Never Dismantle the Master's House." In *Sister Outsider: Essays and Speeches* (Trumansburg, NY: Crossing Press, 1984), 110–12.

8. THEOLOGICAL STRANDS

PROCESS THEOLOGY

God was there in those that fought back.[1]

Process thought identifies *God* and *religion* as an interior calling to a new kind of action and personal responsibility within the individual. Alfred North Whitehead's process thought means that *the many become one, and are increased by one.*[2] This means that many strands of reality come together in one unity. A decision is made and out of that *something*, often *something new*, is contributed back to the world.

Christian process theologian Marjorie Suchocki asks what constitutes a religion and how do we differentiate between religions? This is her approach to systematic theology. First we ask who is God and how did this vision of the world with this God come to be (cosmology)? What does God want in this world and what happens when we do what God wants, and what is the reward (eschatology)? What happens when we don't do what God wants (sin)? What does God believe is our salvation (soteriology)? What about the problem of evil in the world—how can a loving God allow evil (theodicy)?[3] This brief explanation begins to elaborate the categories regarding the creation I call *theelogy*.

1. Process theologian Dr Marjorie Suchocki, public lecture, Claremont School of Theology, Claremont, CA, during the aftermath of the September 11, 2001 bombings on New York City. The above is her answer to the question "Where was God?" when events like 9/11 or the Holocaust happen. Not everyone needs to be participating in a given thought process for it to be in effect. In the gay women's bar, not everyone did "theelogy," but "God was in those who fought back," who *did* do theelogy, fighting back against the shame of the dominant culture by offering community to each other.
2. Alfred North Whitehead, *Process and Reality: An Essay in Cosmology,* Gifford Lectures delivered in the University of Edinburgh during the session 1927–8 (New York: Macmillan, 1929), 21.
3. Suchocki, "Backgrounds in Contemporary Theology".

Process thought states that in every moment each individual takes everything that has come before and also what is possible from this moment, and creates something new. The spark of God is in every one of us. God is calling on the God-self within us—God versus our God-potential. God is not only outside of us necessarily. God is in us and it is up to us to listen to that voice and create the new thing, birth the new thing—rather than do the old thing. However the old way of being presses on us to be reborn again and again. It is the impetus to create the new thing, the small voice inside that asks us to be, in Christian terms "Christian," or the good person who does the action, the one who processes the new birth, connects with the Higher Power, has the wisdom, and then does the thing that is in line with the calling of God towards our God potential.[4]

Process thought depends on concrescence. This term coined by Whitehead in his exploration of process thought is a core concept in process theology, a *process of becoming:*

> Components selected from the past may achieve their unique mode of harmony in the new unit of existence by the introduction of a harmonizing factor never before combined with this particular past. In such a case the novelty created in the present becomes a qualitative leap into that which was beyond the power of the past in and of itself. Yet continuity is nevertheless achieved, since the new quality is used in conjunction with the ... past.[5]

One of the components from the past that did achieve a new mode of harmony, was the pre-Stonewall homosexual community and the ideas they brought *into being* with the embodied lives they lived in the gay bars of mid-century.

LIBERATION THEOLOGY

> Be a lamp unto yourself. Work out your liberation with diligence.[6]

---

4. This is a much reduced version of a complex theological process that is derived from the philosophy of Alfred North Whitehead. Very basically process thought can mean that both God and the world are in process. This process can mean that the presence of God in us, if we listen to it, can birth a new creative and "god-like" event. Process theology also espouses that likewise, God incorporates the world's events into God-self to shape how God calls us in each moment.
5. Suchocki, *God, Christ, Church: A Practical Guide to Process Theology*. This type of "becoming" is also constructed systematically by Carol P. Christ.
6. Siddharta Gautama Buddha, "The Buddha's Farewell." In *The Gospel of Buddha: Compiled from Ancient Records*, ed. Paul Carus (Chicago, IL: Open Court, 1909), http://www.sacred-texts.com/bud/btg/btg94.htm (accessed July 15, 2013).

Although it would take over two decades for gay liberation theology to be articulated, that does not mean that the *lived experience* of those involved in gay liberation movements was not as sacred as those involved in similar movements for liberation (as in the movement *for liberation* on which *liberation theology* was based in Latin America). These connections are articulated in Alma Rose Alvarez's *Liberation Theology in Chicana/o Literature: Manifestations of Feminist and Gay Identities.*[7]

"The Spirit of the Lord God is upon me; because the Lord hath anointed me to preach good tidings unto the meek; he hath sent me to bind up the brokenhearted, to *proclaim liberty to the captives*, and the opening of the prison to them that are bound"[8] God did not *only* come to bring peace, but *also* to bring justice.

Latin American bishops formally supported liberation theology in 1978; the Roman Catholic Church hierarchy condemned the revolutionary movements of which Latin American liberation theologians, and their respective countries were involved until 1986 when they supported a moderate form of liberation theology. The countries involved were predominantly Catholic.[9]

Since I am Catholic, I utilized interviews with Catholics who are involved in using liberation theology within their life work, among them: Father Joe, a priest who found his calling at the Stonewall Riots; Anna Totta, a former nun and now Catholic Charity worker; and Bishop Raul Vera Lopez, Bishop of the Diocese of Saltillo, Mexico who works with a gay and lesbian ministry. At a time when social movements were changing the face of America, liberation theology threatened the Church canons. So much so that in the late 1980s Father Joe, as previously stated, walked into a Dignity meeting of exiled gay Catholics and they adjoined to a gay bar where everyone knew the priest with whom Father Joe attended the meeting. "Church was happening—we were in community."[10]

Liberation theology as methodology for gay religious texts was a natural fit,[11] but this connection was not readily available until the 1990s. Richard

7. Alma Rose Alvarez, *Liberation Theology in Chicana/o Literature: Manifestations of Feminist and Gay Identities* (New York: Routledge, 2007).
8. Isaiah 61:1, italics mine.
9. Catholicism has a history of being redesigned to fit the needs of the poor in Latin America. An example of this is how the Virgin of Guadalupe supplanted the more traditional Virgin image in Mexico after her appearance to Juan Diego in 1531. The Mexican novelist Carlos Fuentes is quoted in Mary Francis (ed.), *A Handbook on Guadalupe* (New Bedford, MA: Franciscan Friars of the Immaculate, 1997), in the essay, "Guadalupe Cult ... In the Lives of Mexicans": "one may no longer consider himself a Christian, but you cannot truly be considered a Mexican unless you believe in the Virgin of Guadalupe", 114.
10. Interview, Father Joe*.
11. Liberation theologians espoused the Church's support of the oppressed and that idea fit into the fabric of the Stonewall revolution—the spirit of the Church was to *proclaim liberty to the captives.* By the 1980s and thereafter gay life would have theological

Cleaver's *Know My Name: A Gay Liberation Theology* was published in 1995.[12] The *Library Journal* wrote of it:

> [This] first attempt to incorporate Latin American liberation theology into ... powerful gay theology ... centers on the call for gay men and for the church to recognize those it has placed on its margins. [It] challenges gay men ... to name themselves ... for such naming secures a social identity that cannot be shattered by the church.[13]

This does not mean however that the theological principles of Latin American liberation theology were not in concert with the principles of Stonewall—at the time the uprising happened—and earlier.

In the 1990s James Nelson's *Body Theology*[14] articulated the work he began in *Embodiment.*[15] *The Library Journal* stated that Nelson's work is "incarnational—and therefore thoroughly Christian" and that it does the revolutionary theological turn of taking both the body and sexuality seriously "as a locus of divine revelation and human growth that seeks to overcome dualism of soul and body, and of spirit and matter."[16] He rethought sexual sin and evaluated, among other things, AIDS. He concluded with two sermons, one entitled "I Thank God for You: A Sermon for Gay and Lesbian Awareness Week," thanking God for homosexuals who helped him address personal homophobia, and explored a contemporary embodied Christ.[17] "I thank God because you have taught me much about our desperate need for more erotic spiritualities and theologies."[18]

MCC set up its first congregation in 1968 in West Hollywood, California and performed its first gay marriage in Huntington Park, CA in 1969. When physical sacred spaces opened up, such developments meant that the bar became no longer "the only space." However, as noted, informant Andi who marched in the arguably first gay rights march with Troy Perry (the first to

---

articulators—among them Troy Perry and Nancy Wilson of the Metropolitan Community Church (MCC). Rev. Troy Perry founded the MCC (a Christian affiliate) with a special affirming ministry for the LGBT populations in Los Angeles on October 6, 1968.

12. Richard Cleaver, *Know My Name: A Gay Liberation Theology* (Louisville, KY: Westminster John Knox Press, 1995).
13. LJ Reviews, "Book Review, *Know My Name: A Gay Liberation Theology*," *Library Journal*, 1995, http://www.amazon.com/Know-My-Name-Cleaver/dp/0664255760/ref=sr_1_2?ie=UTF8&s=books&qid=1271631021&sr=1-2. (accessed July 15, 2013).
14. Nelson, *Body Theology*.
15. James B. Nelson, *Embodiment: An Approach to Sexuality and Christian Theology* (Minneapolis, MN: Augsburg Publishing House, 1978).
16. LJ Reviews, "Book Review, *Body Theology*," *Library Journal*, 1992 http://www.amazon.com/Body-Theology-James-B-Nelson/dp/0664253792/ref=sr_1_1?ie=UTF8&s=books&qid=1271631644&sr=1-1. (accessed July 15, 2013).
17. Nelson, *Body Theology*, 183–9.
18. *Ibid.*, 186.

officially declare gay people fit for "church" community in 1968), told me, "the MCC Church came out of the bars—most definitely."[19]

In fact, the history of the MCC founding is that Perry had a failed suicide attempt, following a failed love affair, and he witnessed a close friend being arrested by the police in a gay bar in 1968. This prompted him to put an advertisement in *The Advocate* announcing a worship service designed for gays in Los Angeles. Twelve people attended. "Nine were my friends who came to console me and to laugh, and three came as a result of the ad."[20] Nonetheless in 1971 the first MCC building was dedicated with over a thousand members in attendance.

Therefore the first gay church came out of a desire for protection of gays and lesbians that was not offered in the gay bar. However, the community had already been founded, as evidenced by Perry's love for his friend and his desire for protection of the community that could not exist within the confines of the gay bar in the way he believed *it might* exist in a Church. His biography is entitled, *The Lord is my Shepherd and He Knows I'm Gay*.[21] And he dedicated a copy to Lee Glaze, manager and owner of the bar The Patch where Perry witnessed his first gay action. Glaze spoke against the arrest of his bar patrons. This act of activism is what Perry credits with giving him the inspiration to create MCC. When I interviewed Glaze, he showed me the autographed copy that Perry dedicated to him.[22]

> The Patch ... was run by one of the most courageous and personable men I've ever met His name was Lee Glaze and he'd run bars in the Long Beach area. The local paper there had done a story on him called, "A Conversation with a Queen." Lee had his own personal civil rights movement going. His attitude was that anybody who got arrested in his bar would be taken care of. Lee would put up bail, pay the lawyers, and fight the case.[23]

Liberation theology had its genesis for gay and lesbian people in the gay civil rights movement, *and* in the lived communities that claimed space for community prior to an actual articulation of gay civil rights—communities that existed in the gay bars. These were contested dangerous spaces throughout the century, but most particularly in the mid-twentieth century when bars were regularly policed and raided.

---

19. Interview, Andrea "Andi" Segal.
20. Kay Tobin & Randy Wicker, *The Gay Crusaders* (New York: Paperback Library, 1972), 21.
21. Perry & Lucas, *The Lord Is My Shepherd and He Knows I'm Gay; the Autobiography of the Rev. Troy D. Perry, as Told to Charles L. Lucas.*
22. Interview, Lee Glaze.
23. Perry & Lucas, *The Lord Is My Shepherd and He Knows I'm Gay; the Autobiography of the Rev. Troy D. Perry, as Told to Charles L. Lucas*, 6.

Queer theologies also had their roots in the roots of other struggles for liberation. Lee Glaze, whose activism on behalf of drag queens in his bar inspired Perry to create the MCC Church, marched in the Selma to Montgomery American civil rights marches/protests in 1965.[24] Joan Nestle, whose essays about the 1950s, particularly her essay on the "sexual courage" it took to be in the gay bars, also marched in Selma. While Joan's work has been widely anthologized and incorporated into queer religious anthologies,[25] Joan herself asserts that she is "nothing if not profane."[26]

People whose actions not only *helped* form later queer religious theories, but *birthed* those later creations, did not themselves consider themselves religious. I call their actions *something theological,* at the time they were birthed—*thee*logical actions, which birthed in later generations *theo*logical actions.

WOMANIST THEOLOGY

In *Making a Way out of No Way: A Womanist Theology,* Monica A. Coleman writes:

> Postmodern womanist theology argues that a black woman is often Christ. The Savior may be a teenager, a person living with a disability, a lesbian woman. We have yet to see how "the least of these" can lead the way ... Salvation is participation in a community that "makes a way out of no way." ... salvation does not need to occur through an institutional faith community. This community can be ... a dancing circle, a coffee house, a book group or a nonprofit agency. But salvation is more than ethical social justice activity. Postmodern womanist theology acknowledges the ancestors and a higher power. They understand their activity as being co-created by the community and God.[27]

This definition of a community-based, workable theology does not exactly fit the mid-century butch-femme bar culture community for the reasons alluded to earlier. It is unlikely that the bar culture participants understood their activity as being, as Coleman writes "co-created by the community and God." Queer theology, which by definition must be postmodern, could also see Jesus Christ as a black woman, or a gay man, or woman, and the Savior may very well be a lesbian. We have yet to see how "the least of these" can be allowed to lead the way with any certainty. A parallel is a question raised

24. Interview, Lee Glaze.
25. Nestle, *A Restricted Country.*
26. Interview, Joan Nestle.
27. Monica A. Coleman, *Making a Way out of No Way: A Womanist Theology* (Minneapolis, MN: Fortress Press, 2008), 170.

by the classic women and religion text, *The Feminine Face of God*, an explication of women's search for the feminist/female God, and God language, or of "the unfolding of the sacred in women."[28] Many of the book's interviews are of women searching for the feminine sacred. Because so many of the ethnographic testimonies talked of the difficulties women had in finding time to search for the feminine face of God while juggling family and work responsibilities, negotiating within themselves whether such a search was a need or a luxury, on reading the book one cannot come up with an actual discourse/theology, or even *thealogy* until women are allowed time to go to the proverbial mountain top and find themselves and "the feminine face of God." The theology espoused in this classic volume then is that women must be allowed and encouraged to search for the feminine face of God and after such time as the search is allowed a discourse will emerge.[29] This is also the thesis in Virginia Woolf's treatise *A Room of One's Own*. If a woman does not have "a room of her own," she will have an almost impossible time creating work or even *the life* that is "her own."[30]

FEMINIST AND WOMANIST

> Don't worship the God of your oppressors.
> Don't let any God colonize you.
> Everyone deserves to worship a God who likes them.[31]

Writer Alice Walker created the term "womanist," claiming that "feminist" carried too much baggage for her as a black woman. She believed in feminist concepts but the house of feminism could not house her. She coined womanist for the black woman who wanted to prioritize both her race and her gender politically.[32] Black female theologians, chief among them Jacquelyn Grant and Delores Williams, then took "womanist" and created womanist theology.

---

28. Sherry Ruth Anderson & Patricia Hopkins, *The Feminine Face of God: The Unfolding of the Sacred in Women* (New York: Bantam Books, 1991).
29. Marie Cartier, "Exploring Conditions Necessary for the Creation of Female Authored Theology." Paper presented at the Women's Spirituality Conference, Lake Forest, OR, 2002.
30. Virginia Woolf, *A Room of One's Own* (New York: Harcourt, Brace & Company, 1929).
31. Alice Walker, "The Only Reason You Want to Go to Heaven is that You Have Been Driven Out of Your Mind." *On the Issues: A Magazine of Feminist Progessive Thinking*, Spring 1997, http://www.ontheissuesmagazine.com/1997spring/sp97walker.php (accessed July 15, 2013). "The Only Reason You Want to Go to Heaven," is adapted from a speech given by Alice Walker at the Auburn Theological Seminary, April 25, 1995. Quote also used in "Sermon by Rev. D.G. Penny Nixon" (Sunday, February 6, 2005), www.mccsf.org/sermons. 2005 #1684. Used with permission of author.
32. Alice Walker, *In Search of Our Mothers' Gardens: Womanist Prose* (San Diego, CA: Harcourt Brace Jovanovich, 1983), xi–xii.

This idea has a history or in this case herstory. It is true that an established term like theology, or feminism, may not have the ability to define, house, and ultimately help a population in which the population does not find identify itself. That population must then create an alternate defining structure to the original defining term or house while at the same time maintaining ties to the instigating house. For example, by its definition *thealogy* maintains ties to the definition of theology and *womanist* maintains ties to feminist/feminism.

BRAIDING

> Womanism is to feminism what purple is to lavender.[33]

Therefore theelogy maintains ties to both theology and thealogy in its definition. It is the discourse used to describe the practice and language of "thee" as sacred (as opposed to "theo" or "thea" as the sacred).[34] While true that "thee" as the sacred partner is not entirely new, it is new as it concerns historical queer community. "Human beings were not born to be alone. God alone is alone. People are capable of falling in love. Illness is not being able to fall in love."[35] Process thought agrees with this, "God alone is alone," and we however are in relation with each other and with God. We are capable of falling in love and illness is not being able to fall in love. It remains to be identified by future researchers to finally and accurately assess (when being queer is no longer against the law) whether or not queer people are "gender dysfunctional" because of societal constraints or genuinely were ill. Of course queer scholars would argue the former. But there is *still* a definition of *queer* as non-normative and an idea that queer people have trouble falling in love because they are mentally deficient. This argument is *still* alive and well in the same sex marriage debates as of this writing. Because queer people were/are not able to fall in love and legalize their relationships in most states in the US, and because they are often prevented from falling in love to this legal extent by the culture at large, I hazard that they were/are not ill or dysfunctional at all—but were/are not *able*—rather than not capable of—falling in love. And this was certainly much truer of mid-twentieth century queer people than it is today.

33. Walker, *In Search of Our Mothers' Gardens: Womanist Prose*, xii.
34. Using the term "braiding" to describe the act of taking several strands of theological discourse, as well as elements of human story and experience, and then creating theology I owe to Monica Coleman and *Making a Way Out of No Way*, particularly as articulated February 3, 2009, at a Claremont School of Theology Process Center Lecture, Claremont, CA.
35. Susan Salter Reynolds, "The Writer's Life: Elie Wiesel's Work Is Never Done," *The Los Angeles Times*, February 22, 2009. The actual quote above by Elie Wiesel is quoted in this article.

9. EXPERIENCE IS PRIMARY

MYRNA'S STORY … CONTINUED

Myrna was married from 1953 to 1968 when she separated, and then divorced her husband in 1970 when no-fault divorce law passed in California. She had terrible insomnia throughout her marriage. "I would get up at one or two a.m. and I would call every gay bar I had the number to from the 1940s. I wouldn't say anything. I would just stay on the phone and listen to the sounds in the background. I would stay on until they hung up, and then I would call another one of my numbers, until I had called all the numbers I had. That was my lifeline."

What did it mean to call those bars and to hear the sounds in the background? "That phone. Those numbers. That was my lifeline." she whispered, and put both hands by her heart. "It meant there was a place somewhere—even if I couldn't go there—that place was out there. I could hear it. Freedom."[1] She called the bars two to three times a week like this—for fourteen years.

Why did hearing the sounds in the background of an anonymous phone call represent freedom? While the communities that coalesced around the gay girl bars in America from 1940–80 can be seen as religious communities through a sociological lens, they also created a community where they developed God and/or the sacred in one another. Three spirals[2] of thought place this community and its gathering spaces—the bars—within contemporary theological method. These spirals are experience as primary; the historical gap in the use of language and a re-examination of the classic "Orders of Theological Construction."[3]

1. Interview, Myrna Kurland.
2. I am using *spirals* as opposed to *lines* of thoughts, as spiraling together makes more sense for this community, than straight lines.
3. Gordon D. Kaufman, *An Essay on Theological Method* (Missoula, MT: Scholars Press for the American Academy of Religion, 1975).

TESTIMONY AND TRUTH TELLING

> What would happen if one woman told the truth about her life?
> The world would split open.[4]

Testimonies of bar women and their use of religious language have been nominally identified in previous studies. For religious language through its illuminative, transcendent nature can well re-frame the gaze on bar women's narratives.

Joan Nestle writes of hearing the gay women's bar narratives of the mid twentieth century, and of how she felt it was time to listen to them in her memoir *A Restricted Country*.[5] She stressed with me that she felt her feminine body was a "portal" to somewhere else—other than the world that butch/masculine women were forced to inhabit. This was the world different from the bar room where the urine from a homophobic man splashed through the door mail slot onto the floor next to where she sat. And this is where she found her sexual self—in that room and also through that portal of her body. That portal offered entrance to an entirely different place. Joan found her sexual self in those bars, with those women, as she believes they found theirs and she felt so indebted to them that saving their stories was the primary reason she founded the Lesbian Herstory Archives (LHA) in New York. She felt that bar women stories were not being heard, and were being lost.[6,7,8]

Nestle went on to become a noted feminist speaker, writer and university professor and was the first to suggest that the bar culture incorporated feminist theories —because gay women's bar culture privileged femme and or feminine desire and butch longing.[9] That a woman's desires were enough reason to drop convention and strive for something different means that this culture should be considered *as part of* feminist history, *not apart from* feminist history. Yes, there was sexism. The bars were four walls situated most often in dangerous urban areas where prostitutes and drug dealers—and gay

4. Muriel Rukeyser, "Kathe Kollwitz." In *Collected Poems of Muriel Rukeyser* (Pittsburgh, PA: University of Pittsburgh Press, 2005). Used with permission.
5. Nestle, *A Restricted Country*.
6. Warshow, *Hand on the Pulse*.
7. Lesbian Herstory Archives, "'Bars'—Subject Files," ed. Lesbian Herstory Archives (Brooklyn, NY). These files represent an ongoing project of Joan's to collect the names of gay women's/lesbian bars, and the stories of women who went to them. Research at Lesbian Herstory Archives conducted in April 2008.
8. Maxine Wolfe, "Invisible Women in Invisible Places: Lesbian, Lesbian Bars and the Social Production of People/Environment Relationships," in *Queers in Space: Communities, Public Spaces, Sites of Resistance*, ed. Gordon Brent Ingram, Anne-Marie Bouthillette, Yolanda Retter (Ann Arbor, MI, Bay Press, 1997), 301–24. LHA subject file material on bars is included in this essay by Wolfe, a LHA board member.
9. Nestle, *A Restricted Country*.

women/lesbians—congregated on corners and in the gay bars themselves.[10] The bars were inhabited by people reluctant to give each other even their real names. If they saw each other in public they would not acknowledge each other, in order to protect jobs and community relations, public or private, outside the bar.

These spaces gay women of mid-twentieth century transformed into *place*, and it conforms to Sheldrake's sense of the place as sacred—as somewhere people gathered to move forward from creating history.[11] Most informants spoke of the bar as "finding home." Sheldrake's conditions are met here for space to become *place*: becoming our potential and community building. "First, 'home' stands for the fact that we persistently need a location where we can pass through the stages of life and become the person we are potentially." The second Sheldrake condition is that "we need a place where we can belong to a community."[12]

I combine these thoughts with traditional gender and women's studies concepts as brought forth in Bettina Aptheker's classic *Tapestries of Life*. Aptheker made three groundbreaking points in this text regarding how we should study women: personal testimony is valid, daily resistance is activism, and art can tell the truth as nothing else can.[13]

Using Aptheker for this point in cultural history suggests that it is appropriate for gays and lesbians to find, to create and to inhabit a place they call home. Since personal testimony *is* valid we must believe the bar women of the mid twentieth century when they assert that the bar was "the only place" and for many "like finding home."[14] This leads us to re-examine the gay women's bar for gay women's/lesbian history as not just a *space*, but a primary if not *the* primary *place*, that a woman of this period had to pass through to become the person she *could potentially* become—a *gay* woman.

Aptheker asserts that in formulating women's history we must realize that "daily resistance is activism." Aptheker is concerned with women's struggles globally stating that for most women to just survive with their family and as part of their people is activism. It is not just the activist struggle in the streets, aka Stonewall, which is activism. It is the necessary day-to-day

10. Penn, "The Sexualized Woman: The Lesbian, the Prostitute, and the Containment of Female Sexuality in Post-War America." Working class populations, among them gay women/lesbians and prostitutes, developed coalitions and friendships because of the proximity of geographic spaces they inhabited. Many gay women/lesbians were prostitutes in mid-century, but coalitions were also formed between straight prostitutes and gay women/lesbians because of the neighborhoods they both inhabited.
11. Sheldrake, *Spaces for the Sacred: Place, Memory, and Identity*.
12. *Ibid*., 10.
13. Bettina Aptheker, *Tapestries of Life: Women's Work, Women's Consciousness, and the Meaning of Daily Experience* (Amherst, MA: University of Massachusetts Press, 1989).
14. The phrases I most often heard from my informants when asked what the bar meant, so much so that the phrase "the only place" was my second choice for a title for this volume.

struggle to keep a people alive—for example, the women in Japanese internment camps who created walls from sheets, and flowerpots from cans, to humanize an inhuman environment for their people to simply be able to go on, after having lost everything. Aptheker quotes the poem from Chicano poet Lorna Dee Cervantes titled, "Para Un Revolucionario," where the poet is listening to her husband planning liberation campaigns in the next room while she washes dishes and she cautions him, "I too am Raza."[15]

Aptheker explains the poet's assertion: the poet "too" is Raza or the struggle. She writes, "Cervantes warns that without her experience, without her knowledge structured out of the dailyness of her life, the dream of liberation will remain incomplete, will remain unrealizable."[16] Can we say then of the gay women in the back rooms in the 1940s–70s gay women's bars that they "too" are Stonewall? In fact perhaps "Stonewall" is part of them and their experience, not the other way around. Stonewall defines a way of being as liberation, but prior to Stonewall the act of daily resistance was to walk from the street into a gay bar. For example, Rory Devine, stuck on a military base in Virginia in 1978, would pay whatever price she had to in order to get to the bar.

> As long as I had money I went to the gay bar every chance I could get. As long as I had money to get there and buy even a drink ... or even if I couldn't buy a drink, as long as I could get there. I was just looking to connect. To connect with women. Because I wanted to have sex ... because then I would have found myself. I used to get there any way I could. I would take a taxi cab. I was in the military and I would get a check twice a month and *all* my money went into taking the cab there and back. The cab was like $50 each way. Shirley's was in Norfolk and I was on the base in Little Creek. The drive there was two hours one way. I was eighteen. What did it feel like when I walked into the bar? It felt like joy ... it was like *opportunity* was finally coming my way.[17]

Without these stories—these experiences and knowledge bases structured out of the dailyness of homosexual lives lived prior to Stonewall and throughout the 1970s and early 80s—any dreams of gay liberation would have been unrealizable.

In order to create a theology people first must find *their home* and then *their potential* in order to articulate anything about that potential. I heard over and over phrases like the above: "I was just looking to connect," "I found myself," "It felt like joy," "like opportunity ... coming my way." We are, after

15. Aptheker, *Tapestries of Life: Women's Work, Women's Consciousness, and the Meaning of Daily Experience*, 26.
16. *Ibid.*, 27.
17. Interview, Rory Devine*.

all, embodied. Whatever else we may or may not become when we leave the embodied home of our actual bodies is conjecture. "The most fundamental fact of human existence is that because people are embodied they are always *somewhere*."[18] If the first step on the journey as an embodied gay being to fulfill one's potential is the gay bar, then that is one's first "somewhere"[19] and then it follows that that step must be honored as part of not just a passage in a historical lineage, but examined for its lessons, in order for any future people of the lineage to realize their own potential.

In order for a space to become home, the second condition of that space is that "we need a place where we can belong to a community."[20] Kathy Rudy writes about "Subjectivity and Belief" in the contested communities of gay places and religion. She notes that secular queer books and conferences never include religious components and "gay and lesbian Christians rarely reach out to include substantial dialogue with non-religious audiences."[21] She feels that bridging this, while it is possible to try to do so, is unlikely to succeed. "Queers inside the church expend much of their energy struggling for recognition within their own denominations, queers outside usually experience the church as an irrecoverable site of oppression."[22] She feels that this is possibly due to racial difference; I agree. She quotes David Roedeiger's studies, which assert that whiteness is "not a culture, but the absence of culture ... the empty and therefore terrifying attempt to build an identity based on what one isn't."[23] Rudy feels that blacks are often able to embrace the divide between belief and non-belief because they share a heritage of being black. She feels that while whiteness dominates queerness in the US, white queers have not embraced spirituality in the same way and with the same necessity as blacks. Although I do not disagree with this statement *per se*, I feel it applies more to upper-class white women's experience, rather than that of the working, or even the middle class. Many of my informants were very connected to their ethnic culture, especially if they were working-class and urban—whether that culture was Irish, Italian, or other deeply felt ethnic identity. Usually that culture was also culturally connected to a religion such as Judaism or Catholicism. Many informants could serve as an example, but Carole S. Damoci-Reed, Italian factory worker, Army officer and butch woman of the 1950s–60s serves well as she was and remains deeply culturally connected and in no way would be able to relate

18. Sheldrake, *Spaces for the Sacred: Place, Memory, and Identity*, 9.
19. In fact, the first gay bar I went to *was called* "Somewhere," in Boston, MA in 1979.
20. Sheldrake, *Spaces for the Sacred: Place, Memory, and Identity*, 10.
21. Kathy Rudy, "Subjectivity and Belief," in *Queer Theology: Rethinking the Western Body*, ed. Gerard Loughlin (Malden, MA: Blackwell, 2007), 37–49.
22. *Ibid.*, 48.
23. David R. Roediger, *Towards the Abolition of Whiteness: Essays on Race, Politics, and Working Class History* (London: Verso, 1994), 13.

to Rudy's definition of "cultural absence" due to skin color.[24] It is this erasure of the difference in class and how class configures identity that is missing in many of the studies that look at *whiteness*. A study such as Rudy's *assumes* upper middle to upper-class white identity, when that represents neither the majority of white experience in the US, nor specifically the experience for the white population I studied—as members of my sample pre-Stonewall were predominantly lower middle-class and or working-class. I find Rudy's comments to be more instructive when she writes, "If we have any hope of addressing the lives of our gay sisters and brothers who have experienced fragmentation at the hands of Christianity, we must begin to reject the privilege associated with whiteness by understanding race and sex struggles (as well as gender and class) as deeply interconnected."[25] The parenthetic uses of "gender and class" are problematic and illustrative of how class is denigrated as not forming a central theme of study.

Mid-century lesbian life studies must consider class *equally* with race. bell hooks argues this when she writes that "class matters." We must begin to look at the matrix of domination as equally weighted in terms of class as well as race and gender, and not prioritize race (or gender) if we are to truly help and understand the underprivileged.[26] The primarily gay women's working-class bar culture will never be understood in all its paradoxes if we don't make a real attempt to understand class. For instance, not one of my informants who identified gay feelings and acted on them prior to Stonewall used the term *lesbian* at the time she came out and very few have ever used that word to describe themselves—unless they entered into lesbian feminism later in the 1970s, which many did not. They felt uncomfortable using that word and for butch women, they often felt disenfranchised from that word. To them it signified not only a sexual identity but a class and political identity to which they often did not have access. As noted, butch women were often asked to leave a feminist-defined space,[27] even if initially they were allowed to enter.[28]

History by necessity is particular. It has already happened. We must find words to describe what happened as accurate historically, but use words that also can be read by the present and future and still maintain historical authenticity. As queers have made more room in the world for ourselves we are not limited to the four walls of the bar. It is tempting to say, as an anonymous source who was initially part of bar culture did say, "I got out,

24. Interview, Carole S. Damoci-Reed.
25. Rudy, "Subjectivity and Belief," 49.
26. hooks, *Where We Stand: Class Matters.*
27. Interview, Falcon River. Falcon was asked to leave a NOW meeting, as were other informants that I spoke with, among them Jeanne Cordova.
28. Interview, Jeanne Cordova.

why didn't they?" in reference to other bar culture gay women.[29] This statement also could be said about those who hold onto religion in the age of queer enlightenment. While it is true that women of the 1950s were deeply affected by being cast as sinners, many contemporary queers feel the way Gerard Loughlin describes in his introduction to *Queer Theology*. "When they (queer Christians) find themselves talked at, but never with—made the subjects of confused and incoherent condemnations—many queer Christians give up on the practices of the church, for who wants to remain in an abusive relationship? But where should they go?"[30]

As has been quoted, the place that gay women went in the mid-twentieth century in the US was the gay bar and it was "the only place," the only place where they were not ensconced in the dominant culture which was for most "an abusive relationship" from which they could not escape, except to the four walls of the bar. However, most women of this generation, who did not have queerness as an option in the wider world, did not find that it was easy to dispatch with religion. In *Boots of Leather, Slippers of Gold*, Davis and Kennedy quote an early 1950s butch informant, who still wore a medal around her neck, getting angry at God because of having to make a choice between God and her sexuality. She said:

> I ripped the medal off my neck and I threw it on the floor and I just thought, "Fuck you God, just fuck you. Just to be who I am, now look what I gotta deal with." My brother and his friends, it would be humiliating for everybody, and it was hard for me to face people. And yet I had to do what I was doing, because I felt it was real for me.[31]

THE SINNER PROBLEM

In 2009 there was much publicity surrounding the Best Actor and Best Original Screenplay Oscars awarded to actor Sean Penn and writer Dustin Lance Black, respectively, for the feature film, *Milk*,[32] about the slain gay rights activist of the 1970s Harvey Milk. In his acceptance speech, Black said,

> Where I'm from in small-town America, they just don't know that there are gay heroes, and they don't know there's other gay people and they don't know there's a potential future, I mean a beautiful future

29. Interview, Anonymous.
30. Gerard Loughlin, *Queer Theology: Re-Thinking the Western Body* (Malden, MA: Blackwell, 2007), 11.
31. Kennedy & Davis, *Boots of Leather, Slippers of Gold: The History of a Lesbian Community*, 356.
32. Gus van Sant (dir.), *Milk* (USA: Focus Features, 2008).

> ... if Harvey had not been taken from us thirty years ago, I think he'd want me to say to all of the gay and lesbian kids out there tonight ... that no matter what anyone tells you, God does love you and that very soon we will have equal rights across this great nation of ours.[33]

In 2009 someone in those small towns across America *might* have turned on the television and heard Black's advice that "God does love you," or even more accepting words. However this is not a given. For instance, Black's acceptance speech was "censored in fifty different Asian nations by pan-Asian satellite TV ... STAR spokeswoman Jannie Poon defended the network's muting of the words *gay* and *lesbian* by stating STAR has 'a responsibility to take the sensitivities and guidelines of all our markets into consideration.'"[34]

In the 1950s, 1960s and geographically in most places into the 1970s, it is unlikely that anyone, even in a gay bar, would say "God loves you."[35] As evidenced in Black's speech the sinner problem is still active for gays, especially those in America's heartlands. It is possible that contemporary gays might hear that it is possible that they might not be sinners,[36] but the exact opposite was true for mid-twentieth-century homosexuals.

To name someone as a sinner is to name them as someone separated by choice from God. When this designation of sinner is made to a people as a whole then that entire group is categorized as without God, a God-less people. In order to understand the mid-century homosexual population, one has to understand the ramifications of being categorized as a *sinner*, rather than *someone who sins*. Stephen Ray explicates this in *Do No Harm: Social Sin and Christian Responsibility*.

---

33. Dustin Lance Black, "The Oscars: Winners," *Los Angeles Times*, February 23, 2009. Black's acceptance speech is quoted in this section, which lists all the winners and acceptance speech quotes.
34. Jared, "Dustin Lance Black's Oscar Acceptance Speech Gets Censored in Asian Broadcasts," justjared.buzznet.com (accessed June 5, 2009).
35. Perry & Lucas, *The Lord Is My Shepherd and He Knows I'm Gay; the Autobiography of the Rev. Troy D. Perry, as Told to Charles L. Lucas*. This would be true until 1968–69, when Troy Perry founded the Metropolitan Community Church in Los Angeles—the first declared minister and church to announce to the gay community that yes, God *did* love them. He confirmed in his interview, and informants also confirmed, that he did "recruit" for his church in bars and was inspired to create his church because of activism he saw in gay bars, particularly that of Lee Glaze and his actions in The Patch.
36. Although Black did not use the word "sinner" in his speech, it was inferred when he made the remark, "no matter what anyone tells you, God does love you." The particular problem that affects homosexuals is that they are isolated by the term sinner and not assumed to be part of the population that "God loves." That Black was allowed to address this on national television in a worldwide telecast was revolutionary in 2009 as was evidenced by the fact that his speech was censored in several countries. This is "the sinner problem" as it affects homosexuals—we are ghetto-ized by the term and not allowed authentic discourse with non-sinners, and therefore left out of the discourse altogether.

> The desolating power of the name *sinner* is one that should be apparent to anyone even vaguely familiar with Christian history. People have been ghettoized, exiled and killed because they have been designated sinners ... Precisely because the church has held such an important place in the development of Western society—and the world by virtue of Western society's global influence—the naming of persons and communities has had the power to legitimate or contest often murderous exclusion. This power has largely been expressed by designating who is a sinner and who is not.[37]

Ray argues for a deep consideration of the harm that the naming of sinner can do—as it can wreak "murderous exclusion." This claim matters to a history of gay and lesbians in many ways, one notable example would be during the height of the AIDS epidemic when gays were told that God was punishing them for their sins by inflicting them with AIDS.[38] Earlier in the mid-twentieth century, America was even more a dominantly Christian country and the ideology *was* that homosexuals were *sinners*, not people *who sin*. Therefore unless homosexuals became something else (that is, straight, which was considered to be the correct path for the homosexual in relation to his or her past), they could not be saved.

From the bar however a gay person might branch out into society within the walls of his or her own individual being as a being without sin. In other words, within the bar it was possible for a homosexual to envision a future where in order to be free of sin she or he did not need to become someone else. She or he could be birthed into acceptance of his or her present self, and this self would have a community. With very few exceptions, the bar was the only place where this process could happen.

AN ALTERNATIVE TO "THE SINNER PROBLEM"

> You've got the look of love
> It's on your face
> A look that time can't erase
> Be mine tonight
> Let this be just the start

---

37. Stephen G. Ray, *Do No Harm: Social Sin and Christian Responsibility* (Minneapolis, MN: Fortress Press, 2003), x.
38. Jakobsen & Pellegrini, *Love the Sin: Sexual Regulation and the Limits of Religious Tolerance*. There are many sources which document the history of the AIDS epidemic (most notably Randy Shilt's work, *And the Band Played On*) and document how religious intolerance fanned the flames of indecent care. Jakobsen and Pellegrini however focus on these issues as well as the logical necessity of loving the sinner if the "sin" is actually *being* homosexual.

Of so many nights like this
Let's take a lover's vow
And then seal it with a kiss[39]

What is the alternative to the sinner problem? The above lines suggest that love can be that alternative, love of self and of the other. How can the effect of sin be mitigated? By finding "god in the self" one can step aside from the designation of sinner when it is unjust—as it almost always is when it designates an entire group of people as Ray suggests.[40]

A majority of the informants used the metaphor "home" to describe how they felt about the gay bar. They described feeling they were "home" being in the gay bar. Falcon said she had never felt home anywhere else and that she went back to the gay bar, despite being taken from there and raped by police. She went because it was *only there* that she found home.[41]

Viktor Frankl wrote in *Man's Search for Meaning* that the Nazis could not take away his "search for meaning." That even in the concentration camps he could still see a sunset against the sky as beautiful—the Nazis could not take that away from him. He postulated a theory of psychology called "logotherapy" that is based on the idea that "man will search for meaning." If meaning is denied them, people will search for meaning until they find meaning in their lives.[42]

The character of Shug seems to suggest the same thing to Celie in Alice Walker's *The Color Purple*—if you can find meaning for your life in yourself, then no matter what someone does to you, you can hold onto that meaning inside of you. For Walker's characters sin was not what we think of traditionally as sin, but sin was not "noticing the color purple." This is reminiscent of Frankl's noticing of the sunset, that in noticing it he was participating in the deep meaning life could have for him, that no one could take away.

> Shug convinces Celie that sex is a Godly act and nothing sinful. Shug continues speaking to Celie about God and her vision of God. She asks Celie what her image of God is, and responds that her own image is not a man or a woman—God is an "it" and wants nothing more than

39. "The Look of Love." From *Casino Royale* (dir. Ken Hughes, USA, 1967). Words by Hal David. Music by Burt Bacharach. © 1967 (Renewed 1995). COLGEMS-EMI Music Inc. All Rights Reserved. International copyright secured. Used by permission. Reprinted by Permission of Hal Leonard Corporation. This song is performed in the film by Dusty Springfield, one of the best-known singers in the UK at the time and a semi-closeted lesbian.
40. Ray, *Do No Harm: Social Sin and Christian Responsibility.*
41. Interview, Falcon River.
42. Viktor E. Frankl, *Man's Search for Meaning: An Introduction to Logotherapy* (Boston, MA: Beacon Press, 1962).

> to be appreciated. Therefore, when she walks by a field and notices the color purple in it, she sees that it is God in the field.[43]

It makes God angry then when we don't notice how a person could make another feel good by running her hand up her lover's leg. Shug explains to Celie that God is *not* an old white man keeping score, but God is all around us, God is us, and if there is sin, it is in *not noticing* the wonder around us, like the color purple.[44]

Mircea Eliade examined the same idea with a religious frame in *The Sacred and Profane*. By studying global cultures, Eliade found that people will create meaning for their lives, and he theorized that this search for meaning was innate (as does Frankl).[45]

The idea that the search for meaning is innate is used so often in contemporary culture that whether or not we can *prove* that the search for meaning is innate, finding meaning in life is essential. We are confronted with various versions of this idea in conversation, and media throughout our daily lives. Our expectations *are that* our lives will have meaning, that they will make sense to us.[46]

In a book review of a biography of the writer Flannery O'Connor, *Flannery*, the reporter writes that Flannery read a lot of theology and suggested that she needed it to help her life have meaning. Flannery said, "It makes my writing bolder." And the reporter added, "she was aware that faith has limits, that everything is up for grabs. And yet ... what else is there? How else do we make sense of who we are?"[47]

HISTORICAL GAP: SPIRITUAL LANGUAGE TODAY *À LA* THE NEW AGE

> God has no religion.[48]

For the gay women's population of the mid-twentieth century, the current language of spirituality, as opposed to the past language of religiosity, does give us a discourse that supports that there was something spiritual, even perhaps religious, going on in the gay women's bar.

43. BookRags, "The Color Purple: Book Notes Summary," http://www.bookrags.com/The_Color_Purple (accessed April 3, 2009).
44. Alice Walker, *The Color Purple: A Novel* (New York: Harcourt Brace Jovanovich, 1982), 73.
45. Eliade, *The Sacred and the Profane: The Nature of Religion*.
46. We in effect have a working Miranda Contract with this idea. Psychology often makes use of the idea, as Frankl does, that our lives must have "meaning."
47. David L. Ulin, "An Alluring Elusiveness," *The Los Angeles Times*, February 15, 2009.
48. Henry Whitney Bellows, *Re-statements of Christian Doctrine: In Twenty-five Sermons* (Cambridge, MA: Press of John Wilson and Son, 1867), 149.

What does it mean to say, "God has no religion?" A long-term study conducted out of UCLA that examined and quantified spirituality and civic engagement based on praxis and a belief set practiced by incoming freshmen suggested answers, as the study was done without necessarily having those beliefs connect to an identified religion. The head of this national study, Dr Lena Astin spoke with me in regards to this study and its connections to my own.[49] The idea that people can have spiritual values and act in service of those, without being connected to a religion *per se*, is an idea that gained currency with the coming of the New Age. The fact that now we (as supported by the findings of Dr Astin's study) can postulate that incoming freshman have spiritual values, without necessarily an identified religious connection, is possible because of the influence of the 1970s—we can have *God* without the rules set forth by a religion. However, when it comes to seeing homosexuals through this lens, this New Age-esque ability to recognize spiritual values of love and community is clouded—sometimes even by homosexuals themselves.[50]

The conflation of homosexual with sinner is historical and has been long lasting. Consider the headline story for New Year's Eve, 2009, which was titled the "The Year in Religion" and "The Battle over Gays." It was one of the *top three religious happenings* of 2009 that was notable. However the "battle over gays" had little to do with religion—except that gays wanted to enter into what is traditionally seen as religious territory, marriage, from which they have been historically excluded. Marriage confers 1,138 civil rights,[51] none of which are marked as supervised by religious institutions, but rather all governed by the state—but the fact that *gays* wanted to participate in a civil rights granting institution such as marriage, which is often (not always) performed in a church meant that one of the top three religious stories for 2009 was "the battle over gays."

> Religious beliefs influenced voters who approved bans on gay marriage in California, Arizona and Florida. Californians overturned an earlier Supreme Court decision legalizing same-sex marriage with a constitutional amendment, Proposition 8, which was supported by white evangelicals, Mormons and socially conservative blacks and Hispanics.[52]

---

49. Arthur Chickering, "Strengthening Spirituality and Civic Engagement in Higher Education." *Journal of College and Character* VIII(1) (2006): 1–5. This article summarizes the statistics found in the Astin study.
50. In fact, Dr Astin did not ask the sexual preference of her survey takers. The restriction was put in place by the Institutional Research Board at UCLA, who determined she could not ask the sexual preference of incoming freshmen; however she was allowed to ask their *feelings* on gay rights issues.
51. Equality Marriage, "Get the Facts: Why Marriage," www.marriageequality.org (accessed may 23, 2009).
52. Cathy Lynn Grossman, "Year in Religion: Political Plays, Papal Visit and Battle over Gays," *USA Today*, December 31, 2008. As of 2013, gays are still denied marriage rights in

During the mid-twentieth century, this view of religion was the only view there was. Religion was connected to a God that was owned by major religions, and whatever spirituality was available,[53] was available only to those who had a place in the major religions. A sense of God and the deep meaning in the world that a sense of God inspires was solely maintained and mainlined through major religions. It was of course available other places—but was not so named, nor was the language available for it to be so named outside of major religions. That is what can be corrected for the mid-century gay women's/butch-femme bar culture her/history by examining its unique friendship praxis as having religious connotations for its inhabitants.

Today's discourse supports that *spirituality* can be something separate from *religion* or at the very least does not need to be connected to a major religion. This idea is available in the general epistemological framework of most Americans. Books with titles like *When God is Gone, Everything is Holy*[54] are not unusual and are displayed at the annual meetings of major guilds in the academic study of religion. In earlier decades this material might have been found in only small specialty shops in the 1970s New Age Movement. Other examples include the book by Ram Dass that appeared in 1978, *Be Here Now, Remember*, with its title printed in a circular pattern on the front cover, which was deemed a manual for the new hippie youth movement.[55] Today this type of book is classified along with religious material, and might be shelved there at an urban bookstore. Spirituality, while not the new religious law, as witnessed by the above newspaper article, is certainly in common use.[56] During the mid-twentieth century, this was not the case. Mircea Eliade's 1958 *Yoga: Immortality and Freedom* was one of

---

Arizona and Florida, however gays can marry in the following US states: Massachusetts, Connecticut, Iowa, Vermont, Washington, DC, New Hampshire, New York, Washington (state), California, Delaware, Minnesota, Rhode Island, and Maryland.

53. As a Catholic youth I can testify to the fact that during this period it seemed that there was a sense of mystery/magic in the world available in major religions, at least in traditional Catholicism.

54. Chet Raymo, *When God Is Gone Everything Is Holy: The Making of a Religious Naturalist* (Notre Dame, IN: Sorin Books, 2008).

55. Ram Dass & Hanuman Foundation, *Be Here Now, Remember* (New York: Hanuman Foundation:, 1978). Originally published in 1971.

56. For a deeply religious New England small town where we were sharply divided between who had gone to Catholic school and who were Protestants, the idea that spiritual life (a key word for finding this text today) could be found outside of a Church—in a book that referenced "be here now" as opposed to worrying about heaven—was revelatory. Most of us were experimenting with the idea that you could live outside of traditional families—as hippies. We were ripe for the idea to *remember* and "be here now." This book passed among us as we sat in tight circles on the football field of my New Hampshire high school. That there was a manual for a sacred life that was *not* derived from the Bible was radically new, not something our parents were passing on, and was deemed something secret. The saying of that time, "Don't trust anyone over 30," meant we were not just in, but felt we *were*, the "New Age."

the first books to identify spirituality as something that could be separated from religion and, therefore, from the world's religions. Indeed someone not connected to the major world religions could attain spirituality through a praxis—for instance yoga.[57] Eliade's book, subtitled "Immortality and Freedom," found that spirituality and "freedom" could be found through the ancient, and exotic to Americans, practice of yoga. In 1959, Eliade published *The Sacred and the Profane: The Nature of Religion*[58] and examined "the nature of religion," providing groundbreaking ideas for the burgeoning religious studies humanities programs in the US.[59]

In *The Sacred and the Profane* he described traditional and modern experience. Traditional humanity is open to the world as sacred. Modern humanity is shut down to this. The sacred is available when it appears different from the profane—and Eliade calls this appearance a "hierophany." Modern humanity experiences all space as the same. But the religious person sees space as qualitatively different, as sacred, and therefore meaningful. Traditional people have trouble living in the profane world, because they cannot find balance. "A revelation of the sacred, a hierophany, establishes a center and that center establishes a world because all other space derives its meaning from the center."[60]

One member of a website discussing Eliade's work suggests that, "The world contains two kinds of people: those who have read Mircea Eliade, and those who should do so as soon as possible."[61] This type of book that was considered radical in its day, and still today as evidenced by this quote, suggested that "modern man," the human of the 1950s, had lost touch with the sacred. Modern humanity needed to get in touch with "his" traditionally religious or primal roots in order to discover what was sacred about his

57. Eliade, *Yoga: Immortality and Freedom*.
58. Eliade, *The Sacred and the Profane: The Nature of Religion*.
59. An editorial review of *The Sacred and the Profane* (amazon.com) describes Eliade as "a leading interpreter of religious experience ... his theory that *hierophanies* form the basis of religion, splitting the human experience of reality into sacred and profane space and time, has proven influential ... his theory of *Eternal Return*, which holds that myths and rituals do not simply commemorate hierophanies, but, at least to the minds of the religious, actually participate in them ... has become one of the most widely accepted ways of understanding the purpose of myth and ritual." See http://www.amazon.com/The-Sacred-Profane-Nature-Religion/dp/015679201X (accessed July 15, 2013).
60. Denis Abellio, "The Traditional and the Modern; Review: *The Sacred and the Profane: The Nature of Religion*," amazon.com member reviews, May 27, 2002, http://www.amazon.com/The-Sacred-Profane-Nature-Religion/dp/015679201X (accessed July 15, 2013).
61. Lawrence Wilcox, "Lost Worlds of the Sacred; Review: *The Sacred and the Profane: The Nature of Religion*," amazon.com member reviews, http://www.amazon.com/The-Sacred-Profane-Nature-Religion/product-reviews/015679201X/ref=cm_cr_pr_btm_link_2?ie=UTF8&pageNumber=2&showViewpoints=0&sortBy=bySubmissionDateDescending (accessed October 24, 2008).

religious life.[62] This book, as opposed to the later *Be Here Now,* was a critique of modernity and its dis-associative effect on all people, rather than a celebration of a culture that had embraced the "New Age."

If today we can talk about God being gone, and still "everything is holy," we have entered a world with an epistemological discourse that lends itself to Jennifer Terry's deviant historiography[63] regarding the sacred and those historical populations cast as deviant. Today's language of spirituality, as opposed to the language prior to the New Age, can be transcendent and illuminative, rather than alienating and exclusive.

NOT "QUEER THEOLOGY," JUST "QUEER"

> We are all in the gutter, but some of us are looking at the stars.[64]

For the pre-Stonewall period for queer people there is no reality/authenticity to the term *queer theology*. Theos—or God, for which logos—or word, could be spoken, had been colonized by the dominant heterosexual Christian community, and was barred from entering the gay bar. Many of us who came out in later decades would literally circle the neighborhoods of urban America trying to find the address someone had scribbled down. In the late 1970s a lover and I did this, finally finding the famous New York City club *The Duchess* with its three-by-five name plate on the building and its small shuttered window opening which only allowed a pair of eyes to peer out at us before we were let in. However, unlike us, God supposedly did not have the address of the gay bar pre-Stonewall. The official God was grounded, owned by the dominant Christian population.

Anna Totta, formerly Sister Peter Marie (of the Sisters of Charity of Leavenworth, Kansas), entered the convent in the 1950s because she wanted to be in a women's community. She exited the convent in the 1990s after a struggle with her emerging lesbian identity. She compared Myrna's story about calling the bars late at night with a person "in prison":

> She was a prisoner in her own home. She could hear the sounds of freedom—just like the Jews in the ghettos and concentration camps could hear the planes overhead of the allies. It gave them hope. That's

62. I use the words humanity and his/her. However, Eliade used "man." Using "man" to refer to all of humanity was *not* only standard English but also somewhat correct—as it did address the people who were allowed to actively participate in the dialogues.
63. Terry, "Theorizing Deviant Historiography: Feminist Theoretical Lineages of Deviant Historiography: A Retrospective Preface."
64. Oscar Wilde, *Lady Windermere's Fan* (New York: Penguin, [1893] 1993), Act III, Lord Darlington.

> what Jesus said—"I came to bring you life." The sound of the gay bars was that sound of life—as she said, "a lifeline."[65]

"Theology doesn't happen and then never changes," said informant Totta and then went on to say that there are very few precepts in the Catholic Church that are *ex-cathedra*, literally "from the chair" of the Pope and infallible. There is a great difference between what the Church teaches and what is actually *ex-cathedra* doctrine:

> If gays and lesbians are in mortal sin, then so also is any couple practicing birth control, anyone divorced—all these people are in mortal sin ... as well as gays and lesbians. The birth rate is the second lowest in the western world in Italy—which is the seat of the Catholic Church, Rome. That is a country that is predominantly—I think 90%—or more Catholic. Are all those people in mortal sin, because they are using birth control—if you look at the statistics? Theology and what the Church teaches, and how it regards things, *changes*.[66]

For pre-Stonewall women with regard to theology as a process/being in process we must consider the demographics of these women. Not one of the pre-Stonewall women I interviewed was *born and identified in childhood* as atheist or agnostic. Not one identified as spiritual—what we today call someone who claims her own spirituality, *à la* New Age, as separate from her childhood religion.[67] They all came from a religious background and could use that as an identifier, as well as other markers, among them the city in which they were born and the age they were at the time of the interview. These were and are markers of identity for them, as they are for many of us. And they change. It is not so easy to identify people according to religion at birth today.[68] For the population that was born in the 1970s and onward, "spirituality" or "no religious affiliation" could be an option for an identity marker as opposed to an organized religious identity. But this was not true for those over fifty years of age—as witnessed by my informants.

Almost all women interviewed believed in God or knew of and were intimately connected with a religion that held a central belief in a deity or supernatural being, both at the time of their interviews, and at the time they were in the gay bars.[69] Although their religions had rejected them, that does

65. Interview, Anna Totta.
66. *Ibid.*
67. To my knowledge. See Appendix A for a list of informants' religions at birth and if those changed significantly during their lives (up to the time of their interviews). Note *pre*-Stonewall population statistics.
68. Again, to my knowledge. See Appendix A for a list of informants' religions at birth and whether these changed significantly during their lives (up to the time of their interviews). Note the *post*-Stonewall population statistics.
69. Again, see Appendix A.

not mean that they had rejected their religions (although many of them did), that they rejected God, or that they accepted or rejected the religious definitions provided by their various faiths that *all* classified them as sinners. What is certain is that they lived at a time and place in history where being gay was considered to be a sin by almost all of the population who were bolstered in that belief by secular authority as well as the higher authority of their religion and its religious authorities. They came into the gay bar from a religious identity that had rejected them. It is not that they did not have a religious identity; rather the religious identity that *all* of them had been born into (with the possible exception of Christian Science)[70] had categorically rejected them. Because of their religious traditions, and because they were gay, they were considered sinners, as well as mentally ill and criminal and thus officially classified as *undesirable* by the society at large.[71]

When R.C. went to register "for weekly envelopes for the Offering" and to be part of the registered Parish when she moved from Hollywood to the Valley in the early 1970s, the priest looked at her and the way she was dressed (pants and white shirt) and said, "Are you a lesbian?" To which she, taken aback, said, "Yes." "He pushed his chair back about six feet and stood on the opposite side of the room from me and said, 'The Catholic Church does not want your kind here.' I stood up and said, 'Father, I didn't know the Church felt that way.' And I left. I didn't return to the Church for twenty-seven years."[72] However, she did continue to "pray" and lead a spiritual life. It was just that, "I didn't go to Church until recently," when she and her partner met informant Father Joe and went to a Parish with an outreach to gay and lesbian people, an official Catholic ministry since 1982.

The women who entered the bar were not necessarily without religion. They all *came from* religions that had *kicked them out* by signaling they were sinners. What they *all* knew about each other was that *no gay woman in that bar was accepted by any religion* during the period of this study pre-Stonewall.[73] They didn't need another supernatural deity. They had a

70. Interview, Rae Hamilton. Of all the women I interviewed pre-1970 only Rae, who was born Christian Scientist, did not feel she was a sinner as defined by her faith by virtue of her homosexuality. Of course many women did not believe their faith's definition of them as sinner, but their faiths still held that view. Rae, however, felt that her faith believed that all are born as "God's perfect children." Since she believed she was born gay, then being gay could not be a sin, since she was born as a perfect child of God. She did not tell her parents she was gay, however, due to societal pressure and the shame of being gay in secular life. Yet she never accepted that her personal religion had turned its back on her because of her faith in the tenets that she espoused as a Christian Scientist.
71. Interview, Judy Grahn. This definition of a homosexual as "undesirable" was actually used as the rationale, and so recorded on the forms, for dismissing gays and lesbians from the military in the 1960s. It was the reason given for Grahn's, and others, military discharge—because she was classified as undesirable, i.e., lesbian.
72. Interview, R.C.
73. With few exceptions—as has been noted, the possible exception was Christian Science.

God—or knew of a God—the God they were born with. What they needed was *a space* that *allowed God* to speak to homosexuals as if they, too, were allowed to sit at the proverbial table. What they needed was the ability to practice *faith through works*.

But how can we speak of faith through works when we are speaking of bar denizens such as drug addicts? alcoholics? pimps? and so on? Totta is succinct, "Jesus said 'Whatever you do to the least of me, you do unto me.' Were there assholes in the bar? Of course. And there are assholes in Church, too."[74]

UTILIZING KAUFMAN'S CLASSIC ORDER AND CONSTRUCTING THEELOGY

First order: what was sacred—then: who was "God"?

Gordon Kaufman wrote, "No theologian will develop a concept of the world completely without regard to the fact that he or she intends to develop a concept of God in relation to that concept of world."[75] He continues saying that, of course, once a concept of God has been furnished then the theologian "will ultimately have to furnish a theological interpretation of that same world."[76] For bar culture women however, the "concept of God in relation" to their concept of the world was only conceived in all discourses surrounding them as sinner to judge. What was furnished for them as "a theological interpretation of that world" was that the discourse (or logos) that would allow them to argue with God regarding the idea that they were unrepentant sinners was blocked because they *were* unrepentant sinners according to the dominant culture—they were and would remain homosexuals. It was a circular and closed argument. In order to communicate with God they could not be unrepentant sinners, that is, no longer be homosexuals. The extreme conditions, in which homosexuals lived in the mid-twentieth century were such that to be in relation with anyone *as themselves—as homosexuals—much less with God* was limited, for most women, to the gay women's bar culture. Literally they had to enter the space of the bar, make of it a place where they could be in relation with themselves, and with someone else, and from there possibly engage in human relations where they were known and not immediately cast as sinners or mentally ill, or criminals. Kaufman advocates "increasing self-conscious employment of methods of imaginative

74. Interview, Anna Totta. This is not to imply that alcoholics and drug addicts, pimps, etc. were "assholes" necessarily. Totta here is making the point that people without good intentions—all kinds of people—exist everywhere, and some inhabited the gay bars, and also inhabit/inhabited churches.
75. Gordon D. Kaufman, *An Essay on Theological Method*, 3rd edn, AAR Reflection and Theory in the Study of Religion (Atlanta, GA: Scholars Press, [1975] 1995).
76. *Ibid.*, 78.

construction," and believes this will "widen the ongoing conversation ... to the full range of issues and problems with which our pluralized world confronts us."[77] He encourages looking at the gay and lesbian population as a population that needs to have a seat at the table of theological discourse.[78] This type of theological consideration was not given during the mid-twentieth century. I believe we must use Kaufman's suggestions and *self-consciously* employ new methods to re-frame the contemporary gaze on this historical community and its activities.

Kaufman discusses three orders in theological method. The first order regards raw experience. "First, there is the raw experience of the individual as the foundation of all speaking, thinking and acting."[79] Because the raw experience of bar culture women was not taken into the imaginative constructions of their day, and in large part also today, I have used ethnographic experience as the starting point in constructing a theology called "theelogy" useful for this culture and historical period.

Second order: what was done about the sacred—then: what was "thee"logy?

Kaufman's second order moves from raw experience to reflection upon experience. "Second, the individual reflects upon or thinks about this experience."[80] I constructed "theelogy" to describe the bar culture women's experience. Its genesis comes from my training in liberation theology and process thought/theology. The experience of these women, and their praxis—although unarticulated as religious language—was in fact process thought in action: they were in relation to, and with, the praxis of liberation. Theological discourse as it stood did not fit the experience of the bar culture women; nonetheless, it helps us to see the possibilities of religiosity in bar culture community.

A new word or house is needed to articulate what these women were doing for each other. I call this new word *theelogy*, in honor of the concept of friendship, and friendship's ability to see the humanity, or the sacred, in each other and in our shared community members. Since there was no authoritarian intermediary for these interactions, the authority to name the sacred, that is, humanity in each other, rested with the bar patrons themselves. In the period between 1945 and 1975 when homosexuals were kicked out of all major religions and deemed sinners because of their self-identification as homosexual, the communities in the bars were the only places where most

77. *Ibid.*, xv.
78. *Ibid.* In this revised volume, Kaufman mentions gays and lesbians throughout, but particularly in the last section.
79. *Ibid.*, 6.
80. *Ibid.*

women experienced this sense of shared humanity. Theelogy was practiced by all women in all religions who entered the bar with the hope of salvation, baptism as *friend,* even though they were homosexual. Therefore, theelogy was practiced by Christians, Jews, and other religious practitioners, or non-religious practitioners. Although theelogy was unnamed as such at the time, it was the only *religion* this population was able to practice during this historical time period in which they did not first, just by virtue of their being, have to identify themselves as sinners. In the lived praxis of *theelogy* they were first able to identify *as gay women* and then also as friends, as community members and as lovers.

Third order: what can we say to others about this sacred—then: could pre-Stonewall women say it? No.

Kaufman's third order is the last of his points of order. While I am not, *per se,* doing third order theology (nor were these women) it is important to examine the construction in its entirety within the three orders. Kaufman's order moves from personal reflection to shared communication with others. He writes that the third step is when, "he or she may finally choose to communicate that experience and reflection to other persons through language, participate in a ritual, or take up a role in an institution."[81] He is very clear that without the language to describe our experience we will be limited in its description by what we can say about it. Therefore, if one does not have access to religious language, one will not be able to name personal experience as religious.

> The language in which we think, the traditions we have inherited, articulate certain connections between concepts and certain relations between words and ideas; it is in terms of these connections and valuations and interpretations that we focus our attention in experience, divide it up the way we do, and see in it what we can. It is, thus, the availability of our language of words like "infinite," "holy," and "God," that gives our experience in its religious aspects its peculiar quality and shape.
>
> It would be truer to say that the language we speak provides a principal foundation for our religious language than to hold that some preconceptual, pre-linguistic raw experience is the principal foundation of our theological language and thought.[82]

Mid-century bar culture gay women did not speak the language of religiosity because they had been branded by all of the major religions as sinners.

81. *Ibid.*
82. *Ibid.*, 7–8.

Thus they would not have named their experiences in the bars as "religious" experience. Hence theelogy, through the methodology of deviant historiography used in creating religious discourse as history, employs ethnographic method and process/liberation modalities to create a framework *for today's populations* to view the populations of the past as religious. However, even here, in order to create an adequate language for the population's lives to be re-framed authentically I must abandon the terms "theology" and even "thealogy"[83] and the concept of an overarching big "G" God and instead focus on "thee," the small "g" god. Hence, the language created names the *experience* of these women authentically, employing their lived experience of community as sacred.

Kaufman writes, "Only if one is aware of certain important values which 'God-talk' can provide, and certain serious dangers against which it can help protect, will one feel impelled to move beyond anthropology and cosmology to theology."[84] This is compelling when one considers how "God-talk" has been used against gays and lesbians. For instance, when remembering Fred Phelps and his group holding "God hates Fags" signs across from Matthew Shepard's 1998 funeral,[85] one realizes not only the harm that God-talk can do, but the *agency* that the belief in "God-talk" can inspire folks to act with—for either good or evil. I move therefore into and then beyond a social constructionist reading of religiosity regarding butch-femme bar culture and into theology in order to take hold of "God-talk" and have used it in service of this population, and to give the population itself the tools to help protect their members. Queer people, especially pre-Stonewall people, were disenfranchised from religion and "God-talk." Theelogy attempts to rectify that, even if in the historical record.

THE CONCEPTS AND REALITIES OF SPACE AND PLACE

Ordinarily sacred—space and place

The *ordinarily sacred* in space and place was noted earlier, as was the idea that place defines an individual because one takes up space in that place. It

83. Christ, *Rebirth of the Goddess: Finding Meaning in Feminist Spirituality*. There are several goddess spirituality scholars who use this term; Christ is considered the first to position it within a full text and flesh out the concept of a *thea*logy.
84. Kaufman, *An Essay on Theological Method*, 60.
85. Matthew Shepard's funeral, Friday, October 16, 1998, found a new controversy. Rev. Fred Phelps of the Westboro Baptist Church (Topeka, Kansas) started organizing a protest over Shepard's funeral. In his fax announcing this, he urged people to arrive with signs containing messages such as *NO TEARS FOR QUEERS*, *FAG MATT IN HELL*, and *GOD HATES FAGS*. Phelps also started a website with the domain name of www.godhatesfags.com. See Southern Poverty Law Center, 2013, "Fred Phelps," http://www.splcenter.org/get-informed/intelligence-files/profiles/fred-phelps (accessed September 27, 2013).

is repeated here to underscore what place should give for it to be considered transformative. In order for space to become place, then space must become *a* place in which one feels the things that *place* should give a person by definition: community, affirmation of the sacredness of a people, and human capacity for transcendence. These three transformative things, for pre-Stonewall women, were often provided by the *space transformed to place* of the gay women's bar.

If the gay bar was the only place where they could feel these things, then for them we must consider this place *was* sacred, whether or not it is so named sacred by all of those who utilized it. It is a given that the gay bar was *the only space* where *a place* was established for gay community. Within the four walls of the gay bar was the only secure space where gay women could know for sure that they had encountered other gay women. They created and maintained the only place where they could meet someone else like themselves. This latter statement affirms the sacredness of the people within the walls. Why? There was no other place where gay people could even be acknowledged.

THE EMBODIED BODY—FROM SPACE TO PLACE

In terms of process thought, *the past,* for most pre-Stonewall homosexuals in dominant culture, held the relation of sinner space and the shame of inhabiting such space. Theories of space and place imply that the body, the actual physical body of pre-Stonewall homosexuals, had to become *space* before they could inhabit bar culture and make community there—and then a *place* after inhabiting bar culture and creating community. Remembering that the body is a space first, and a space that many take for granted as their own, we begin to see how the bar functioned as transformative. We cannot transform space into place unless we begin with space helping to shape our personal identity and then community. In the final stage of transformative place, the place that we inhabit helps us, the community gathered within it, to go forth and make history with our lives.

When women of this generation say that the bar was "the only place" for them, they are saying that the bar was the only place that could serve the function that space transformed into place serves for others, the dominant culture, and that *in* the dominant culture they did *not* experience inhabitation of space/body that helped others to create personal identity. The gay bar then, for most of these women (and men), *did* provide that place where they might actually experience this first stage of inhabitation of space—that of creating personal identity, in which they might identify the actual Self.

10. WHAT IS *THEELOGY*?

GOD?

> It is in this century misunderstood, so much misunderstood that it may be described as the "Love that dare not speak its name," and on account of it I am placed where I am now.[1]

Ginny's story, highlighted earlier, illustrates the love that dared not speak its name. Both her and her partner were teachers and were friends with another female couple, with whom they often had drinks, however they did not discuss that they were all gay. "That was just the just the way it was back then. We never talked about that."[2]

> Butch-femme women made lesbians visible in a terrifyingly clear way in a historical period when there was no Movement protection for them. Their appearance spoke of erotic independence, and they often provoked rage and censure both from their own community and straight society.[3]

The only sacred accessible to the bar culture women was the possible self that might, despite the odds, be able to identify herself as sacred, for she was inhabiting the place where such a self could be seen. If the self, *her self*, could do this, she might then be able to see that type of self in someone else. The gay women's bar then was perhaps a God-less place but not necessarily a god-less place.

1. Oscar Wilde, "Testimony of Oscar Wilde," http://www.law.umkc.edu/faculty/projects/ftrials/wilde/Crimwilde.html (accessed April 17, 2010). Oscar Wilde spoke this famous line to the court when he was on trial for homosexuality in 1895. The quoted line is from a poem by Wilde's lover, Lord Alfred Douglas, "Two Loves," published in *The Chameleon*, December 1894.
2. Interview, Virginia "Ginny" Borders.
3. Nestle, *A Restricted Country*, 108.

Theelogy then is the discourse of the sacred that was created in the gay women's pre-Stonewall bar culture rather than theology because it is only in retrospect (through the methodology of deviant historiography) that we can assume that there *was* a "God" greater than the self inhabiting the world of the bar. In the world of the pre-Stonewall gay women's bar, a woman was first so isolated she did not know herself; if lucky, she came to know herself as herself and then in community with others like her, and she could help someone else make this trajectory. The idea of these women creating a "God" in the bar is not probable. What happened is that they created friendship and in the rarified air of the bar, that was sacred enough. It was sacred enough to get arrested for, to get raped for, and to fight for. But it was not larger than the self, *per se*, because these women were stretching to encompass a definition of self first. As the authors of *The Feminine Face of God* attest, often women who have been divorced from the ability to create discourse of the sacred must first find their actual selves, before they can find and articulate theories of "God."[4] First a woman must find herself. Only then can another discourse, that of "God-talk," be created. Women must first go to the proverbial mountaintop and find the inner self which is so often denied them. For bar culture women then, I believe the gay women's bar was that proverbial mountaintop—the place where they began the search that would lead to self-definition. This search I call theelogy.

When Marcella Althaus-Reid chose merely to put a picture of the statue of Jesus with the sacred heart blazing as the provocative cover on her 2003 text *The Queer God*, one understands how radical the idea and visualization of God as a God *for* queer people is, or the notion of God *as* a "queer God."[5] Coleman writes that the Savior can be a black woman or a lesbian—God can be different from what the dominant culture imagines.[6] However it is important to add that this postmodern imagination is postmodern and can only operate *today*, and it is dangerous to place any ahistorical rendering of this theological interpretation on historical cultures. Deviant historiography maintains that we must carefully consider the historical realities of a people while we re-frame the way we *gaze* at them from a contemporary position. God in the postmodern world can only be discussed, as Althaus-Reid does brilliantly in her introductory essay where she specifically discusses theology, in "other contexts" as in gay bars and their connection to a "Queer God."

That "Queer God"/accepting God was not, however, to be found in the 1950s gay bars, except as a gay person might be able to see god in the other, the *you*. In this period it truly was, as ntozake shange notes, a question of

4. Anderson & Hopkins, *The Feminine Face of God: The Unfolding of the Sacred in Women.*
5. Marcella Althaus-Reid, *The Queer God* (London: Routledge, 2003), 1.
6. Coleman, *Making a Way Out of No Way: A Womanist Theology.*

finding "god in myself"[7] and "loving her." The gay people of this period began to see god in each other and more importantly, by being in community with each other, they were able to find god in themselves.

Theelogy is relational by its very definition.[8] Theelogy was practiced by all women in all religions who entered the bar with the hope of salvation, being baptized as *friend* even though they were homosexual. Therefore, theelogy was practiced by exiled Christians, Jews, and other religious practitioners, as well as non-religious practitioners. Thus *theelogy* could baptize one into true friendship.[9]

Theelogy is a non-hierarchal religion that witnesses the presence of God without an intermediary and sees God in each other. It is the religion of community. This connects to the theological framework espoused by McFague in *Metaphorical Theology,* articulated earlier, where she proposes the model for religious language of "God as friend," as opposed to God as "father."[10]

Theelogy defines its conditions for membership first as being part of the historical mid-twentieth-century gay female population. These women, having been cast out *of church*, went to find meaning in some other space, creating *a place* for themselves in the gay women's bars. A woman had to find herself *first*, and be *baptized* into her definition of self, outside of traditional religious structures. Therefore the creation of the religious community in the bars was necessary as the bar was "the only place" where a gay woman could identify herself as herself, a gay woman, in community with other gay women. Thus, the gay women's mid-twentieth century bar can be seen through this re-framed gaze as a possible *religious community*. Theelogy was trans-religious, so we cannot say that the bar was a church *per se* anymore than a temple, but the structure of the bar did provide in essence that house of worship for this religious community, in the same way that such structures provide physical spaces for communities of faith to gather.

It is because I believe, as a theologian and a historian, that there are certain important values that "God-talk" can provide in terms of looking at this particular culture, that I invested this ethnographic, historical project with theological language. However, taking into account the ethnographic lessons provided by examining this culture has necessitated the move from theology to the move of creating and advocating the use of theelogy. Theelogy is the discursive *place* where the important values of small "g" "god-talk" can

7. shange, *For Colored Girls who have Committed Suicide, When the Rainbow is Enuf: A Choreopoem*.
8. Whether or not a claim can be made that theelogy *is* theistic is arguable, but beyond the scope of this project.
9. This does not mean that the women themselves practiced third order theology in terms of advocating others to believe as they believed. It means that I, *here,* am advocating, through *naming* their practice as theelogy, that we today can view this historical population and its practices differently.
10. McFague, *Metaphorical Theology: Models of God in Religious Language*, 177–92.

be provided as we re-frame the gaze on mid-twentieth-century gay women's bar culture, and move away from the very serious dangers[11] that traditional theology has created in past discussions.

Mid-twentieth-century gays and lesbians in the US made sense of who they were by inventing and living an unnamed theology that I name theelogy. Theelogy is not just the ability to see God in the other, the "you" in "Baby, *you* are my religion." It is also the ability to place you, the self, as the viewer who will make that statement, and who will choose to be in community with others where that kind of statement can be spoken. Faith in everything, not just God, does have limits—but what else is there? For mid-twentieth-century gay women there was the gay women's bar. For many, that was *all* there was, for that was the *only* place there was.

Theelogy then *is* the reflection on the god that is the beloved—it is the "you" in "Baby, *you* are my religion." The community inhabiting the bar culture—from the people who looked into Beverly's eyes, the upper class librarian who never felt seen except in the bar; to the voices Myrna heard, as she listened to the voices in the bar from her end of the phone in the heterosexual marriage that she could not leave without losing her children; to Falcon's bar community, a community that allowed women to feel "home" where they had never felt home anywhere else—all of these reflected a possible "god" back to these people. To all of these women and more, that "you" saw them as something *other than* sinner/pervert/criminally insane/felon. That these people might see someone like themselves, that "you," as something other than the dominant definition of the discarded "you" who they were *supposed* to be, for all of these, the bar was the location that sparked the birth of a part of themselves that until that point was unknown even to themselves.[12] In other words, the bar provided the miraculous option of being a space in which women might be able to create a place where they could be something other than what society ordinarily deemed them to be—worthless.

In "theelogy" it is acknowledged that since this theelogical/theological discourse is written as originating from an analysis of the mid-twentieth-century gay women's bar population, there is no big "G" God to which one can be connected. Any connection with God was probably severed in order for the gay woman to enter and participate in the gay culture in the first place. Of course there may have been the unusual woman who knew God to be an all-loving being who still loved her no matter what.[13] My research,

11. Ray, *Do No Harm: Social Sin and Christian Responsibility.*
12. Judith Butler, *Undoing Gender* (New York: Routledge, 2004), 132. In queer studies terms, this is reminiscent of Butler's writing on the gaze—the subjectivity and *possible* transformative nature of the gaze.
13. Interview, Rae Hamilton. For instance, Rae, who was brought up Christian Scientist, was brought up to believe that God loved her no matter what.

however, has revealed that most women felt their lives must lean towards the secular if they were to be gay. Even if they maintained cultural ties with their religion, as did Joan Nestle who always identified strongly as Jewish culturally, most responded as she did to the question of whether her cultural association with Jewishness implied that therefore she was religious. She said that definitely she was not. She told me, "I am nothing if not profane."[14]

Theelogy, then, is that *search for god*, that *finding of god*, and whether or not named, that ability to *see and call the "you" beloved*, whether in lust or love. This kind of naming, so foreign outside of the gay bar, began the search for something named and sacred, something akin to Buber's *I–Thou*.

It is only through a postmodern theorizing, such as the lens provided by deviant historiography, that we can theorize a theelogy that operated to sacralize the community. Defining this way *of relating* as theelogy suggests that this community saw God/god in each other and were able, and we today are able, to name the "you" in "Baby, *you*" as "religion."

What many bar culture women were practicing was *theelogy*, or love of *other*, even love of *otherness* or the queer, as much as was possible.[15] My thesis is that bar culture gay women lived theelogy within a public setting. It does not, however, follow that theelogy has been practiced solely by this culture. Theelogy, as I name it here, is the first theelogical/theological discourse that we articulate as beings searching for meaning in our lives. This is in line with the theories explicated earlier by Frankl.[16] We must find meaning in our lives. If the context for meaning is taken from us, we will find and create another context for deep meaning.

If women were barred, from discourse with a transcendent God but wished still to live a sacred life or a life with deep meaning, the choice for the mid-twentieth-century homosexual in the dominant culture was to *become* someone else, as opposed to *do* something else. This *something else* meant she would not answer the call of God within her to be her Self. She would not answer the call to be in relation. Process thinkers believe all of creation is in relation. The dominant culture chose to identify all homosexuals as people who could not be in relation without doing damage—and had to become someone else. This someone else would be someone who fit the dominant culture's definition *and* carried a past identity, that of reformed sinner. This was required for the pre-Stonewall homosexual to be in any kind of meaningful, socially constructive relationship. For the homosexual to be able to see *the possible future* of being a homosexual in relation and

14. Interview, Joan Nestle.
15. Logos means *study of*, and philia means *love of*. Because in religious studies we *study* theology, I named this practice which originates in my own study of the culture, *theelogy*. Perhaps in their raw experience we could speak of the bar culture women *themselves* as practicing *theephilia*, from which I then have constructed theelogy.
16. Frankl, *Man's Search for Meaning: An Introduction to Logotherapy*.

moving forward in relation *as homosexual* was to question the authority of the time (religious, medical, legal, social) and to answer the call of, if not big "G" God, then small "g" god—the "god in myself." That "god" is the god whom shange also finds.

While theories embedded in liberation, queer, feminist, and womanist theologies helped me re-frame the gaze on the pre-Stonewall period differently, ultimately I concluded that it was necessary to name the sacrality of bar culture women as something *other than* these processes. However, if not for these processes and working through their lenses I would not have had the agency or language to create theelogy. While in the actual language and usage of theelogy I lean towards space and place theory[17] and the process of becoming as elucidated by process theology, my acquisition and deployment of these constructions depends on, is informed by, and made possible by these formations of theologies that were "liberated" from traditional theology. These are those theologies that came after and were formed by the gate of liberation theology: among them feminist and queer theologies.

Theelogy is not liberation or queer theology, because that would imply that the women using this theory had access to "God-talk." They did not. But I have access to it, and those reading this have access to it. Through the method of deviant historiography, we can re-frame our gaze on this culture and see a possible sacrality at work. In that historical re-framing then, theelogy becomes *a kind of* libratory queer theology, as it is the precursor to and births future queer community and framings that would *result in* queer theologies. But, in its time and place *it was theelogy*, the language of friend as sacred, not theology, the language of God as sacred.

The progression of contemporary post-Stonewall thought then that created the space and parents the place where theelogy as an idea can be birthed—the process of becoming that happened for bar culture women that I call *theelogy*—was preceded by the butch-femme bar culture praxis of mid-twentieth century America.

BUTCH-FEMME BAR CULTURE OF MID-TWENTIETH-CENTURY AMERICA: THEOLOGICAL REFLECTIONS AND CONVERSATIONAL PARTNERS

> Why indeed must "God" be a noun? Why not a verb—the most active and dynamic of all.[18]

I begin here with Mary Daly and her concept of moving "beyond God the Father." I posit it as a possible trajectory, using deviant historiography, as the

17. Sheldrake, *Spaces for the Sacred: Place, Memory, and Identity*.
18. Daly, *Beyond God the Father: Toward a Philosophy of Women's Liberation*, 32.

realized future 1970s feminism birthed from the butch-femme gay women's bar culture community.

When Mary Daly first published *The Church and the Second Sex*, she considered herself a Christian, albeit a radical Christian. When she re-issued the text seven years later she considered herself a "feminist post Christian." This is somewhat like, but also unlike, the original text for *Beyond God the Father* and its re-issue twelve years later. At the time that *Beyond God the Father* was published, Daly already identified as "post Christian" and when she re-issued the text with an "Original Reintroduction" she discussed how she still related to the woman who originally wrote the text as herself, only now at its re-issue she was older and could add to what she originally wrote. Whereas when she wrote the "Feminist Post Christian Introduction" to *The Church and the Second Sex*, she wrote that she considered the original author (herself in 1968) someone admirable, but so separate from the self she had become in 1975 that she could no longer say it was part of her. The titles of these texts are instructive as well. In 1968, Daly's groundbreaking text addresses the Church and the problems she believes it had because it had (has) "a second sex," and she called out the Church on its bad behavior. By the time the next text came out, Daly was through with chastizing the Church. She, along with many lesbian feminists, would be "beyond" God the Father. However, for Daly there was a lineage there that she would not disavow; it was no longer she, *herself*, that was part of the Church's "second sex."

The Church and The Second Sex[19]and *Beyond God the Father*[20] and their original introductions and then their "re-introductions" on successive re-issues ("Feminist Post Christian Introduction" to the re-issue of *The Church and the Second Sex*,[21] and "Original Reintroduction" to *Beyond God the Father*[22]) are good places to think about the lived possibilities of a working liberation theology permeating the butch-femme culture of mid-twentieth-century America. As Mary Daly wrote her "reintroduction" there was a lineage to which she owed her thinking—even though her thought was so radically different as to be called "post Christian." Although Daly does not say this, this type of radical theology can be found in the original butch-femme bar culture, and then the ensuing women (or "womyn") only lesbian feminist movement. "Womyn" were beyond masculinity, yet they embraced traits that had been called masculine prior to 1970. Did the ability to claim the notion of "womyn" owe itself to the butch and femme women who traversed their gender in order to live difference within their biological bodies, so that they lived the feminist principle of proclaiming that biology is not necessarily destiny? Yes, I believe so.

19. Daly, *The Church and the Second Sex.*
20. Daly, *Beyond God the Father: Toward a Philosophy of Women's Liberation.*
21. Daly, *The Church and the Second Sex.*
22. *Ibid.*

I am not the first to suggest a connection between Mary Daly and liberation theology. Althaus-Reid made this connection within "Class, Sex and the Theologian: Reflections on the Liberationist Movement in Latin-America."[23] She wrote that not only have generations of oppressed people identified with the Exodus narrative in the Bible, and with being able finally to flee "lands of injustice," but also that Mary Daly put out the "early feminist theological call" that urged "women to abandon the patriarchal churches, and the Latin American poor have all identified themselves with the Exodus narrative."[24]

In its original incarnation, Althaus-Reid reminds us that:

> Liberation theology did not set out chairs for poor women or poor gays—at least it never did so willingly. The inclusive project affirmed itself by exclusion policies which determined the identity of the poor. The poor who were included were conceived of as male, generally peasant, vaguely indigenous, Christian and heterosexual. In fact, militant churches would not have needed many chairs around the table of the Lord if these criteria had been applied. It describes the identity of only a minority of the poor. The poor in Latin America cannot be stereotyped so easily and they include urban poor women, transvestites in poor street neighborhoods and gays everywhere.[25]

This connection was illustrated succinctly at the 2008 National Association of Catholic Diocesan Lesbian and Gay Ministries (NACDLGM) conference aboard the ship the Queen Mary in Long Beach, California, when Bishop Raul Vera Lopez, Bishop of the Diocese of Saltillo, Mexico gave the closing plenary address.[26] He talked at length about the three levels of his own history and how he came to be the plenary speaker at such an event as a conference for gay and lesbian Catholic ministries.

His first level, as he described it, was to come to grips with his first ministry assignment. He was assigned to work with the rural poor. When he broke them up into groups for biblical discussions, he looked around at his poor community and thought, "Who am I kidding? These people cannot intelligently discuss the Bible!" He realized that in order to "follow in Christ's footsteps" he would have to get beyond who he thought he was. He would have to lose his privilege and become like the rural poor. In so doing, he realized the rural poor were living more the life of Christ than he could ever have imagined. "If they had the least crust of bread, they would share it with each other. I had never seen their type of generosity and commitment to values and kindness." By the time he left that ministry for another assignment, he

23. Althaus-Reid Marcella, *Another Possible World* (London: SCM Press, 2007).
24. *Ibid.*
25. *Ibid.*, 27.
26. Vera Lopez, "Closing Plenary Speaker".

said he wished he could "kiss the feet" of every person there—that's how much they had taught him. One of his next challenges was on assignment from Rome to go to a "political" Church and get the parish priest there to stop being so political or against the ruling government. He was not supposed to give support to the anti-military forces that resisted the rules. But when Father Raul went there he realized that the poor who were coming to that Church were more on the side of Jesus than the Church hierarchy was. The poor had come to hear him speak at great sacrifice to themselves, taking up to a day-and-a-half to avoid the para-military forces that were surrounding the Church, rather than the shorter one-hour route they would take if they could. How could he deny these people their sacrality? "They were living Christ and I was not. I had to stand with them." Because he did this, he was castigated by the Church and lost much of his prestige. But, as he says, coming in line with the way Jesus lives "is more a letting go of what you have and coming to embrace the real values of community and love ... People asked, 'How are you, your Excellency?' [common term used to address a bishop] And I would say, 'I don't know how he is, but I'm fine. My name is Raul.'" And slowly he created community with the people he served, and learned from them.

Within the last decade he was assigned to Saltillo and there he met the lesbian and gay population to whom he now ministers. "You," he said as he addressed the lesbian and gay Catholic attendees and their allies at the conference, "are my ticket to heaven."[27] Bishop Raul said that the gay and lesbian ministry has grown in Mexico and now has a week-long festival that many community members attend. He is also sponsoring a neighboring city in setting up an outreach program to gay and lesbian people. In his eyes there is no difference in his ministry to the poor in the city, his past ministry to the rural poor, and his current ministry to the city's homosexual population. Liberation theology should be defined in his lived praxis as a theology liberated from the Church dogma that would castigate him for political involvement and would ask him to hold the Church party line that says homosexuals are living in sin. There is no conflict for him, when he evaluates his history, of how he came to develop a passionate ministry to homosexuals that is in line with his passionate commitment to the poor. Neither of these ministries came with implicit blessings from Rome; rather he lost stature being involved with these ministries. He suggested that the parable that best describes his commitment is the one of Jesus with the money lenders. Jesus threw the money lenders out of the temple and said, "It is harder for a rich man to enter Heaven than for a camel to pass through the eye of a needle."[28] How you live is important—not how you think or preach—if the latter is not connected to and interwoven with the lives of those you serve.

27. *Ibid.*
28. Mark 10:25; Matthew 19:24; Luke 18:25.

He told a joke about a priest and a taxi driver in Mexico where a cab ride on its deep winding roads can feel like taking your life in your hands. The parish priest and the cab driver end up at the Pearly Gates:

> Saint Peter sends the priest to Purgatory and lets the cab driver into Heaven. But the priest won't go—he is astounded! The priest pleads, 'The cab driver gets in, and I don't? St Peter, I am the priest!' St Peter goes to his computer and does some calculations just to be sure of his decision. "Well," he says, "Father, the truth is that when you were preaching, most of the people fell asleep. But when he was driving ... all of the people were praying!"[29]

What is important in ministry is to be with the people and be of the people—and if people are sleeping through your sermon then you are not "with the people."

The subtitle of Mary Daly's book *Beyond God the Father* is "Towards a Philosophy of Women's Liberation." Because she was a religious writer and her first book came out at the same time as liberation theology was being developed, I situate her as part of liberation theology. Although she divorced herself from "Christianity" she did not divorce herself from the sacred. This was true for many lesbian feminists who desired to be "beyond God the Father," for there was no *saving* a Christianity that insisted that women could not move beyond their place as "the second sex."

Liberation theology was not conceived originally as a theology *of liberation* for a specific people as much as liberation *of theology itself* and a re-connection of theology with ethics. Liberation theologians believed Jesus' lived teachings were committed not only to bringing peace, but also justice.[30] *Liberation Theology at the Crossroads* critiques liberation theology's involvement with revolution and asks liberation theology to see democracy, rather than Marxism, as the solution.[31] The *Harvard International Review* stated that the work succeeded in proving that "democracy stands as the only logical—and theologically correct—alternative for contemporary liberation theology."[32] This view restricts liberation theology to one type of political regime, then diminishes its importance and is in conflict with Althaus-Reid who asserted that "without another understanding of God, without different religious practices and different theologies, another possible world cannot be built."[33]

29. Vera Lopez, "Closing Plenary Speaker".
30. Boff & Boff, *Introducing Liberation Theology*.
31. Sigmund, *Liberation Theology at the Crossroads: Democracy or Revolution?*
32. *Ibid.*, back cover.
33. Althaus-Reid, *Another Possible World*. This is a published report of work presented at the World Forum on Theology and Liberation, Brazil, 2005 in which contributors believed that "another world is possible—one where justice will reign."

The idea that "another world is possible" is also behind Daly's work—and inherent in *Beyond God the Father* and its subtitle *Towards a Philosophy of Women's Liberation*. Liberation theology operating as a liberated theology means that theology is liberated from dogma.

> A friend usually has things in common with her friends, beyond compassion. Jesus must have had something of the sinner and prostitute too within himself if he enjoyed their company. At least he must have felt that they had things in common, ways of thinking or laughing or befriending ... Sinners and prostitutes are human beings like anyone else ... Jesus kept going to them with the obstinacy of the Argentinean gays who kept going to the few gay clubs in Buenos Aires during the years of the dictatorship. The call of love and intimacy is always stronger than anything else.[34]

Liberation theology exists not only to serve a specific oppressed people, but it exists as a liberated theology that can serve all oppressed people. And it arose from the lived struggles of a people—be they Latin American peasants, gay men in the middle of the HIV/AIDs crisis, or women coming to consciousness in the early and mid stages of the Women's Liberation struggle. It also existed as a *lived theology,* without a named God, in the bar culture of butch-femme in mid-twentieth-century America.

> In 1961, the Mattachine Society's nationwide membership was 230; Daughter of Bilitis' was 115. Fewer than a thousand people (including several FBI agents) read their magazines. In contrast, tens of thousands of lesbians, gay men, bisexuals, transgendered people, and straight tourists flocked to lesbian and gay bars that year. Notwithstanding police raids and liquor license revocations, those bars proliferated after World War II. Most major American cities had a variety of bars that served as the foundation for local lesbian and gay communities and subcultures.[35]

The reason William Eskridge includes detailed accounts of bar culture lesbians in his book on sodomy laws in America from 1861–2003 is because he is documenting how laws against homosexuals were made and how they were *changed*. I argue that bar culture lesbians, gay women, butches and femmes, and street dykes were not proto-political as others have argued, but simply *political*. One of our rights as Americans is the right to public

34. Althaus-Reid, *Indecent Theology: Theological Perversions in Sex, Gender and Politics*, 113.
35. William N. Eskridge, *Dishonorable Passions: Sodomy Laws in America, 1861–2003* (New York: Viking, 2008), 131.

assembly; our first Amendment gives us the right to freedom of assembly. Freedom of assembly is the right to come together with others and express, promote, pursue, and defend common interests. The right to freedom of association is recognized as a human right, a political freedom, and a civil liberty. Freedom of assembly is guaranteed in the Constitution of the United States and it means both the freedom to assemble and the freedom to join an association.[36]

Eskridge cites Davis and Kennedy's Buffalo study as the best account of a bar-based subculture, and one which demonstrated that:

> bars were the terrain where a modern lesbian identity was shaped ... Buffalo's bars drew women from all over northern New York and even Canada. While most of their patrons were working class, others were teachers or owned their own businesses. What they found in the lesbian-friendly bars were places where they could make friends, meet potential sexual partners, and claim public space that had traditionally been denied to women in America. The prevailing lesbian social script in the 1940s and 1950s was the butch-femme one ... many couples readily displayed affection in public. In the bar or on the street, a butch-femme pair was therefore recognizable as a homosexual couple ... [The] astounded police harassed and sometimes brutalized these women ... [it was known that] female couples were violating New York's sodomy law,[37] [however] butch lesbians were usually arrested [instead] for cross-dressing, public indecency or disorderly conduct. At the height of this harassment emerged the street dyke, a full-time bar queer who appeared in public in jeans ... often with a pretty girl on her arm and always prepared to fight off fag-bashing bullies and police. While polite society—including the Daughters of Bilitis—disdained the street dyke and the stone butch, they were heroes in the bars.[38]

It is not that I want to take away the distinction of the Daughters of Bilitis as being the first lesbian rights *organization*.[39] But the numbers are so small that to credit it with the social change that then became the gay rights movement, without crediting the "tens of thousands" of gay women, particularly butches and femmes who created and maintained the public presence and the public spaces from which the small DOB women birthed themselves and

---

36. Webster, "Freedom of Assembly," http://www.websters-online-dictionary.org/fr/freedom+of+assembly.html (accessed April 16, 2010).
37. Just by appearing queer in public, female homosexuals violated the sodomy law, but it was not enforced as was the code for men. What was enforced for women was masquerading, or dressing *as a man*.
38. Eskridge, *Dishonorable Passions: Sodomy Laws in America, 1861–2003*, 132.
39. Gallo, *Different Daughters: A History of the Daughters of Bilitis and the Rise of the Lesbian Rights Movement*.

later emerged is historically inaccurate. Kennedy and Davis argued in *Boots of Leather* that the butch-femme bars of mid-century were political. As Gallo states in her subtitle of *Different Daughters*, DOB precipitated the "lesbian rights movement."[40] The problem is historical/"her"storical and semantic. "Lesbians" were not usually called "lesbians" prior to the 1970s, especially in their own friendship circles. "Lesbian feminism" was an invention of the 1970s, and its radical political tone was a moniker for its varied cultural groups—and so lesbian became tied to feminism. Butches and femmes were for the most part completely disenfranchized from any system other than the organizational system they themselves created in the bar. They were not connected to feminism *per se*, unless they came out as feminists in the 1970s, and disowned or moved away from a defined butch-femme lifestyle. Having come out as gay and/or butch or femme or gay women in previous decades, that is the identification that most of them kept, and so they often felt they were not "lesbians." So, I agree with Gallo's title that DOB was intimately connected with and part of what birthed the "lesbian rights movement." But the decades prior to Stonewall were not lesbian identified, they were butch- or femme-identified. The community created in the bar by butch and femme women was the first time for almost all of these women that they were able to be in community. They would later be categorically excluded from most lesbian rights organizations and castigated as mimicking heterosexuality and accused of role-playing. In changing the name of what a female homosexual was from gay female or butch or femme *to lesbian* within the culture itself, butches and femmes and gay women's bar culture did lose *their* historical place as actually *being* the birth place of "lesbian rights," and in a very real way by being the birthplace of DOB itself.

Know My Name: A Gay Liberation Theology is a "contribution to a gay, white, male ... theology of liberation, nothing more. I cannot claim to speak for lesbians or gay men of color. Much of our experience is shared, still more is familiar, but much remains distinct if not estranged."[41] The 1995 text was written specifically for gay men. A theology of liberation for lesbians must look back at bar culture and re-frame the gaze on that culture in order to include in it the history that moves from bar culture through lesbian feminism like Daly's work and then into new readings of theology like *Know My Name*.

40. I don't mean to question the impeccable scholarship of this volume. But, I want to clarify the semantics of the use of the word "lesbian" and "gay women." How history is made when a word is coined or used in popular life that heretofore has not been used that way is that there is a possibility of erasing the history of those who were part of this populace prior but not identified with the *new name*. Hence the *history* of the people who are called *this new name* does not necessarily include the *prior* populations who did not identify with this name, but do (and still often will) identify with the old name. However, they *are* part of the historic lineage of this newly named group.

41. Cleaver, *Know My Name: A Gay Liberation Theology*, vii.

Theelogy helps with that re-framing. Liberation, feminist, or queer theology has significance for marginalized populations who try to own a discourse with God as friend, rather than foe. Contemporary queer populations can manipulate the discourse of the sacred; this was not true for queer populations of the mid-twentieth century. These adjectival terms do not work for this culture to identify their experience, because that would assume they had access to the workings of theology—the discourse about God. They did not; they were outcast from traditional religious communities.

Theelogy contributes to the ongoing constructions of feminist, queer, and other libratory theologies. It provides the birthing point for these later theological constructions. By adding theelogy as a tipping point we have a place to situate these constructions' beginnings and to re-frame the her/historical importance of the period.

HERE IS THE CHURCH, HERE IS THE STEEPLE, OPEN THE DOORS ... WHERE ARE THE PEOPLE? OR ... WAS EVERYONE IN THE BAR DOING THEELOGY?

Was everyone in the bar culture practicing theelogy? Or love of the other as possibly sacred, that is, a possible friend? Seeing the value in the other person, the possible Christ? Absolutely not. Not the straight man looking for the gay female prostitute—perhaps. Not the cops looking to destroy gay bar culture, or being paid off by the Mafia and conducting bar raids that kept everyone on edge—perhaps. Not the butch who pressured the femme to be a prostitute—perhaps. Not the Mafia watering down the drinks—perhaps. I add "perhaps" because my informants have said that all of these interactions were contested. For example, there were interactions with straight men, particularly the bouncers and owners of the bar that, while conflicted, also validated the humanity in each other.[42] *Perhaps* many people in bar culture were there for reasons other than creating community, affirming humanity, finding someone in themselves to love and someone outside of themselves to love, and giving that love to themselves and to the other, perhaps for the first time, this being the only *place* or site/body where that could happen. But this can be said of all major religions that are housed within a church structure. People gather in such structures for many different reasons. Just as

42. Interview, Joan Nestle. Joan Nestle told me she felt very conflicted about her relationship with Vinnie the bouncer at The Sea Colony, the bar she went to most frequently in New York City in the 1950s. He was Mafia; she knew that sometimes the men who worked there ridiculed the women who went there, but at the same time, the men who worked there offered protection to the women there and helped create and maintain the place where this community could actually partake of community rituals. Finally, not friendship but elements of friendship existed between the Mafia workers and the bar women—elements of friendship and community that were not offered to these women in any other place.

everyone knows, whether or not they are religious, that they have entered a religious space when they enter a church or temple (etc.) where the religion the structure houses is at least *acknowledged* and acceptance of it is *encouraged*—so did every person, whether a cop, a member of the Mafia, a homosexual, an alcoholic, a prostitute, a drug dealer, a straight man, and so on, know that when they entered the gay bar they had entered the space where gay female community was acknowledged and community was encouraged at a time when there was no other such space. This then was the space that became a place where gay love and life was established and practiced. This is where theelogy was practiced, where the *you* was seen, and *perhaps* loved and worshipped in the way the beloved can be loved and worshipped.

Process thought believes God is in everyone and everything. God was in everyone in the bar—those who *formed community* became metaphorically in accordance with God's call for art, adventure, beauty, and friendship. Where can we say God was then in the gay women's bars of mid-twentieth century? God-self *enacted* was in those who established community, who looked at a newcomer and made her feel, as so many informants said they were made to feel, "at home" for the first time or rather *seen*.

Theelogy in the bars employed traditional theological practices: baptism, Eucharist, ecclesiology, and salvation.

Baptism

(Initial entry to the bar and finding one's self and one's community.)

In Christian terms baptism signifies that those who are baptized are able to leave *sin* behind, for a new place—a possible Heaven in the afterlife, and a path to walk in this life. Baptism is supposed to help humanity make a way in the profane world. It also gives us agency in this world. We are baptized, and can say we have an investment in this doctrine and way of living and can help to name or define it because of an investment and indoctrination into it. We become part of the Church and have ownership in it because we are baptized into it. I have said that I am baptized Catholic. As a lesbian woman I believe that the Church cannot get rid of me. I have said I am, "Catholic ... like Madonna,"[43] and that the Church has to accept me in their membership. *I am baptized*. Luther, when creating Protestantism from Catholicism, also used this argument—he had been baptized. He had a stake in the tradition.

> Halting the sacrament's gradual slide into obscurity in the middle ages, Luther injected a vitality into baptism. No longer was this merely the

43. The singer/entertainer Madonna Louise Ciccone.

sacrament of infancy. Luther saw baptism's significance extending beyond the momentary rite at the font. Baptism permeates the entire life of the believer, and therefore plays a large role in Luther's theology.[44]

> Sacraments can only be spoken of in *relational* terms ... the sacraments effect a deeper "relationship" ... with the Church. Baptism happens not only to the individual, but also to Christ's body, the Church. ... we celebrate Baptism in the Christian assembly, with the community present and actively participating. It is the community ... who is welcoming the new members, journeying with them, providing models for them, supporting and nourishing them.[45]

In the gay women's bar communities, baptism meant leaving the slavery of sin behind. When they were outside of the bar they were considered sinners; inside the bar there was a chance that they would not be—there might be, inside those four walls, the freedom of a Promised Land. Baptism is the first sacrament and is therefore often considered "the door" to the other sacraments. "The Sacrament of Baptism is often called 'The door of the Church,' because it is the first ... not only in time (since most Catholics receive it as infants) but in priority, since the reception of the other sacraments depends on it."[46] Walking through that door and entering into community with other gay women allowed most gay women the first opportunity for baptism into gay life. This was the first time that they had an assembly with which to celebrate. Falcon said that when she entered her first gay bar she felt that, "I had never fit anywhere before, and I fit there—for the *first* time I *fit*. It was home."[47]

Beverly spoke of how she heard about the bar in the mid-1940s as a place where people who were deviant went. She knew that she belonged there. But first she went several times just to walk around the neighborhood, not daring to go in.[48] Many women spoke of this fear of entering this space—of having to go several times, before they dared to enter. Passing through the door—the first entry point—would be a baptism into gay life and was not taken lightly, but as a ritual of crossing over into gay community. This was necessary because everything else could only be accessed by crossing through that door for the first time.

---

44. Mark Tranvik, "Luther on Baptism," *Lutheran Quarterly* XIII (1999), 75.
45. Sandra DeGidio, O.S.M., "The Sacrament of Baptism: Celebrating the Embrace of God" *Catholic Update* (2009), www.americancatholic.org (accessed June 12, 2009).
46. Scott P. Richert, "About Baptism," About.com: Catholicism (2009), www.catholicismabout.com (accessed June 12, 2009).
47. Interview, Falcon River.
48. Interview, Beverly "Bev" Hickock.

Eucharist

(Breaking bread in community with others—often this was having a drink, as is done on the altar of the Catholic Mass.)

In Christian terms Eucharist signifies:

> ... ritual commemoration of Jesus' Last Supper with his disciples, at which (according to tradition) he gave them bread with the words, "This is my body," and wine with the words, "This is my blood." The letters of the Apostle Paul demonstrate that early Christians believed that this institution included a mandate to continue the celebration as anticipation in this life of the joys to come in the Kingdom of God.[49]

In the gay women's bar communities, Eucharist was this breaking bread and/or having a drink with someone, often for the first time, when someone else knew who you were—a homosexual—and was willing to break bread with you *knowing* that was who you were. The tradition of having a drink (alcoholic or non-alcoholic) in community with someone else was continued in order to keep the community alive in anticipation of "joys to come." These joys might be a possible relationship, continued community, or the simple joy of helping to keep the bar open so one would have a space/place to return to.

Although Beverly was a college student and later a high-profile government librarian, who created the materials and library which instructed those who built California's freeway system, she felt that the only people she could be in real community with were the women in the bars.

> They were the only people who saw me. When I was at the bar and someone looked into my eyes, I felt like I was really seen. That had never happened before. It didn't matter that we were different in what we did outside the bar. Inside that bar, being there with each other, feeling like someone could see you—we both knew that we were both gay. That was enough.[50]

Ecclesiology

(Taking risks in order to create community, fellowship, and shared traditions of faith.)

49. Encyclopaedia Brittanica Online, "Eucharist," *Encyclopaedia Brittanica 2009* http://www.britannica.com/EBchecked/topic/194799/Eucharist (accessed June 12, 2009). The story of the institution of the Eucharist by Jesus on the night before his Crucifixion is reported in all four books of the New Testament.
50. Interview, Beverly "Bev" Hickock.

In Christian terms ecclesiology signifies, as formulated by Karl Barth "an academic discipline primarily of the church: what it is, how it is organized, what it does, and what benefits it provides. In the Christian faith it is also the church that is the Body of Christ who is still alive and rules the church, [and has] activity with our present world through ... Church [empowered by] the Holy Spirit."[51]

In the gay women's bar communities, ecclesiology was the actual process by which gay women needed, and so studied and created, communal spaces. Nancy Valverde helped transform the then straight bar, Redz, into a gay women's bar in the 1950s by telling straight men that they could not come in. Nancy was arrested throughout the 1940s and 50s for "masquerading" or dressing in men's clothing. She spent numerous nights in jail, had her clothes taken away, and was roughed up severely on several occasions.[52] She filed a law suit against the city and won the right to wear men's clothing,[53] because she argued she needed it for her profession—she was one of the city's first female barbers. By finding and creating a community space where she fit she could create a self-searching place where she could be and do the work of her community, or the ecclesiological work of community building.

Salvation

(Authenticating each other as fully human; that is, perhaps finding friendship and even love.)

In Christian terms salvation means the "liberation from evils ... into a state of freedom and security. As sin is the greatest evil ... Scripture uses the word 'salvation' mainly in the sense of liberation of the human race from sin and its consequences."[54]

In the gay women's bar communities salvation is, using theelogy, finding one's self as a homosexual in the bar—as it was "the only place," finding community with others in the bar culture for one's self, *and* helping another woman to do the same. These are traditions important in all church communities. Process thought demands commitment to the formation of self, in creation and community. This is the primary function that the gay bar carried out for many, if not all, women who went there. It was in fact the "only place" for many of them, where they had a chance to fulfill the function of relationality that we are called to do here on earth.

51. Karl Barth, "The Nature of the Church," www.jsrhee.com/QA (accessed June 2009).
52. Panotchtitlan, *The Barber of East L.A.* In 2008 her story was immortalized in a performance opera by a Los Angeles trio of butch performance artists. The bar Redz still exists as a gay women's bar as of this writing.
53. Faderman & Timmons, *Gay LA: A History of Sexual Outlaws, Power Politics, and Lipstick Lesbians*, 95.
54. Kevin Knight (ed.), "Salvation," www.newadvent.org/cathen/13407a.htm (accessed June 19, 2009).

Process thought defines our role as one in which we are called to be in relation and to authenticate ourselves as fully human *in relation*. Having done this we can give testimony to others and help them in their journey towards their own religious experience. Again, the only place where most bar culture women might have the experience of being able to testify to *the good news* that they were fully human *as gay women* and were not immediately lost was in the gay women's bar. Having had these experiences they could then pass them on to others so that others could own their homosexuality in community, not necessarily as sinners (or mentally ill, deviants, or criminals) but as participating relational humans in authentic relations with others in community. Theelogy articulates and provides a language for this praxis.

However these women usually did not first go to the bar hoping to find others; they went first to create the baptism of *finding and naming self*—an acceptance we sometimes are able to find in religious community, if that community recognizes our personhood as valuable and not inherently sinful, as no religious community did at this time for gay women. In religious community we hope to find connection with others that will illuminate and accept that part of ourselves that is most deeply felt and which we most want to feel acceptance for, so that we can be part of, and partake in, the joys of community. Since the gay women's bar was the only place for most of these women where this kind of community praxis could take place, the bar *structure itself* became the community place; and it is only through a process like deviant historiography that one can name the interactions that took place in the bar as having any religious significance, or call them as I do, theelogical.

THE SEARCH

In theelogy, God is the *you* as in "Baby, *you* are my religion," and the community "god" exists within. God is the beloved, the other. The world came about because God made us, homosexuals, too, and said, "Whatever you do to the least of me, you do unto me."[55] So in loving "you," one loves god/perhaps God, and sees god/God/the sacred/"you" *in you*. And so, if that is what was done in the service of god/God in that historical moment—to see the "you" *in you/the other*, despite society's proclamation of you as sinner—then one saw the "you" *not* immediately as sinner, and was therefore then practicing theelogy.

How do I love thee?

I name and so elevate that form of loving in the 1950s to *theelogy* because it *did* happen; the women of the period *allowed* it to happen at that place and under those conditions in which it was forced to happen.

55. Matthew 25:45.

11. FOUR TENETS OF THEELOGY

What does God want? To love. The God of *thee* wants us as homosexuals and wanted then for historical bar culture gay women: (1) to have each other, (2) to see each other, (3) to love each other, but more importantly (4) to see the other, especially to see the other in ourselves *as an other*, in contrast to the self, by which, then, the self can be defined. The ability to see the homosexual as something *other than* the sinner was only available for most women in the gay women's bar.

"I love thee to the depth and breadth and height my soul can reach." I love thee in the dirt as I pick you up from the straight male assault or rape. I love thee as I straighten your tie, the butch who has had the cop thrust his hands down her shirt and grab her breasts, taunting her, and saying, "So, you're a man, right?" I love thee as I bail you out of jail for being a gay woman and for loving me, or my community, enough to simply stand as one of us. I love thee in the way I keep the bar community alive with my presence, I love thee in the way that I tell straight people that this is a women's bar in 1950s in East LA and making it so. I love thee as I create space for thee, and make a possible *we* out of *you and me.*

Theelogy meant that during the period between 1945 and 1975, in any urban center in the US a gay woman could walk into a gay women's bar, the way an alcoholic could walk into a meeting anywhere in the US and be recognized and find her Higher Power, however she defined that, and take the next step in accepting herself by being around others like herself. Not everyone at an AA meeting will stay sober. Not everyone in a gay bar will come out of the experience with a heightened sense of self or community—but many *did,* and *do.*

How do I love thee? Let me count the ways.
I love thee to the depth and breadth and height
My soul can reach, when feeling out of sight
For the ends of Being and ideal Grace.

I love thee to the level of everyday's
Most quiet need, by sun and candle-light.
I love thee freely, as men strive for Right;
I love thee purely, as they turn from Praise.
I love thee with a passion put to use
In my old griefs, and with my childhood's faith.
I love thee with a love I seemed to lose
With my lost saints,—I love thee with the breath,
Smiles, tears, of all my life!—and, if God choose,
I shall but love thee better after death.[1]

I LOVE THEE WITH A LOVE I SEEMED TO LOSE/WITH MY LOST SAINTS

Theelogy is that *search for god*, that *finding of god*, and whether or not named, that ability to *see god* and to *name the "you" beloved*, as god. This kind of naming began the search for *something named* and sacred. This kind of search was, for most women, foreign because it was inaccessible, outside the gay bar.

I believe that the bars practiced *thee*logy by seeing the homosexual as a self that did not need to become the past but could be birthed into a new relational future. This new future remarkably could be relational without being tarnished with the cast of *sinner* within the walls of the bar.

FOUR TENETS

1. To have each other
2. To see each other
3. To love each other, but more importantly
4. To see the other, especially to see the other in ourselves, as an other

Mid-twentieth-century homosexuals brought with them ideas about community, love and liberation but also, and in a much more basic sense, the idea about the right to be—to take up space, and therefore name place. The harmonizing factor never before combined with this particular past was the formation of public urban space that could be animated by this populace, thereby creating place. Doing so created the qualitative leap into what was beyond the power of the past. That is, it created the publicly accessible gay women's community, which connected to the isolated past of the individuals. As noted in process thought we discuss "the many becoming one, and

1. Elizabeth Barrett Browning, *Sonnets from the Portuguese* (London: J. M. Dent, 1894), #43.

increased by one," by which many ideas and actions from the past come together in this moment to create this new singular moment that now creates the new reality. Before this moment is created, there is an idea that perhaps this possible future that had not existed before, could exist *now*.

Faith, for process theologians is the belief in the power (God) of a relational past coalescing towards a new future that can relegate the past to the past. The past is not inherently bad. Some part of the past/tradition should and is carried into the future. The gay women's bar of the mid-twentieth century was just such as idea. It was a *birth* place which the individual entered and "there was no other place" where this could happen according to my informants. It was a genesis or birth into the homosexual self, the *probable future* an individual might be able to grasp and move into from the many who had come before into this space, now place.

I call these gay women's bar communities and their rituals of the many becoming one and then again the many becoming one *theelogy* not only because the bar was the birthplace of gay women's civil rights in that it was the first place to claim public space but also because the bar gave birth to the *individual herself* as a gay woman.

This happened because many isolated homosexuals came into a space, transforming it into a place—

(1) To have each other.

Have

Nancy Valverde speaks of "taking over" Redz in the 1950s, turning it from a straight bar into a gay women's bar so that the women of East Los Angeles would have a gathering space. This bar is still in existence today as a lesbian bar.[2]

And then they were able to identify their actual selves as gay—

(2) To see each other.

See

June, a self-identified femme, spoke of seeing butch gay women on the street corner outside of a bar in the 1940s and knowing finally who she was and who she was attracted to. A light bulb went on, she said, when she saw the women gathered in front of that bar. She realized that she too, could have the feelings others talked about, but she had not experienced—desire and

2. Interview, Nancy Valverde.

sexual attraction. She was afraid she would never feel those feelings, and then she *did* feel them for the first time, when she saw the butch women.[3]

And saw the gay person and identified her in each other—

(3) To love each other.

Love

Bev, although an upper-class librarian who came out in the 1940s, never felt "seen" or in community/friendship with anyone outside the gay bar. It was *only* in the gay bar where she felt she was seen by anyone truly—because she knew they saw her as gay and did not reject her, but accepted her. Although there were immense differences between Bev and other bar patrons, she felt it didn't matter. At that time what did matter was the fact that in that space they accepted each other as gay women, and did not turn away from each other, as the entire rest of the culture did.[4]

And then repeated that process with someone else—

(4) To see the other, especially to see the other in ourselves as an other.

See the other in ourselves

Joan Nestle spoke of how a butch came into the bar having been badly beaten. It was inside the bar that she was seen and tended to. "She was one of our own," Joan said.[5] What little could be done in the confines of the four bar walls was often done, so that someone coming into this space had a good chance of being helped by someone else into the process of feeling seen and connected to community. They could then in turn do that to someone else.

Theelogy is the basic relation between the gay woman self and her world. Catherine Keller writes in *From a Broken Web* that connections must exist in community and the self in relation in order for a person to feel whole. Lacking these connections the self emerges from a broken web.[6] The ability to see the disenfranchised self as a self worthy of identification as *the* self and then with others like the self, thereby forming community, was what the bar culture was able to offer women.

3. Interview, June Loewy.
4. Interview, Beverly "Bev" Hickock.
5. Interview, Joan Nestle.
6. Catherine Keller, *From a Broken Web: Separation, Sexism, and Self* (Boston, MA: Beacon Press, 1986). While Keller does not speak directly to my construction of theelogy, her thesis of transformation in connected community or disconnection from self (for her, that would be sexist community) is important to consider in my construction.

Is goodness without a named God good enough? Scholars debate "faith, secularism, and ethics" in *Is Goodness without God Good Enough?* One thinker re-phrases the debate question as "Can those who do not believe in God be good?" and answers affirmatively. "Although the ethics of secular humanism ... may not satisfy those who hunger for salvation, it nonetheless has much to commend for those seeking the good life for themselves and their fellow human beings."[7] Whether or not we agree that goodness without God is enough, we can see that goodness without God is still debatable today.[8]

Was goodness without God possible for the homosexual in 1950? Yes, it was possible and was practiced. Was it recognized as goodness? No, it was not recognized as goodness by the outside-of-the-bar world—goodness with or without God was not the question to the outside world as they had already named the women as sinners. But for the inside-of-the-bar world, *goodness* was *enough*. And *goodness* had the power to lay claim to the *discourse* of God for future generations.

Suchocki explicates a similar process explaining community formation from a process perspective. The individual becoming is a process whereby "the power to grasp a sense of what one might become through unification of the past" combines with "the feeling towards what might be" and this then is "the aim toward individual becoming."[9] Concrescent creativity is the occasion that "culminates in the satisfaction, which then generates transitional creativity."[10] Suchocki notes that this transitional creativity also creates not only "one more impulse of energy—the many become one" but importantly for theelogy and community "in so doing the many have been increased by one."[11]

Thus theelogy gives a language to the process whereby *possible* gay women entered the gay women's bar, were recognized and supported in their baptism towards *becoming identified* gay women, who could then in the ecclesiological tradition help others in so naming themselves and joining the community.

In doing this, the many became one self and then the many were increased by one, and so on—creating church. They were then seeing god "in each other" and practicing *theelogy*.

---

7. Paul Kurtz, "Ethics without God: Theism Versus Secular Humanism." In *Is Goodness without God Good Enough?: A Debate on Faith, Secularism, and Ethics*, ed. Robert K. Garcia & Nathan L. King (Lanham, MD: Rowman & Littlefield Publishers, 2009), 212–13. The work has nine contributors—six theists, three non-theists—but one non-theist agreed to take part in the dialogue in order to clarify "his position."
8. Immanuel Kant, *Foundations of the Metaphysics of Morals and, What Is Enlightenment* (Chicago, IL: University of Chicago Press, 1949). While this question is still important today, the idea of a possible "goodness without god" dates back to at least Immanuel Kant's enquiry in 1785.
9. Suchocki, *God, Christ, Church: A Practical Guide to Process Theology*, 245–6.
10. *Ibid.*
11. *Ibid.*

12. CONCLUSION ... LAST CALL!

Last dance
Last chance, for love
Yes, it's my last chance, for romance, tonight[1]

I'm not religious, but I like God and he likes me.[2]

The research for this volume ends approximately with the 1990s. This is primarily because, as an *illegal* identity, the gay women's bar culture that predominated the female gay landscape and experience from 1945–75 did not, for the most part, survive past the 1980s. For some this experience ended in the early 1970s, for some bar attendees the bar remained "the only place." However for gay women "coming out" in the mid-1970s and beyond, the lesbian bar was no longer "the only place," nor was butch-femme the primary organizing principle for gay women.

This work is a beginning history of butch-femme culture, its primary meeting and organizing space, the gay women's bar, and its meaning.

How do you sleep when the rest of us cry?
... What kind of father would take his own daughter's rights away?
And what kind of father might hate his own daughter
if she were gay?
I can only imagine what the first lady has to say.
You've come a long way from whiskey and cocaine.[3]

1. "Last Dance". Words and music by Paul Jabara. © 1977 (renewed 2005) EMI Blackwood Music Inc. and Olga Music. All rights controlled and administered by EMI Blackwood Music Inc. All rights reserved, international copyright secured; used by permission. Reprinted by permission of Hal Leonard Corporation.
2. Tony Kushner, *Angels in America: A Gay Fantasia on National Themes,* 2 vols (New York: Theatre Communications Group, 1993), part 2, *Perestroika.*
3. "Dear Mr. President". Words and music by Alecia Moore and Billy Mann. © 2006 EMI Blackwood Music Inc., Pink Inside Publishing, Sony/ATV Music Publishing LLC, and

The fact that in 2008 a major label female singer, Pink, prominently made clear that she was playing with a female band, in which the members were lesbian and well-known as such, was not unusual, and *that was the point.* The Indigo Girls happened to be a lesbian duo, one the very out and proud Amy Ray.[4] That they joined together *to critique the then president of the US* showed just how far gay culture had come since the Inquisition and Lavender Scare of the 1950s.

The gay bar was for many a space between a rock and a hard place that eased after the advent of lesbian feminism. The feminist movement itself also ensured that women (however not necessarily butch- or femme-identified women) had more *spaces* they could enter other than a bar. Lesbian feminism and women-only spaces ensured that women had spaces they could transform to places for religion, health, news, and more that were inconceivable to the women prior to Stonewall, who in order to just be around other women socially had to go to a bar (as informant Linda Lack reported[5]).

The gay women's bar was rich in community and ritual, a home for many, and for most their only sense of a "home" place where they could develop a queer self-identity. These are concepts of place that we attribute often to religious places and religious experience.

The 1980s birthed a different culture for gay people. The bar culture did contribute to its birth, even though it was replaced by something else. *Baby, You are My Religion* brings a lens to this culture that created something else, but also *was something notable in and of itself* and which operated in almost every urban area from the 1940s through the 1970s. This then supports a reframed gaze of this culture.

There was something meaningful and historic *and* religious going on for many of the bar attendees of mid-twentieth-century gay women's America. The fact that this type of experience became more articulated and more publicly lived after Stonewall does not mean that that prior secret bar culture did not birth the latter.

The Catacombs of Rome were underground burial places near Rome, Italy. The burials began in the second century, due to a shortage of land as well as a need for persecuted Christians to bury their dead. Although they are most well known for Christian burials, it is also true that pagans and Jews

---

Turtle Victory. All rights for Pink Inside Publishing controlled and administered by EMI Blackwood Music Inc. All erights for Sony/ATV Music Publishing LLC and Turtle Victory administered by Sony/ATV Music Publishing LLC, 8 Music Square West, Nashville, TN 37203. All rights reserved. International copyright secured; used by permission. Reprinted by permission of Hal Leonard Corporation. I listened to this in the gay coffeehouse, Hot Java, Long Beach, CA, in which I was writing, June 23, 2008. "Dear Mr. President," is sung by Pink and noted on all media as "featuring the Indigo Girls."

4. Kathy Belge, "An Interview with Amy Ray: Amy Ray Tackles the Tough Stuff," About. Com: Lesbian Life, http://lesbianlife.about.com/od/lesbianmusicians/a/AmyRay.htm. (accessed April 18, 2010).
5. Interview, Linda Lack.

buried their dead in the catacombs as well. Therefore these very first Christian communities were persecuted and were diverse and included those who were not exactly like them, and who were not accepted by the ruling society, had customs considered barbaric by the ruling society, and did not have accurate records written about them at the time in which they were forming their belief system and community. Some of those who *attended* these rituals were believers—and some were responding to a land shortage.

The most well-known source about the Christian community is of course the Bible. The earliest printed edition of the Greek New Testament appeared in 1516 from the Froben press, by Desiderius Erasmus, who reconstructed its text from several recent manuscripts of the Byzantine text-type.[6] The fact that written accounts of the early Christian gatherings did not come into existence for probably a century after their occurrence and not in any general sense for over a thousand years does not make the catacombs and their history of Christian civil disobedience any less significant. The fact that once more stable, comfortable spaces such as churches were created to house the once deviant and underground Christian populace, and the fact that the new populace went to those above-ground respected places for Christians once they existed, does not mean that the underground group was less respected.

The butch-femme bar culture was in a sense the *catacomb culture* of gay and lesbian civil rights history. Butch-femme culture maintained meeting spaces for the gay women's populace throughout the mid-twentieth century. Out of these spaces would arise the activism, the religious movements such as MCC, and also the politicizing and the love that would sustain the coming generations of gay women that would become *lesbians*.

"Baby, you are my religion," a woman once said to me, a butch woman. Her ability to articulate that in 1997 had roots in a historical lineage that stretches back through a history of butch-femme women, their culture and environs—primarily the gay women's bar culture, "the only place." We as lesbians come from a *place* and we must return to that place—and know it—perhaps for the first time. We, as a queer culture, deserve to celebrate and take pride in the gay women's bar culture, which is our lineage, our members and our accomplishments—our historical *place*. It is time to be proud *of* our history, rather than *search for* a history we can be proud of.

As Tony Kushner said, "I'm not religious, but I like God and he likes me."

And so, too, the gay women of the mid-twentieth century. They weren't practicing religion the way we have come to expect religion to be practiced. Most of them had given up on the idea of religion and some of them were not doing anything religious at all. But for some of them, there was something more. *Baby, you are my religion* ... perhaps they, too, liked "god" and I believe ... she liked them back.

6. Kenneth Scott Latourette, *A History of Christianity* (New York: Harper & Brothers, 1953), 661.

APPENDIX A
DEMOGRAPHICS

BREAKOUT DATA

List of informants: 93 women, 8 men, 1 transgender; 102 total
(note: *all* gender and sex definitions self-identified as such by informants)

The tables below include the following data:

Decade: time period in which gay feelings were first recognized and acted on.
Age: at time of interview.
Race: self-identified.
Identifier: self-identification of gender/sexual expression *for time period discussed in interview.* (If identification changed significantly at a later time, and was self-identified as such, then identification is followed by the new identifier in parentheses *in the chapter biographical identifications of informants*—but it is not indicated here. If there is a backslash then the informant held both identities throughout—but first most significant and so indicated here.)
Religion: self-identified as *birth religion.* (If this changed significantly at a later time, and was self-identified as such, it is followed by another religion in parentheses *in the chapter biographical identifications of informants*—but this is not indicated here. If there is no parentheses, but a slash, then the informant held both religions throughout—but the first was most significant and so is indicated here.)

Number of informants by decade

Decade	Women	Men	Transgender
1940s	14		
1950s	21		
1960s	22	6	1
1970s	24		
1980s	12	2	

1940s

There are 14 interviews for the 1940s (14 women, 0 men, 0 transgender)

Age at time of interview	
76–80	2
81–85	10
86–90	2

Race	
Caucasian	11
Mexican	1
Pacific Islander	1
Caucasian/Spanish	1

Identifier	
Androgynous	1
Butch	6
Femme	1
Gay	4
Homosexual	1
Kiki	1

Religion	
Catholic	4
Christian	2
Christian Scientist	1
Jewish	3
Methodist	1
Presbyterian	1
Unknown religious identity	2

1950s

There are 21 interviews for the 1950s (21 women, 0 men, 0 transgender)

Age at time of interview	
61–65	4
66–70	12
71–75	4
76–80	1

Race	
African American	3
Caucasian	16
Mexican	1
Mixed race	1

Identifier	
Androgynous	1
Bull Dagger	1
Butch	7
Femme	8
Gay	3
Kiki	1

Religion	
Baptist	1
Catholic	4
Christian	2
Greek Orthodox	1
Holiness Sanctified Church "Holy Roller"	1
Jewish	5
Methodist	1
Native American: Creed Of White Buffalo	1
Protestant	1
Southern Baptist	1
Unitarian	1
Unknown religious identity	2

1960s

There are 29 interviews for the 1960s (22 women, 6 men, 1 transgender)

Age at time of interview (all)	
51–55	2
56–60	6
61–65	10
66–70	7
71–75	4

Race (women only)	
African American	3
Caucasian	17
Chicano	1
Caucasian/Native American	1

Identifier (women only)	
Butch	10
Femme	11
Lesbian	1

Religion (women only)	
"No specific religion"	1
Baptist	1
Catholic	10
Christian	2
Jewish	2
Protestant	2
Spiritual	1
Unknown religious identity	3

1970s

There are 24 interviews for the 1970s (24 women, 0 men, 0 transgender)

Age at time of interview	
46–50	3
51–55	8
56–60	5
61–65	5
66–70	1
71–75	1
76–80	1

Race	
African American	2
Caucasian	17
Chicano	1
Caucasian/Filipino	1
Filipino	1
Mexican American	1
Spanish	1

Identifier	
Butch	7
Butch lesbian	1
Butch/Lesbian feminist	1
Feminist	2
Feminist/butch	1
Feminist/femme	1
Femme	2
Gay	2
Gay/butch	1
Gay/lesbian	1
Lesbian	2
Lesbian feminist	3

Religion	
Atheist	2
Catholic	8
Christian	1
Jewish	4
Methodist	1
Presbyterian	2
Protestant	1
Spiritual	1
Unknown religious identity	3
Wiccan	1

1980s

There are 14 interviews for the 1980s (12 women, 2 men, 0 transgender)

Age at time of interview (all)	
36–40	2
41–45	4
46–50	1
51–55	4
56–60	–
61–65	1
66–70	–
71–75	2

Race (women only)	
African American	1
Caucasian	9
Mixed race	2

Identifier (women only)	
Androgynous	2
Butch	4
Femme	4
Gay	2

Religion (women only)	
Atheist	2
Catholic	3
Jewish	2
Presbyterian	1
Unknown religious identity	4

Class (women only)

Note: Class identification was assigned by author and not self-identified. Designation is based on information provided and should be considered approximate, rather than exact data.[1]

Class identification of women respondents (93 women)

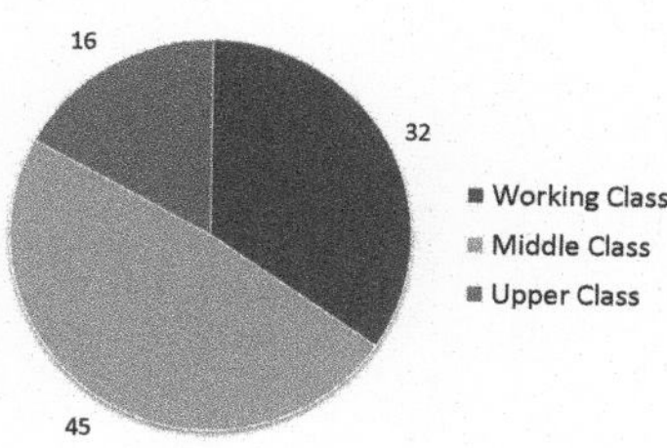

Class identification by decade—1940s

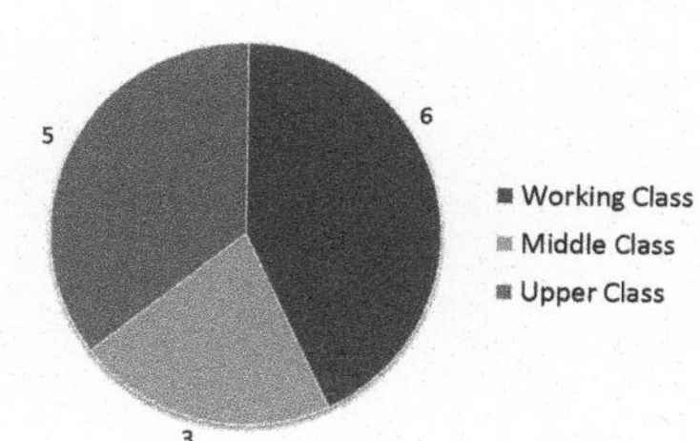

Class identification by decade—1950s

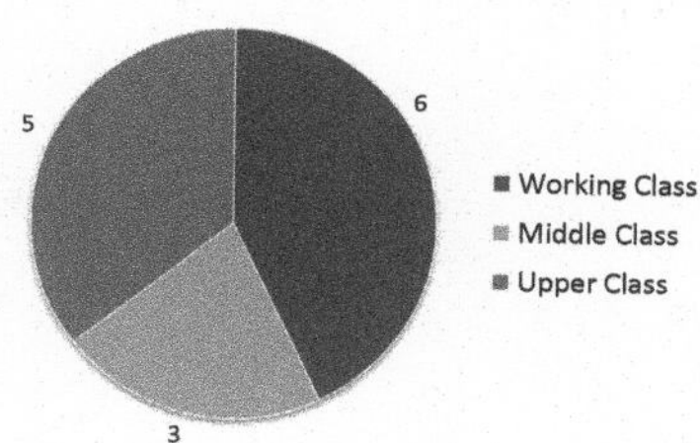

Class identification by decade—1960s

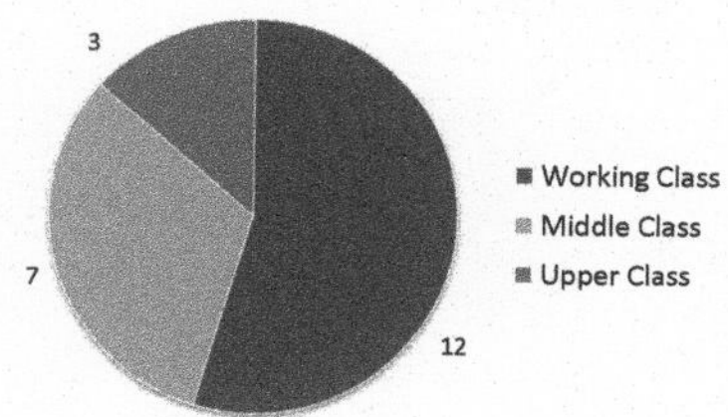

Class identification by decade—1970s

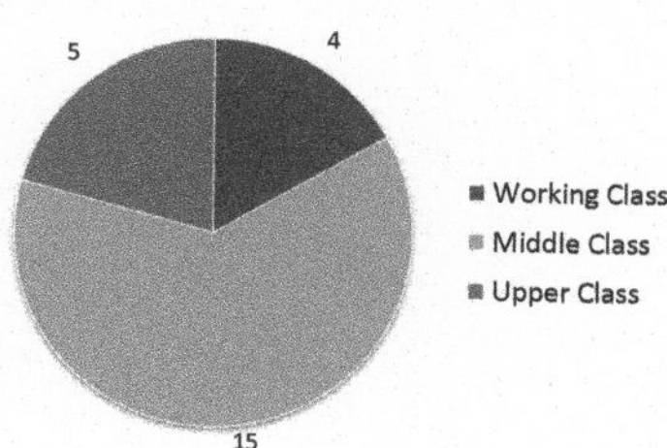

Class identification by decade—1980s

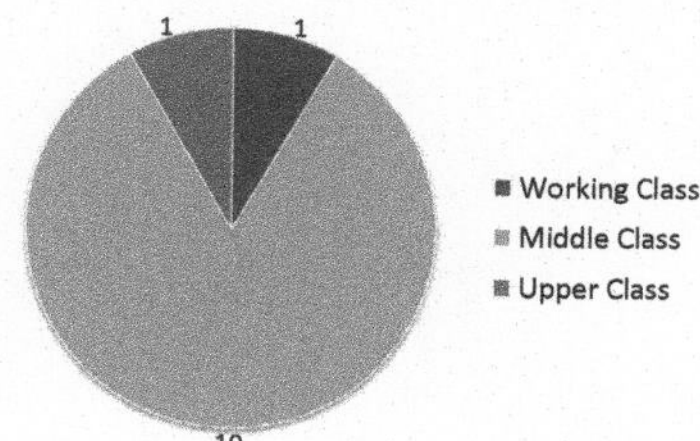

1. Charts, illustrations, and table graphics by Kimberly Esslinger.

APPENDIX B
SOURCES

PRIMARY SOURCES

Oral history interviews

All interviews were conducted by the author.
List indicates: informant name, place(s) of interview, date(s) of interview.

Alexis Del Lago, Hollywood, CA; October 22, 2008
Alice Meyers, Hollywood, CA; July 20, 2008
Andrea "Andi" Segal, Hollywood, CA; May 28, 2008 and October 21, 2008
Andy, Los Angeles, CA; August 1, 2008
Angela Brinskele, Long Beach, CA; December 10, 2006
Anna Totta, Long Beach, CA; October 7, 2008 and October 15, 2008
Anonymous, Long Beach, CA; May 11, 2009
Armina, Sweden; June 18, 2008 (email)
Auntie B. (William Huff), Long Beach, CA; December 1, 2008
Ava, Chicago, IL; August 2, 2006
B.R., Costa Mesa, CA; April 7, 2007
Barbara Kalaish, Long Beach, CA; July 7, 2007
Beverly "Bev" Hickock, Los Angeles, CA; August 2, 2008
Bishop Raul Vera y Lopez, Long Beach, CA; September 21, 2008
Bobreta Franklin, North Hollywood, CA; September 5, 2007
Bren*, Northridge, CA; Various dates, fall, 1998
Bronco Alda Moonwater, Burbank, CA; October 21, 2008
Carole S. Damoci-Reed, Anaheim, CA; March 19, 2007 and March 21, 2007
Carolyn Weathers, Long Beach, CA; June 16, 2007 and January 18, 2008
Chris Schumacher, Huntington Beach, CA; June 8, 2007
Cynthia Robinson, Northridge, CA; April 23, 2008
D.A.M., San Bernardino, CA; October 14, 2008
Darlene, Long Beach, CA; June 11, 2007
Deborah Edel, New York City, NY; June 5, 2008
Delia Silva, Torrance, CA; June 27, 2007
Doreen Brand, Los Angeles, CA; August 2, 2008
E.C., Pasadena, CA; June 12, 2007
Ellen Ward, Signal Hill, CA; July 17, 2007

Evelyn Basa, Seal Beach, CA; June 6, 2007
Falcon River, Pacific Palisades, CA; September 21, 2007 and Northridge, CA; February 20, 2008
Father Joe*, San Bernardino, CA; August 28, 2008
Flo Fleischman, Reverend, West Hollywood, CA; September 1998
Fran D.*, West Hollywood, CA; May 20, 2008
G.J., Long Beach, CA; July 27, 2007
G.K., Pasadena, CA; June 12, 2007
Gypsy Powers, Santa Cruz, CA; August 22, 2007
H.C., Long Beach, CA; May 30, 2007 and June 5, 2007
H.M., Long Beach, CA; August 29, 2008
Hazel "Ev" Everette, Long Beach, CA; June 20, 2007
Heather Hamm, Long Beach, CA; June 27, 2007
Helen Factor, Long Beach, CA; July 16, 2007
Irene "Tally" Talbert, Brooklyn, NY; May 11, 2008
Ivy Bottini, Los Angeles, CA; March 15, 2008
Jane Scott*, Claremont, CA; July 25, 2007
Jayne Doolittle*, Garden Grove, CA; June 8, 2009
Jeanne Cordova, Alta Dena, CA; May 22, 2008
Jewel Thais-Williams, Los Angeles, CA; September 5, 2007
Jo Duffy, West Hollywood, CA; Various dates, 1997–2008
Joan Nestle, New York City, NY; April 4, 2007 and April 11, 2007 (telephone)
John Garcia, Long Beach, CA; December 8, 2008
Judie Jones/Miss Judy, Long Beach, CA; August 28, 2007
Judy Grahn, Santa Clara, CA; March 23, 2009
June Loewy, Seal Beach, CA; June 6, 2007 and July 16, 2007
Karen Kahn, New York City, NY; May 10, 2008
Kate Flaherty, Long Beach, CA; June 13, 2007
Ken Davis, Long Beach, CA; September 8, 2008 and April 17, 2009
Kim Palmore, Long Beach, CA; April 27, 2008
L.N., Huntington Beach, CA; June 8, 2007
Laura Hill, Long Beach, CA; June 20, 2008
Lee Glaze, Hollywood, CA; December 3, 2008
Lillian Faderman, Fresno, CA; April 12, 2007
Linda Garnets, Santa Monica, CA; April 16, 2007
Linda Lack, Los Angeles, CA; July 23, 2008
Lisa Samson, North Hollywood, CA; April 1, 2007
Madeline Davis, Brooklyn, NY; May 9, 2008
Mari Lamy, Seal Beach, CA; June 6, 2007 and July 16, 2007
Maria Doest, Long Beach, CA; October 1, 2008
Marie McPherson, Valley Village, CA; September 3, 2008
Marilyn Taylor, Seal Beach, CA; May 18, 2007 and July 17, 2007
Marj Johnson, Anaheim, CA; August 2, 2007
Mary, Long Beach, CA; June 20, 2008
Mary Martinez, Long Beach, CA; September 21, 2007
Melanie DeMore, Oakland, CA; April 14, 2008 (telephone)
Minnie Bruce Pratt, Claremont, CA; April 20, 2007
Miss Rosie (Wayne Blaum), Los Angeles, CA; June 8, 2008
Myrna Kurland, Los Angeles, CA; October 9, 2008
N. Amazon*, Long Beach, CA; April 27, 2007
Nancy Valverde, Northridge, CA; April 23, 2008, and Hollywood, CA: May 28, 2008 and October 21, 2008